KISS FOOT, LICK BOOT

KISS FOOT, LICK BOOT

Foot, Sox, Sneaker & Boot
Worship / Domination Experiences
Vol. 1

Edited by Doug Gaines / The Foot Fraternity

Leyland Publications

San Francisco

First edition 1995.
Front and back cover photos and interior photos copyright © 1995 by The Foot Fraternity
Cover design by Rupert Kinnard
ISBN 0-943595-57-6

Leyland Publications
PO Box 410690
San Francisco, CA 94141
Complete illustrated catalogue available for $1 ppd.

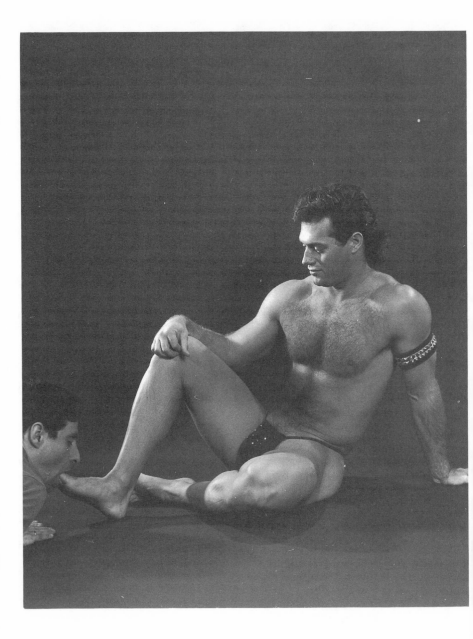

"SUCK, SLAVE. I WANT CLEAN FEET."

"I could sure use a good foot lickin' from you right now. Come on, you know and I know that you're into feet, man. Get your ass over here and do it to me, honey!" he told me. He was so handsome with those sexy, commanding eyes. I moved toward his beautiful manly feet, reached out and touched them. My hands trembled with excitement, as I slowly traced their meaty shape. "Look at 'em, man. Feel 'em. They're sexy, just like the rest of me. You want them, dontcha?" he asked with a sexy tone of excitement in his voice. "Ohhh yes, yes I do." I moaned my excitement over their beauty and strength. He grinned at me with an ornery expression on his handsome face. "Kiss 'em!" he told me, priding his dominating sexual hold over me. I bent down and began kissing along both his beautiful strong athletic feet. I was wild with euphoric pleasure in kissing such a handsome stud's feet. He was preying on my weakness, my homosexuality, with the sight of his nudity. He now preyed upon another of my weaknesses, my sexual fetish for his feet. He was sexually talented and intelligent. In such a short time, this first time together, he observed and knew me even as a stranger. Already, so shortly after exposing himself to me, he had chosen the first action to be at his feet and I was tracing their lengths with kisses in homage. Their wetness of sweat was filling my nostrils with his raw masculine pungence, as the taste of his sweating flesh caressed my lips. He seemed to know all I wanted, all I needed, with his feet. His legs were bent at the knees and his hot sexy feet rested inches away from his flaccid hanging cock and huge heavy balls. It was a sight to behold and smell, as the heat of his sweating crotch, legs, and feet bathed my head with a rush of raw masculine, sexual-erotic, male-animalistic aroma of sex to be had.

He watched and felt in silence as I kissed at every inch of his manly feet and toes for him. When I finished, he rose to his feet and turned to walk away from me. After several steps, he turned his head back to look at me staring in confusion at his beauty. Those sexy eyes pierced my own. He was so handsome, wearing only a red bandana about his head. He had stopped walking. "You want more of my feet, dontcha?" he asked enticingly. "Oh, you know I do," I answered him on my knees, as I stared into those knowledgeable, sexy, commanding eyes. There was always a certain hint of dominance in his eyes. "Then crawl into the house for them," he said calmly, then disappearing, himself, through the door. One who is weak must learn to play another man's games and for him I would have crawled anywhere for such a reward as his feet.

When I crawled into the house, I saw him perched upon a stool covered with red vinyl in all his naked beauty awaiting me. I crawled across the wrinkled slickness of the vinyl tarp on the floor till I lay flat on my stomach, prone at his feet. I clenched both his feet with my hands behind them and again began kissing them in homage.

"You are enslaved to me and cannot resist my feet, can you?" he asked down at me. That dominant eroticism was in his voice, yet it was spoken with calm deliverance. "You have a power, a superiority, beauty I cannot resist," I said speaking at his feet and not up at him. I kissed his foot before continuing. "You are a sexual god to me. I worship you at your feet," I told him, excited by the whole fantastic sexual fantasy happening. He raised one foot up to the tarped stool he sat on, resting the heel of it on the stool's edge, leaving his other foot for me to touch and adore. "Lick my foot!" he commanded with a soft sensual tone in his voice. With hungering desire I obediently began licking the tasty salted sweat from his foot on the floor. "You are such a pig, slave," he called me. "You have a tendency to make men detest you for your perversity. You are such a pig to lick my sweaty stinkin' feet like that," as I lapped wetly at his flesh.

"You are the real low-life when it comes to being a man. You are good for nothing but being used and abused by other men. Like me!" he said. "And you like that. Look at you, yer a pig faggot licking all over my dirty sweatin', stinkin', smelly feet. Lick between my toes, you pervert, and taste that crusty ole toe jam that's there," he instructed with a masterly tone. Obediently I slushed between his toes, greedily lapping for the tangy raunch deposit of dried sweat. My saliva ran out my mouth to solidify the crusty raunch so I could suck it into me to swallow. "Ahhh . . . you dirty, sleazy, raunch-eatin' foot freak!" he sneered at me, feeling my spit, tongue, and sweat sucking mouth on his foot. His dirty, sweat-smelly sexy foot was so erotic and tasty to me that I wildly lapped and slobbered my spit between his manly toes; then

I licked and sucked the sweaty toe jam out from between them into my mouth. The taste of his raunchy raw jam was every delicious yield a man's sweaty feet could be to me. While lapping his foot on the floor, he spit all over the foot that rested on its heel at his crotch on the stool. Then he spit on me like the low-life fag foot slave I was to him.

"You're filthy, man!" he told me. "You're a sleazy, raunchy, dirty assed, subhuman, pervert scum who eats the feet of real men. Get your fuckin' ass up here on my other foot, you sissy-assed queer and lick it for me," he demanded. I got up on my knees and surrendered to his spit-slimed foot. The B.O.ed stench aroma of his heated crotch and foot filled my nostrils. This was true raunchy-funk sex, and I began slurping the spit off the veined top of his foot. "Ah, baby, go for the scum, spit, and foot cheese. Eat that B.O. off my foot. Be sleaze, man!" he enticed. Oh, I was there, sucking onto more of his sweaty smelling raw tasty toes.

"Practice on them toes, fag, and I'll let ya suck on this big dick of mine," he told me. "Then I'll come all over that foot of mine and yer face. Ahhh, you'd love that, huh? Lickin' my sperm off my feet like a pig?" he teased at me.

Oh yes, I thought to myself as I sucked his tasty, round hard toe in my mouth. He sat stroking his hot, horny meat as he watched me blow his toes. This was why he came to me. He needed the raunch perversity of it all. He liked being dirty B.O.ed raunchy and making me smell, lick, and eat it off his body. No perfumes or soft bodies or gentle sex with a woman. Just raunchy raw dirty sex making a queer worship and do him. This was ego-sex! Domination, verbal abuse, humiliation, degradation, he inflicted upon another man, a queer, into his raunch. A low-life feet-licking body-worshiping cocksucker down on his knees blowing on his toes with that wet sucking mouth of his. My toe-sucking felt so good he wanted to feel my mouth on his big horny dick. He dropped his foot from my clutches to the floor and stood up. He grabbed my head of hair in one hand and guided his thick monstrous cock to my lips.

"From toe job to blow job, you cocksuckin' feet lover!" he jeered, as he thrust his hips forward forcing his cock into my mouth past my wet lips. "Ummmph . . ." I humped onto the huge meat that forced open my mouth. "Suck a penis, you cocksuckin' whore! Pig out on meat, and I'll cum all over yer face and

9

step on it," he boomed at me. Feverishly I began sucking his throbber. The thought of him splashing my face with cum and smearing it all over me with his feet ignited my mind with lust. This had to be everything I wanted and more. In short time he cummed on my face with gob after gob, wad after wad, of thick-creamy slimy-cum. I rubbed my face all over his blasting, hot, throbbing dick, as it oozed jism all over me. I wanted it all on me so he would slime my face with his big feet. What I couldn't wipe off onto me, I sucked off his cock and swallowed. When he finished I went to the floor on my back as he sat down. Then came his big feet stepping onto my face. "Ahhhhh . . ." I moaned in ecstasy. The big meaty soles and heels of both feet slid onto my face, squish-smacking the creamy thick jism between them.

"That's what yer all about, sleaze," he spoke down at me, as I slurped the cum on his feet into me. "You're slave, man! Naked, raw, savage, man-eatin' pig-slave! You eat my spit, my sperm, my sweat off my big feet, man," he told me. His cum was thick, pungent-tasting and his feet smelled of his sex. My mouth salivated with drooling, hungered lust as I feasted on his cum-slimy feet-flesh. I licked clean the bottoms of both his feet at his soles, heels, and bottoms of his toes. And now I was sucking on his sperm-coated hard round toes, and lapping at the jismic drippings between them. Man cum was spunk-starchy tasting and addictive to me. And with the taste of his feet flesh it was twice the delicious taste of man combined.

"Suck, slave! I want clean feet," he demanded. Ahhh, how I liked to appease and please him. I lapped inch by inch, toe by toe, their bottoms, their tops, their sides, till all his sperm was off his feet and into me. It took a long time, but he was patient and cooperative yielding his feet to me. When I had finished and his feet sheened clean with wetness, he pulled them from my face and stood up. I lay contented and enjoyed having such feet. I stared at his whole naked beauty and knew I worshipped this man standing over me.

"Get up on your knees, pig!" he commanded and obediently I got up. He then bound my wrists together with a wide leather belt-strap at the front of me. He sat before me and stared into my eyes, as I remained kneeling before him. He spit into the palm of his hand and lifted it out, holding it at my chin. I bent my head to his hand and lapped his spit into my mouth, swallowing it.

"You're mine! *You are slave!*" he told me. I stared silently and obediently into his sexy, commanding eyes. "You're my pig, man!" And you will learn me, my body, my big cock, and my feet," he told me as he brought one of his feet up and pressed it firm on my chest. "You're my low-life, man! You're my raunch fag to do with what I want. Do you understand me?" he asked. "Yes," I answered humbly to his beauty and commanding dominance. Slowly, he slid his foot down my stomach and rested it atop my bound wrists on the belt. "You worship my feet, don't you, slave?" he barked at me. "Yes, yes," I answered, feeling his toes against my groin. "You've smelled my feet," he said sexily. "You've tasted my sweat, and spit, and my cum off my feet," he said, grinning at me. "Ahhh, yes and I worship them," I couldn't help blurting out to him. "I know, man," he told me with arrogance and that ornery, sexy look in his eye. He dropped his foot from my wrists and stood up.

"And I want even more of your feet-lickin' and toe-suckin', ya know?" he enticed. I was staring straight up as he stepped close to me, pressing his flaccid cock against my naked chest. My chin touched his hard muscled stomach. "Lick my stomach!" he told me. I could smell his sweaty flesh and pressed my face onto his hard belly, licking into his navel. With both hands he grabbed behind my head and pulled me hard against him.

He moved and ground his belly against my face, wetting me with his slippery sweat. I groped my own balls and cock and began stroking myself with my bound hands, as I felt his stomach's mounded muscles stroke my face in sweat. His cock began to harden as he fucked against my chest. "Ahhh yeah, pig. Don't stop lickin' my stomach till I tell ya to get down on my feet again," he instructed as I licked his muscles, tasting his flesh. His belly and my face, his cock and my chest, my cock in my hand, all squish-smacked loudly in sweat-fleshed rhythmic, pulsating sex.

Then suddenly it happened; his chest-hard fucking cock erupted in a forceful hosing rush of warm piss. It gushed up onto my neck and flowed down the front of my body. Instant wetness flowed over my chest, stomach, hands, crotch, and thighs, then onto his feet.

"Ahhhohhhhh," I shrieked in gasp-moaning ecstasy against his stomach, as my cock erupted in blasting climax sending splay af-

11

ter splay of cum onto one of his shins, only to ooze down his leg toward his foot. Piss bathed my flesh and flowed down me to his feet. I lapped at his sweating belly, cummed all over his shin, and showered in his piss all at the same time. Still splaying piss he shoved me down to lay in puddles of his piss on the vinyl tarp to lap his feet. His foot was wet with piss and my dripping cum.

"Do it, pig! Lick my fuckin' feet!" he demanded as he pissed all over my back side. I obeyed him.

LICKING MARINE BOOTS

The relationship that developed between myself and my "nephew-in-law" was definitely an unexpected one. It began when I was living in Oceanside, California (about a year-and-a-half ago). David had just turned twenty years old and had been recently promoted to the rank of Corporal in the U.S. Marine Corps. We had first met when my niece brought him over to my place for a night-long game of cards, beer drinking and music playing (on the stereo). I remember thinking, how does she (my niece) do it . . . David was very handsome, I thought. His eyes were piercing . . . his attitude was typically Marine-like, something like a high school jock who finally realized that he really is better than other people . . . and the jogging shorts he was wearing revealed the hottest pair of tanned legs I've ever seen. That first night, and the next six months, all I did was look . . . Although David knew that I am gay, he wasn't bothered about it and talked about it freely whenever the subject came up. With him being a Marine I was somewhat surprised by this, and at the same time I was relieved.

When Christmas came around I was bold enough to give him a Christmas gift that I figured he could (and would) really use. The fact that it would be giving me a closer contact with him was a formidable bonus. I gave him a card with a separate note enclosed. The note gave him a full six months of Boot Shining service. When he read the note he looked directly into my eyes and then down at the muddy Marine boots he was wearing. He looked back at me and said very seriously, "I hope you know that I wear two pairs of boots everyday, and both of them will have to be shined before

I leave for work the next morning." He was so matter-of-factly serious in his tone of voice (at twenty years old) that I got a flutter of nervousness and my heart skipped a couple beats. I assured him meekly that I was willing and prepared to shine them as often as he thought it was necessary. He laughed out loud and informed me that he expected me to come to his place every evening in order to keep up with the work. From the first moment after David read that note inside his Christmas card I knew he was going to enjoy the fact that he had a boot shiner under his control. And from that moment, our relationship changed dramatically. Before David left my place that evening, he made it clear that he would be expecting me to make a boot shining visit to his apartment before the next morning. I waited (partly out of embarrassment) until I thought my niece was in bed (she always went to bed early), and I prepared myself, trying my best to not be nervous, got in my car and drove to David's.

When I arrived, David was sitting in his favorite chair. He was still dressed in his Marine "cammies" (camouflage shirt and pants) and the same muddy Marine boots he had been wearing at my place. I was about to sit down and watch TV for awhile when he said, "You'd better get started on my boots if you expect to be home before morning." I was a little startled at his directness, his commanding tone. At the same time I was relieved that he had taken charge. I really didn't know how to break the ice (so to speak). David told me where the boot shining kit was. I went to the hall closet to get the boot polish, brushes and other paraphernalia. With the shine kit in my hands, I looked down at the floor and saw ten boots (five pairs) in various stages of being scuffed and muddied. It was then that I heard David call from the living room. "Oh yeh, you might as well bring my other boots in here while you're at it!" In a split second I realized that perhaps I had gotten myself into more than I could handle. It was already nine-thirty in the evening, and if David expected me to shine a total of six pairs of his Marine boots before I went home, it was going to be very late by the time I got into bed.

I had assumed I would sit on the sofa with the boots and shining equipment arranged on newspaper on the floor. I had envisioned myself being able to watch television with David, drink some beer and one by one clean, then shine each of his boots. (I thought he had maybe three pairs, not six). As I began getting

13

things set-up David asked me what I was doing. I told him and his response was much more than I had ever anticipated. "No, no, no, no!" he said rapidly. "I want you to get down on your knees here in front of me and get my foot gear cleaned and shined where I can watch." I was at the same time horrified and excited. The thought of being forced to my knees by the order of a twenty year-old Marine was something out of a fantasy. David held up the note I had placed in his Christmas card. He took a long drink of his beer. "According to this Christmas present you gave me I get six months of service to my boots *and* my shoes, and I get it any way I want it! And I want to see you do it while they're on my feet. So, get on your knees here in front of me and get to it!" I could tell that David had consumed more than one beer. He was definitely getting into the fact that he could tell me what to do and be certain that I wouldn't argue with him.

After I had prepared everything within reach of where David was sitting, I knelt down slowly and looked up at him. He had crossed his right ankle over his left knee so that my face was just inches from the toe of his dirty boot. He leaned back comfortably in his chair, which pushed his foot forward. He bent the ankle of his right foot just enough to push it firmly against the side of my nose. He gave it a quick shove and laughed as he ordered me to get up and "fetch" him another beer. I got up and obeyed David's order, then resumed my place kneeling at his feet. David's usual friendly hospitable manner was gone and showed absolutely no signs of returning. I was shuffling things around trying to decide how I was supposed to get the mud off David's boots. I glanced up at him just as he was taking a swallow of the cold beer I brought him. My mouth was dry. I looked into David's eyes, and asked him if I could have a beer before I got started cleaning his boots. He lowered the half-full bottle from his lips and told me "You think you're here to enjoy yourself? Huh, answer me." "No," I answered. "Damned right! You're here to do your daily duty on my boots—not to drink my beer, and don't think you're going to get out of cleaning my tennis shoes." He laughed, a kind of sadistic chuckle. He placed the toe of his boot against my nose again, took another swig of beer and told me to clean the mud off his boots with my *mouth*. I couldn't believe that he was ordering me to lick his boots. But that's exactly what he expected to watch me do. . . .

14

David placed his right foot on my left shoulder, letting the entire weight of his leg rest heavily; he twisted his heel from side to side grinding the sole of his dirty boot into my clean white shirt. He applied more pressure, forcing me to bow down before him. "Start licking, boot licker!" he commanded. His boot was dirtier than any I had ever imagined. I extended my tongue to its full length and drew it slowly around the edge of that muddy boot. I could feel David's toes wiggle inside the warm, dirty leather, and I could smell the leather and boot polish made stronger from the sweaty foot resting inside the tightly laced boot. While I wasn't too surprised that David had readily accepted the Christmas gift I offered, I must admit to being shocked at finding myself shoved to David's waiting foot, and there, under his ever watchful eye, eating the dirt and scum from his worn boot. Continuing to let his right foot rest comfortably (and weightily) on my shoulder David occasionally chuckled and laughed at my perpetual struggle to keep his right foot elevated at the level I had been ordered to and yet keep my head low enough to facilitate placing my tongue firmly on the dirty leather of his left boot, licking it clean. My tongue was beginning to get pretty sore, and I wasn't (even) finished with the first boot! When I had finished licking the top portion of his boot, David tilted his foot back, rocking it on the heel of that licked Marine boot and raising the toe into an upright position and said simply, "The sole's dirty too, clean it off!" "Yes Sir," was my reply. David laughed and added to the order by telling me to lift his foot off the floor and hold it in my hands while I licked the sole clean. He extended his leg to its full length, forcing me to crawl backwards in order to obey his command. I had to keep one hand on the floor to keep from falling over on my face (with his other boot still on my shoulder).

After I had cleaned both of his boots to his satisfaction, David told me to take his boots off from his feet and "for a change of pace, go get my tennis shoes out of the closet, you can clean them while your wet tongue marks dry off from my boots." I got up and walked to the closet, rubbing my shoulder and massaging my sore tongue on the roof of my mouth, which was gritty with the dirt from David's boots. I returned and knelt before him with two pairs of leather tennis shoes (*one* pair of high tops) in my hands. I sat them on the floor and started loosening the laces on David's left boot (the first one I had licked clean for him). I was interrupted with an order to "fetch" him another beer. I obeyed, and returned to what I had been doing. David's legs were extended and his left foot was crossed over the top of his right one at the ankle. David ordered me to lift his feet up with one hand and keeping my other hand behind my back, loosen his boot laces with my teeth.

Though I'm certainly not a weakling, holding both of David's feet off the floor (about 2½'–3' high) was very difficult and before I finished loosening the laces of one boot my arm was beginning to tremble from the weight imposed on it. I was told to bend my arm at the elbow and hold my wrist turned upward about 1½' out from my waist. David then rested his feet directly on my wrist, digging the heel of his boot into the tender flesh. Holding his feet up in this position forced me to place my neck over the toe of his boot in order to loosen the bootlaces. David moved his foot back and forth slightly, just enough to jam the toe of his boot into my neck rubbing it cruelly and quite firmly directly on my "adam's apple." David laughed at the sight of his uncle struggling to obey his commands.

When I had finally finished removing David's boot, he told me that the ball of his foot itched and that as part of my service to him I was responsible for his total foot care. I was stunned when he told me to press my face against the sole of his socked foot and rub it in order to take care of his "itch." I looked at his dirty, white cotton sock. He'd been wearing it all day. It was full of sweat from his masculine, size 9½ foot. David bent his toes backwards extending the ball of his foot. "Get to it, faggot. Rub my foot with your face . . . and I want to hear you breathe nice and loud through your nose!" I have to admit that my heart was pounding harder than I can ever remember before. From the position of my face in relationship to David's sweaty foot I could already smell the odor of dirt, Marine-boot leather and foot sweat. In compliance with David's order I moved my face closer to the bottom of his waiting foot. As I was just about to make contact with that sweat-filled sock David laughed again and said, "That's right, do what I order you to do . . . come on, boy, smell my sweaty foot." I inhaled loudly as I pressed my face firmly against the bottom of his foot. I could feel the moist ridges of his dirty sock. The smell of David's dirty sock was completely intoxicating. He pushed his foot harder into my face and told me to open my eyes so that I could see how much I was at his mercy . . . how total my submission to his will.

Although I had silently admired David's feet ever since I had met him, I had never imagined that he actually wanted me to *worship* his feet. I had never allowed myself to think about the possibility that David would enjoy humiliating me. Truly, things had progressed much farther than I had expected. And now that I was on my knees with David's foot in my face I wasn't at all certain that I wanted to be there. In fact, I was beginning to feel very uncomfortable. Nevertheless, the power that I had already given to this teenage Marine was more than I was able to control. David didn't give me very long to think about how uncomfortable I was, or about whether or not I *wanted* to be his foot servant. David pulled his foot away from my face and quickly thrust it forward, smashing it hard against my nose and then twisting it from side to side. ''I told you to rub my foot, cunt face, and I want to hear you smell my dirty sock. Now do as you're told, faggot!'' He repeated the kick to my face and with that I knew there was no turning back for me. I was totally and completely subject to his will.

Keeping David's feet held up (like his personal, human foot stool) was extremely difficult to do while massaging his foot with my face. Every time I let them drop too low, or raised them up too high for his comfort I was rewarded with a kick . . . not hard enough to break anything, or draw blood, but plenty hard enough to make my eyes water. The pungent smell of his sweaty sock was beginning to be more than I could take. I pulled my face back, breaking contact with his foot just enough to catch my breath. This act (of self-preservation on my part) was met with a controlled rage on David's part. He pulled his feet away from my face and ordered me to get the ''polaroid.'' When I returned with the camera he proceeded to take pictures of me with his feet in my face and his socked foot shoved in my mouth. He then told me that unless I obeyed him completely he would show the photos around . . . letting everyone (family and/or strangers) know that I worshipped at his feet and that I had tasted his sweaty dirty socks while they were still on his feet. David knew this would be too embarrassing and humiliating for me to endure and that rather than be exposed by him in such a manner I would indeed do as I was told!

Before that first night was over I had been subjected to every humiliation imaginable while kneeling at David's hot feet. I had completed the original assignment of cleaning (with my tongue) and shining five pairs of his boots and two pairs of his tennis shoes. Just before he told me to leave (for the time being), he made me remove his dirty socks. After I had pulled them from his feet he ordered me to kiss each of his toes and say thank you. David then wadded the pair of socks he'd tortured me with and shoved them in my mouth telling me that I was to keep them there all night. To make sure I had obeyed he stopped by early the following morning (on his way to work). I answered the door with his smelly socks still packed in my open mouth, and his foot sweat dripping down my throat.

MY SEXUAL FETISH FOR FEET

My name is Alex, and I'm obsessed with this homosexual fetish for other men's feet. I can remember back as far as when I was 15 years old, and discovering my interests in other boys' and men's bodies.

I was an only son when my mother remarried to a man who also had an only son. I think I was as sexually attracted to my stepbrother and stepfather as much as my mother was to the latter.

My stepbrother's name is Shannon, and he was three years older than I. Shannon was handsome, and a well-built athlete who was the pride of his father.

I became so attracted to him and his beautiful body so obviously, that one day soon after my 18th birthday he enticed me and seduced me. From that day on, for months, he dominated and used me until he reduced me to total sexual dependence for his body.

Shannon was egotistical and dominating, like his father. He had lots of girlfriends, and prided himself in seducing them, then forgetting them.

Unlike his girlfriends, Shannon used me for his kinky, sleazy desires for the perverted sex he couldn't have with the girls. He called me his *queer*, and never treated me like a brother. He treated me more like a slave to him, like his dad treated my mother. Mom and I became weak and obedient to them.

It was Shannon who first delighted and enlightened me to my sexual fetish for feet. Shannon was an all-state high school athlete in his senior year. His feet were as strong and beautiful as the rest of his body.

One night, when home alone together, Shannon made me go down on his feet as he lay naked, watching a college basketball game on TV.

I had always been comfortable whenever I serviced Shannon's body sexually for a long period of time. My first time down on his feet was no different.

Shannon lay full-length on the sofa with his head propped on a pillow on one arm of the sofa; his feet crossed, one on top of the other on the back of the sofa where I was sitting at the other end facing him. His feet were face-high to me. It was my first time to see and examine, touch, and to feel, smell, and taste my first pair of male feet. So it was, at age 18, I became enslaved to other men's feet.

The sight of Shannon's feet was erotic and sexually attracting to me. They were strong, and possessed their own kind of dominating magnetism that made me react to them. They excited me—making my heart pound, my mouth water, my own cock grow stiff. They compelled me to touch them, feel and respond to them with exploring hands and face, so I moved in on them.

Ahhhhh . . . the joy I experienced instantly with Shannon's feet was sheer ecstasy. The masculine, raw aroma of their sweating, meaty flesh filled my head, igniting a passion and lust I never had for feet before.

I inhaled and stroked their shape, and began kissing them with a responding adoration for my masterful stepbrother's all-powerful, masculine, athletic feet.

At first, there was no reaction from Shannon as he lay there, deeply engrossed in the game he watched on the TV. His disinterest offended me, yet had an exciting effect on my sexual masochistic psyche that I didn't understand at that age. It was as if I didn't exist to him. I was secondary to his ballgame on TV. Mentally, it was a put-down in reality that I have since grown to know, understand, and need. It was also good in the sense that I was alone with my affections and my new-found sexual discovery for feet.

I drooled with a hunger to taste, driving me insanely greedy for feet. My sexual fetish was reality, and I was—and still am—sexually captivated by man-feet.

It was on that day that I became addicted to Shannon's feet with a homaging, worshipping desire, which made me ejaculate with no assistance, but my excitement for feet.

My tonguing also began to excite Shannon to a stiff erection from this new-found perversion he enjoyed as I sucked his toes, one by one.

By the game's halftime, Shannon was so turned on by my feet licks and sucks, he made me suck his cock. And it didn't take long before he was filling my mouth and throat with another one of his thick, slimy, tasty sperm loads. From that day on, Shannon added his feet to his other enticements to prey on my homosexuality to dominate and control me.

I never knew at the time, but Shannon had told everything about me to his dad. My stepfather favored Shannon over me. He knew his son wasn't a queer. When together alone, they often joked about my mother and me as the weak half of the family. It served their egos that each of them controlled one of us.

One day, when Shannon was out of state, checking out a college for next year, and my mom was working, my stepfather came to my room. He was shirtless and barefooted, wearing only a pair of Levis.

"Ya know, kid, it ain't often you and me ever get to be alone together. I understand you been queerin' Shannon since your mom and I got married," he told me.

I was shocked he knew, and sensed his presence as one with sexual intent. I was scared and afraid of him, yet I was excited by his mature, hard body. He sensed my fear.

"You wouldn't be tryin' to influence my son to be queer, now would ya, boy?" he asked.

"No, sir. I've only done what Shannon makes me do," I answered.

"You're his faggot?" he asked.

"Yes, sir," I answered him.

He unzipped his Levis, and ripped open his fly. He wore no underwear, and exposed his huge man-cock to me.

"See this dick, kid? It was this dick that made Shannon. If it wasn't for this big piece of fuckmeat, you wouldn't have my good-lookin' son to play with," he told me.

He was so strong and powerful-looking. Not at all like my real father looked. I could see the sexual attraction my mother must have for him.

"I take good care of yer mother with this fucker, kid. And I'm your daddy now," he said. "Git yer little fag-ass over here, son! You got plenty of reason to appreciate this dick. On yer knees, boy!" he demanded.

I was scared to do anything, except obey him. I knelt at his naked feet, and lifted his heavy cock with my face. I kissed it for all the reasons he said, and more. I had never had an older, adult man beyond Shannon's age.

My stepfather was all muscle and grit. He had just come home from work, and still reeked with that sweat and masculine B.O. He and his son were physical, both good at giving off those raw-sexual, manly raunch smells.

"Yeahhh, kiss it, boy! Smell, and lick on it like a big, meat lollipop," he teased down at me.

Ohhhh, how I kissed and licked that man. I lapped on his big, meaty dick, and rubbed all over it with my face as he stood, staring down at me, watching and feeling me.

"Ahhhh . . . you little cocksucker. You're hungry for it. Get on it!" he ordered. "Suck me!" he commanded.

I sucked onto my stepfather's cock—my first older, adult cock, a *man's* cock. It was huge, and a real jaw-splitter for me. It was warm and sweaty, and a wild, hard, meaty cock! It filled my mouth with the first half of its length, and I sucked on it.

"Heeyyyy, kid, taste it. You're on a man now. Show me how good you suck, boy," he enticed me. "I wanna feel that mouth . . . I wanna feel it suck on me," he said.

Ohhhh, I bobbed on him, wanting him . . . sucking me a *man's* dick.

"Suck, boy! You need that fucker, just like yer mother does," he intimidated. "You're my queer boy now, kid. You'll never forget my cock, or my body," he told me as I sucked. "You suck good, kid. You deserve big dick . . . and I like gettin' sucked on by my hungry little faggot boy," he excited me with his talk and dick.

Never had I experienced such power, strength, and hugeness all in one man. His cock was so alive and throbbing in my mouth. He was completely different from Shannon.

Shannon was youthful, an Adonis, an athlete with a smooth, well-defined, muscled body I worshipped. His father was mature, rugged and raw, hard, tough-muscled, experienced body. They were the best of each generation . . . they were studs . . . and I belonged to them.

I slurped and sucked on a master's cock. I inhaled him and tasted him, and never wanted to stop sucking him.

"I'm gonna hose you, boy! I'm gonna feed you a man's load," he told me. "Suck for it, boy!" he demanded. "I'm gonna baptize you! I'm gonna feed you my 'fuck,' my slimy sperm, kid!" he told me. "Suck!" he demanded.

His big hand gripped the top of my head, and he wrapped his other hand around the base of his cock.

"Ahhhh . . . eat me, kid!" he moaned as he exploded into my mouth with the thickest, most unbelievably pungent, delicious, creamiest cum ever to fill me . . . so quickly, I couldn't take it all. I opened my mouth wide, and he slid his cock out atop my tongue.

"Uugghhh," I gasped as I swallowed gulp after gulp of his tasty, all-man sperm . . . and still he kept milking more and more of it into me.

"Take it, boy! Ain't nobody cums like me. Eat it all, and you'll always want more of it," he said, looking down at me as he blasted his last over my tongue, teeth and gums. He shoved into my mouthful of cum. "Suck! Clean it off, boy! You're gonna be my fag-boy from now on. Taste yer new ol' man's big, drippin' dick," he told me.

My stepfather was a treasure to me. I remember how, after I sucked his hugh cummer clean and he pulled it from my mouth, I had clung—hugging—to one of his powerful legs. I was a frightened 18-year old boy, and, never having had such a powerful, authoritative adult figure who impressed me so much, he seemed like a giant to me, and so out of place in my small, confined bedroom. I kissed his leg.

"Please," I remember practically begging him, "let me be your son, too. I need a father to love."

I remember almost crying. He reached down, and picked me up off the floor . . . lifting and swinging me with ease, till he held me cradled in his powerful arms, and carried me out of the room.

He took me to his and my mother's bedroom, and laid me on

their bed. He stripped off his Levis, and climbed in bed, beside me, and began to roughly take off my clothes.

"You little bastard. There's somethin' about you bein' so damn willing," he said as he pulled me atop him, and his hands explored my naked body.

I began licking his massive chest, smelling his masculine, sweating flesh and feeling his hard, muscular body with my hands. He excited me, feeling his nakedness against me. He let go of me, and folded his arms behind his head, like Shannon always did, yielding his body to me to explore.

"You want a daddy to love, Damien? OK, boy. But I'm a strict father, and I'll expect ya to be an obedient son," he told me.

"Ahhhh, I will, I will!" I moaned happily as I buried my face into his wild-smelling, wet-soaked, pungent, man-sized armpit. I became wildly excited by its smell, and found myself fucking against his groin with my stiff cock.

I rubbed my face in his pit, getting it wet with his sweat, and began licking it into my mouth. I slid my hands up his huge, rock-hard, bulging, flexed biceps . . . feeling their veined strength.

"Taste and feel me, son. Give yer ol' man a bath," he told me.

Ohhhh, how I licked that man! Smelling and licking his B.O.ed, muscle flesh. I lost myself to his massive, all-male body. I licked his rock-hard body from veined biceps, neck, shoulders, and chest to suck on his nipples.

"You're like yer mother, kid. Ya love this big, man body of mine," he said. "Tell ya what we'll do here," he said as he reached into the drawer of the nightstand beside the bed, and pulled out a tube of something. "Shannon tells me that you like to lick his feet. You wanna lick yer ol' man's big, smelly feet?" he asked.

"Ahhh, yes, I do," I said excitedly, sitting up, straddling his body with his cock stiffly pressing the length of the crack of my ass.

"I want you to turn around, boy, and straddle my hips. I wanna see that nice, pretty boy-butt of yers," he instructed me.

I did what he told me, as he lubed his big dick that I was kneeling directly above. Sliding his feet back, his knees rose before me.

"Grab onto my knees, boy," he instructed as I felt his lubricated fingers lubing the crack of my ass. "Never had me a young boy-ass before," he told me as his finger probed into the opening of my hole.

"Relax, boy . . . yer daddy don't want to hurt you," he told me. "Just gettin' ya all loosened up so ya can sit on my big dick while you bend over and lick my big feet," he told me.

Ohhh, the idea really excited me. He took his time, and worked my ass with probing fingers, talking me into relaxing to the joy of a probing fuck.

Time and effort paid off as his big, greased cock entered me, and he was talking me onto it.

"Ohhh, yeahhh . . . slowly, boy . . . take what you can and relax . . . then take more," he talked me on, filling my ass with minimal pain as I sat on his big throbber. "That's my boy! You're takin' it, kid. Feel that hot cock in you," he enticed me.

I gripped his knees and shoved down, sheathing that huge phallus. Wanting it *all* inside me. It split me open, and pained me for each inch I conquered, until I finally felt his rough, sweaty pubic hair against my ass.

I had it *all* inside me! I sat still on it, letting it swell and settle in my tightness. Slowly, he sat up, his knees falling off to opposite sides.

My hands slid on his hairy lower legs, and gripped around his ankles, as I bent over onto my elbows to accommodate his move.

There they were below me—his big, beautiful feet with the arches of them facing up at me. He sat, resting the weight of his upper body on his extended arms.

"OK, kid. You like lickin' on big, smelly feet . . . go ahead!" he said. "Lick daddy's feet, and fuck on my cock with that pretty boy-ass," he told me.

I'll never forget the experience all my life, and beyond. My young ass filled by his huge man-dick, and that warm, sweating scent of his big man-feet filling my nostrils.

"Ohhhh, daddy . . ." I almost cried from ecstasy never before felt as I pressed my face onto one foot, while my ass moved up his cock.

My stepfather had it all. He was a master of sex, and knew how to manipulate and take who he wanted to get what he wanted.

His cock and feet took me over, driving me insane with passion, lust, and greed. I fell into an ecstatic, wild rhythm—fucking back and forth on his cock as I inhaled his foot odor, and licked at their wild, meaty flesh, tasting the sweat into me.

"Ahhh, yeahhh, fuck on me kid! Lick them big, smelly feet!" he commanded me. "Yer little boy-butt sucks up yer ol' man's dick just like yer mouth did, kid. Only, it's deeper . . . and warmer . . . and loves my meat like a cunt," he told me as I rocked back and forth in loud, greased fucks on his monster cock.

Ohhhh, it was sheer, wild ecstasy plunging my insides with stretching sensations that drove me insane to make passionate love to his big, meaty foot. I rubbed and caressed its huge shape . . . sliding my face over its wide, meaty bottom as I kissed, licked, and slurped . . . and sucked the sweat off it into my mouth.

My new daddy was amazed at me. I was just a cute, 18-year old boy, riding his cock with reckless abandon, as I sucked with wild, queer perversity and worship on his feet. I was far more sexual than he had thought I'd be. A queer boy was turning him on, and he was enjoying it.

"Damn, boy, fuckin' my dick and suckin' my feet . . . you *love* yer daddy and his big, muscled body and raunchy sweat," he enticed, yet teased me too. "Ahhhh, ride me, boy . . . suck on my toes, you sexy little faggot," he taunted me.

He was one big, hot man! With one invading cock that ripped pleasure into me, and tasty toes that filled my mouth with a shape that I couldn't stop sucking on. I couldn't have been more sexually turned on in my entire boyhood than I was at that time. The combined pleasures were beyond description. I was a boy lost to the hugeness of manhood. Lost to my two greatest sexual passions—cock and feet!

My daddy sat, leaning back on his powerful, muscled arms, letting me do it all to him. Ohhhh, that cock up my ass! Those big, beautiful, hunky, sweaty, wild, raw-tasting feet of a man I was loving. I never wanted to ever stop . . . pleasure dominated it all.

My ass sucked his monster meat to surpass the tolerance as his foot succumbed to the sensations of wet, slurping sucks flaying his toe.

He threw his head back, and closed his eyes, and yielded his pleasures to his boy's hot, loving ass.

Thick, creamy sperm flushed my whole insides! Warm, forceful man-cum shooting into every internal channel and void in my ass. I shoved back against him, holding his all inside me as he hosed.

I held his ankles, and buried my face between the meaty bottoms of both his feet, inhaling their sweating sexuality, and moaned my joy while he flooded my insides with fatherly juices of love.

"Ahhhhh, son!" he called me in ecstasy. I kissed his feet in adolescent homage.

PUNK SLUT WORSHIPS FEET AND SNEAKERS

"You're a fuckin' 'punk,' man!" he told me. Then he spit in my face.

"You're dirt . . . you're fuckin'-assed scum. You disgust me and everybody else around here. Ya wanna suck my dick, punk? I got a nice cock you can take in yer mouth. Yeahhh, look at this horny piece of meat, punk. Ya wanna mouth it?" he teased and enticed me.

"Get down on yer back, asshole!" he said, shoving me to the floor.

He straddled me above my chest, with his cock inches from my face. He spit in his hand, and brought it down to my face.

"Lick it off!" he demanded.

Obediently, I licked it off. He then shoved his forefinger into my mouth.

"Suck on it, punk," and I sucked it as he probed inside my mouth with it.

He leaned forward and spit in my face again. I could smell his warm crotch, and knew he hadn't showered all day. He was raunchy, and his B.O. intoxicated me like an aphrodisiac. He pulled his finger from my mouth.

"You like my cock, faggot?" he asked.

"Yes," I answered, inhaling his raw, raunchy crotch.

"Kiss it for me! Yeah, that's it . . . kiss it all over, you cocksuckin' punk. Kiss that meat like you want it. Kiss my balls, and smell that hot meat of mine. You like that, do you?" he asked down at me.

"Ohhhh, yes, yes," I moaned, kissing, breathing and inhaling him into me.

"Would you like my dick in your mouth, punk?" he teased.

"Ohh, yes, yes!" I answered.

"Ya want it bad enough to beg for it?" he asked.

"Ohhh, pleeaasse, I beg of you . . . please let me have you in my mouth. I beg to suck you, blow you, give you good 'head.' Please, make me suck you," I begged him.

"You don't deserve my cock. You know that, don't you? You're a fuckin' faggot, and that makes you scum low-life. You're a 'sissy'! Just a fuckin' punk sissy slut that begs for raunchy, sweaty cock. You better give me good head, you dumb fuckin' bastard. Gimme yer mouth, sissy!"

He grabbed my head in his hands, and straddled over me, on my back. He forced his hot, horny meat into my mouth. He had total control of me as he shoved his cock into me and pulled my head onto it. I had to only smell and inhale up my nose his raw B.O., and taste that wild, round, sweaty, hot meat in my mouth, and I was "there."

Another conquering, hot, sweaty male cock fucking into me, violating my face, taking me. He knows what I am, and he uses me to unleash his hatred. He becomes a human raw-sexual animal that feeds my perversity.

My whole wet mouth and tongue sucks every inch of his sensitive, throbbing, roundness as he controls the rhythm.

"Ohhh, yeahh . . . suck! Taste it, you *fuckin' slut*. Suck dick!" he demanded of me with contempt.

I obeyed with hungry greed and abandoned care. I was lost to my own lusts, sucking on another man's cock, as he verbally raped at my mind and violated my mouth. Soon he was holding my head steady, and pumping his vicious load of cum into me.

"Damn, man! How can you do that? How can you eat another guy's fuckin' sperm?" he asked, shoving my head off his cock.

"Because he's a girl, man. A whore girl in a male's body. Ain't ya, honey?" came the reply from another naked man, walking over to us. "I'll take the fuckin' punk for awhile," he said to his friend, who gladly gave me up and left the room, disgusted with me.

The blond-haired, blue-eyed Adonis stood high above me, straddling my face, his feet on each side of my head with his toes touching my shoulders. I lay on the floor naked, on my back, sprawled out before him. I looked straight up at his firm ass and huge cock hanging down at me over his balls.

27

I could smell his body, and observed the beads of sweat glistening on the blond hairs of his muscled, tanned legs. He was an athletic hunk of a man.

"Like what ya see, girl?" he teased down at me. I didn't like his accusation, but knew to argue or correct him would be fruitless. I reached back, and stroked each of his hard, sweaty calves.

"Yes," I answered with a sudden inhaled gasp at the feel of him.

I turned my head to one side, and kissed the inside of one of his feet. My kiss amused him. Slowly, he lifted his big, smelly, sweaty foot from the floor, and I could feel the calf flex in my hand from the shift of weight onto his other leg. I turned my head, following his foot as he shadowed my face and stepped onto it. With both my hands, I grasped it about the ankle.

"Kiss it, ya fuckin' whore! Or I'll crush that pretty-boy head of yers like a grape!" he demanded.

His foot was heavy and so meaty. I kissed for him to feel as he pressed hard to exert his authority. I inhaled this wild, raw-sweaty, masculine aroma that excited me. And my cock began to grow. He slid the foot off me.

"My smelly feet excite you that much? Or is it me you like?" he asked, with a nonchalance as he eased into a chair close by.

The taste of his feet-sweat was on my lips as I ran my tongue over them. I rolled over on my stomach, and crawled to his feet. I kissed each one of them.

"You!" I answered.

"But you like my feet, too, dontcha, girl?" He seemed to enjoy belittling me. "I mean, my feet are big . . . and must smell pretty raw. Why do you kiss another guy's feet like that?" he asked with a soft voice, somewhat sexy. I inhaled the sweaty aroma from their closeness. They *did* excite me, and my heart pounded.

"They're so big and strong . . ." I began, with some difficulty at getting the words out. I stroked at one foot with my one hand as I held it with the other. "They seem very dominating, like you. When I smell and kiss them, I get all mouth-watering and aroused . . . as if they had power over me. They make me want to lick them . . ." I said, gasping for air, and filling my lungs. I was breathing erratically from smelling and feeling them.

"You wanna go down on my feet, or get fucked, punk?" he asked.

28

"Your feet," I answered.

And he fucked me.

That's right! He came out of that chair, spit on his cock, and roughly violated my ass. I could do nothing, but take the pain and pleasure with moans, groans, and sighs.

Once inside me, and fucking me like a stud, I was begging for his cock. And he delivered like a butt-fucking champ. He filled my ass with cum, then lay full-length atop me on my backside. His head rested against the side of mine. He breathed heavily into my ear.

"You're one tight butt-fuck, girl. And I'm gonna bring that female out of you. You're a cunt! And as long as you hang out around here, I'm gonna prove it to everybody, punk!" he said. He then got up, and left the room.

I hated him.

* * *

I lay in the room, on the floor. I waited. For whom and what, I didn't know. An hour passed, then a third stud entered.

He was 6'5" tall and 210 lbs—lanky, solidly well-built, muscularly-framed, wearing a jockstrap, sneakers, and thick drooping old sweatsocks. He was handsome, with brown hair and green eyes. For being so tall, it was his lanky, agile, long, tapering, muscular frame that made him so beautifully sexy. His shoulders were broad and round, and although his bare chest seemed hard and sunken, it was supported by a massive, strong upper back. His stomach was long, hard, and flat . . . yet accented with abdominal muscles. There was smooth, flat flesh from his navel to his crotch. Part of his pubic hair showed out of the top of the jockstrap, which seemed to be bulging from being over-stuffed with meat and balls, but not clearly visible since he was not yet aroused. His legs were long and sinewy, and very proportionate. His feet had to be size 16 and wide in his huge sneakers.

"You must be the punk everybody's talkin' about. I understand you're into guys, is that right?" he asked, entering the room and sitting down.

"Yes, sir," I answered, drinking in his long, beautiful body with my eyes.

He scooted down in the chair until he sat at its edge, and laid back with his hands behind his head, exposing his body to me. "Come on up here, and kneel between my legs," he said. And I obeyed him. "Now, sit back, and look at this body of mine, and listen to me," he said.

I sat back on my feet, and he lifted one big foot, and set it atop one of my thighs.

"Unlace my sneaker, and give it to me," he instructed, and I obeyed. "Now, get up here where I can reach yer face." I knelt forward, and he grabbed me behind my head with one hand, and shoved the opening of his sneaker over my mouth and nose with his other hand. Instantly, the raw rancid stench of old, worn sneaker filled my nostrils. It was raunch from months of sweating feet.

"Smell it!! Whiff the dirty stink out of my sneaker, baby. Lick and taste that funky raunch from months of my sweatin' feet in 'em! Ohhhh . . . you *love* that scuzzy sneaker. It's dirty, filthy, stinkin' . . . just like your mind is," he said, sliding the back of the sneaker over my chin, and forcing as much of my face into his sneaker as he could.

I licked the dirty raunchiness of the inner sole, thinking of all that sweat from his foot that saturated it for months. The aroma was gagging, raunchy stench that made my eyes water and blood rush my brain with excitement.

"Ohhh, you filthy sneaker-whiffin' asshole faggot. You're the most disgusting human being I've ever met," he sneered with disgust, and tossed his sneaker over the back of his chair. He placed his hands behind his head again.

"Ya like raunch, homo? Lick out my stinkin' fuckin' armpits, ya scum-freak!" he demanded me.

I was turned on by him, his abuse, that sneaker, and his hot body . . . all at once. I buried my face into his wet, wild, smelly, erotic, raw armpit. The sweaty aroma was far more ecstatically intoxicating than his sneaker! I sucked on the hairy, soft flesh, drinking his wetness into me, and swallowing its salty raw taste.

"Ahhh, damn . . . suck it out! Eat my B.O.! Ahhhh . . . lick it out! What a fuckin' filthy bastard you are! *Do it!* Eat stinkin' fuckin' armpit, ya filth-lovin', scum-eatin' faggot!" he abused.

Ohhh, he was right. I *am* a sleaze. And I *loved* smellin' and slurpin' out his B.O. I lapped one armpit clean, and licked across his chest, and into the other. And I ate it out just like the first one.

When I finished, he shoved me off him to sit between his spread legs. He lifted his other sneakered foot to my lap, and I unlaced it wide because I *knew* now what he'd do with it. I slipped it off his foot, and handed it to him. He sat up, grabbed me behind my head, and pressed the opening over my face.

"Lick it out, scuzzball! I want the whole insides cleaned," he said, shoving that dirty, gagging sneaker onto me.

I inhaled and licked at the raunch in them. A couple guys walking past the door had quietly stopped to watch the big guy degrade and belittle me in awe.

"You like dirty, smelly raunch off guys? I'll give ya plenty, asshole. I played basketball all mornin', and I reek with B.O.! And I'm gonna make you lick me clean. Just whiff and taste that sneaker, creep, and you know that it's gonna be a job eatin' my stink! And you and I both know it's exactly what a sleazeball like you really wants. Am I right, faggot?" he asked, pulling away the sneaker and tossing it to the floor.

"Ohhhh, yes. Don't stop, don't ever stop making me lick you! You're hot! You know me perfectly!" I said, rubbing his long powerful thighs with my hands.

I then spotted the other guys at the doorway, just before his big hands grabbed my head and pulled me down, burying my face into his bulging jockstrap.

The aroma of his sweaty, hot crotch and moist, rancid, stained, dirty jockstrap warmed my face and filled my nostrils. And again, the surge rushed my body with erotic excitement for his raunch.

"Lick my dick right through my jockstrap. Let me feel that faggot tongue of yers! Yeah, that's it, lick out my dirty funky jockstrap, homey. I ain't fuckin' washed it in weeks," he chided, making me know what I was licking.

I wetly tongued at the moist pocket that held his manhood inside. I breathed his hot crotch, and couldn't ask for better aroma off any man.

"While you're lickin' my sweaty ol' jockstrap, reach down there and peel off one of my socks, stupid," he instructed. I did what I was told, and handed it over my head to him as I tongued the cotton pouch in his crotch.

He turned the sock inside-out, and slid his hand inside it. He then grabbed my hair, and jerked my head back. He then began wiping my whole face with his sock-covered hand. The moist stink of sweaty sock was euphoric! He held his hand over my mouth and nose, allowing me to inhale its ranky incense.

"Open yer mouth!" he ordered, and stuffed my mouth with his sock-sheathed fingers to suck on.

As I sucked on his rancid sock, he made me remove his other sock from his other foot, and hand it to him. He then turned that sock inside-out, and removing the sock in my mouth, he slid it off his hand. He folded the two socks into a ball, and stuffed as much of them as he could into my mouth.

"Chew 'em!" he demanded.

As I chewed the rancid, raunchy, raw flavor of his feet from the socks, he stood up before me. He fingered the waistband of his jockstrap, and slowly slid it down over his thighs.

Right before my eyes, while I knelt in front of him—my mouth stuffed with his dirty socks—I watched him unveil ten inches of thick, round, flaccid, hot cock. It hung in beautiful erotic dominance over his huge, swollen, tight balls.

He slid off the jockstrap, and replaced his socks with it in my mouth, and he sat back down. I sat between his legs on my feet, chewing his dirty, stained, ranky-tasting jockstrap as it hung from my mouth.

"You're one fuckin' pig-slut, man," he said as he leaned back in the chair, and lifted one of his long, powerful legs high up one side of me to rest atop my shoulders at mid-calf.

"Spit that fuckin' jock outta your mouth!" he said, and then raised his other leg to rest it on my other shoulder.

"You'd make a good footrest for this room, fag. How good are you at lickin' a guy's dirty, sweaty ol' stinky feet?" he asked as he slowly slid one leg back towards him until his huge, size 16 foot was resting atop my shoulder.

"I'm real good. I'd worship you at your feet. Please, I beg to clean your dirty, hot, big feet for you," I said, reaching up and stroking its hugeness.

He lifted it off my shoulder, and pressed it to my face. My hand automatically took him around the ankles to support it for him.

My vision of him, the room, even the guys watching at the door, disappeared from the big meaty sole of his foot covering my face.

I inhaled the sweaty aroma, and pressed my lips to the meaty flesh, kissing it. Ohhh, finally . . . a man who knows how to use me . . . feeds me his feet.

The guys at the door watched in awe as I began licking the huge foot of the good-looking athlete using me as his footstool. And I hoped they were taking note of it for when they'd get around to me.

I wetly tongued his heel, and lapped up the tasty raw sweat off his sole. His foot-flesh yielded its wild, sweaty odor that ignited that sexual hunger in me. I licked at the lengths of his toes, and drove my tongue between them to taste their yields of sweat. Locking my lips around them, one by one, I sucked their lengths with hungry, passionate lust.

"Ya know, I *could* appreciate a sleazy faggot like you. But I don't. I wouldn't let anybody I liked eat out my sneakers, socks, and jockstrap like you did. But you're a punk pervert, and that makes you something to use. Use to suck on my toes, and clean my stinkin' feet with yer mouth. You're a freak, man. A queer! Hey, come on in here, guys, and watch this sleazeball lick my feet," he said.

The guys entered the room to observe closer the action I gave at the big stud's feet. I didn't care. I was "high" on his huge foot, sucking lovingly on his delicious, long, hard toes. One guy, wearing only gym shorts, stripped them from his waist. His cock was hard, and he began milking at it.

"Hey, big guy, I'm horny. Ya care if I jack cum all over that big foot of yers he's lickin'? I'm sure the fag will clean it off for you," he said.

"Go ahead," the big athlete approved. "How about you, buddy?" he asked the second guy.

"Hell, yes," he answered, pulling down his pants, and taking a stand on the other side of me.

The whole scene was wild. As I licked on a big, meaty, size 16 foot of one hot jock, two more were milking their cocks inches from my face.

Soon there was cum all over my face and the foot I worshipped. And I greedily licked and sucked on the slimy, cum-drippin' feet of a man!

"Punk slut!" I heard someone say with disgust.

"SMELL THEM RAUNCHY, FUCKIN' DIRTY OLD SOCKS"

So many times I've been alone. Alone at work with many employees around me, or at singles bars and gay bars with all kinds of people around me. I am good-looking, and I'm in my mid-twenties. My body is hard and I am often cruised socially by both women and men. I socialize, but usually resist romanticism.

I'm lonely because I have homosexual tendencies and desires that make me vulnerable to certain dominating types of men I want and need, but resist because of the danger involved.

I fear sexual male dominance and crave it at the same time.

I'm sexually attracted to the hard, muscular-bodied male who most often has that super ego that accompanies his superbly developed body. Even harder for me is the fact that the ones I become attracted to are usually heterosexual, and I crave that, as well.

So one can understand the sexual predicament and dangers involved of a queer having the hots for a straight hunk tough enough to rip my head off. And that's why I'm lonely a lot.

Oh, I trick at the gay bars for one-night stands. And I enjoy the sex. But I still have my weakness—that craving desire to be *found out* by a straight, male, muscled Adonis who'll take advantage of me and my homosexuality, and use me for his own sexual satisfaction without inflicting bodily harm to me. However, I do crave the mental pleasures of his verbal abuse, such as humiliating and degrading me as inferior to him. I am so alone with only the fantasy of it all. I only look at such men and fear the results of any approaches to them.

It was the middle of the week, and I got off work and didn't want to go home. I stopped for a beer at a mediocre bar.

When I entered, it was full of the usual trades patronage of jock-macho construction workers and laborers. And like such other bars I've been to, I knew I would stay and fantasize over a certain few of them till they would leave.

Sports, women, and work dominated most conversations. I sat quietly and just enjoyed the views. I was alone, again, in a crowd.

At the time, I did not know a pair of eyes was observing me as I observed certain muscular hunks I fantasized over . . . one of them being him.

As the after-work, early-evening crowd began to dwindle to go home to wives, kids, and dinners, I was just beginning to get a slight buzz on.

He took the stool beside me and ordered himself another beer. I could smell the raw aroma of his big, hard-muscled body from the sweat of a day's work. I also felt the heat of his presence, and the rush it made me feel inside. His leg touched mine and didn't move. I didn't react because I liked it against me. I didn't know he was testing me.

He struck up a conversation with me, and he easily dominated my attention with his body. After a half hour, I felt relaxed with him, and had a buzz on that helped overcome my shyness.

He was divorced, an ironworker, a bodybuilder, was 30 years old, and talked about his women friends and sex with them. Occasionally, he'd touch me when making a point, and the touch would send a warm shock wave through my body.

He learned I was single—as he expected I was—and after learning I had my own place, he suggested we pick up some beer and drink cheaper there. I agreed, and we left.

At my place, we talked, had dinner, and somewhere during that time, his shirt came off. And later, drinking beer, he asked me if I wanted him.

I did, and wasn't shocked. I did want him, but I was afraid to ask. I wanted to resist him, but the sight of him excited me. His body preyed on my weakness. I stood there, looking at him, unable to speak.

"That's what I thought," he said, assured that I was queer. He stepped in front of me, and putting his hands atop my shoulders, shoved me down on my knees.

"Hell . . . go for it!" he told me. I reached for his crotch and he grabbed my hands. He lifted them to his hard, rippling, muscled stomach. "Feel!" he said. And with fingers and palms, I felt the hard abdominal muscles of his hard, beautiful belly.

"I want you so bad. I want to please you, worship you . . . and I'm scared," I said with a broken voice, and trembling in my hands as I rubbed his stomach flesh.

"Lick it!" he demanded, and I knelt straight up and licked his belly. "Kiss it!" he ordered, and I obeyed. "Go on . . . feel all up my body and kiss and lick that hard stomach," he enticed me. My arms reached, and hands explored the hard, vast muscles of his upper body. I kissed and licked at his salt-tasty, sweated flesh, and inhaled the raw, masculine aromas of his body. I meshed my wet tongue into his hard navel.

"Mmmm . . ." he moaned, "You like my hard-muscled body, *faggot*? Ya like the taste of my sweaty stomach, do ya?" There was a teasing tone in his voice.

"Ohhhhh, yes . . . yes!" I moaned excitedly, lovingly licking all over the muscled mounds of his abdomen.

"Get down on the floor and lick my boots like a dog!" he demanded. I obeyed him, and began licking his dirty, worn, old workboot.

I had never licked dirt off a man's boot before. And even though I didn't like it, there was a certain thrill to being obedient to such a powerful man.

"You got every reason to be scared of me, homo. You just do what I tell you and we'll get along fine. I *want* to be worshipped by a faggot, and I'll treat you like one, too! Like lickin' the dirt off my boots," he teased at me with abuse. The more he talked, the more I licked at his boot. It *was* worship . . . and I was at his feet, eating the dirt I lapped off his filthy boot like the low-life I wanted to be to him.

Shoving the coffee table up against the front of the sofa, he sat down on the sofa and crossed his legs out across the coffee table so his booted feet hung over the edge.

"Take off my boots!" he ordered, grinning at the sight of a ring of dirt around my mouth from orally cleaning his boots. "I figured I had me a scum-scuzzy faggot when I saw how ya liked starin' at the guys in their dirty work clothes, and closin' your eyes every time you could smell their B.O. whenever one would get close by you. Now I'm gonna give you somethin' really smelly—my dirty, sweaty, stinkin' feet and socks!" he said as I removed the second of his boots.

He was right! I was already feeling the warm, rising, rancid, smelly aroma of his feet and socks at my face.

I reached up and took his feet in my hands, leaned forward, and for the first time, I touched and smelled another man's socked feet. I had no idea, till this moment, the unbelievable joy I was getting from feeling and inhaling the strong, raw-masculine, sweating scent of a man's stinking socks and feet, just unsheathed from his boots.

I moaned my excitement as my eyes and mouth watered from the heated stench, and I pressed my face to them and inhaled.

"Oh, yeah. You like that smell alright. Smell them raunchy, fuckin', dirty ol' socks, homo! Smell 'em and bite into them and taste the sweaty, raunchy-stink," he grinned. "Then chew 'em off my feet," he added.

I had fantasized meeting such a straight male of powerful build who would dominate and abuse me verbally and sexually. But I never fantasized it in quite this way. A straight was teaching a gay a real experience with boots, socks, and his feet that really excited me.

To smell and inhale, chew and taste this muscular Adonis' dirty-greying, filthy, stinking socks was wildly euphoric to me. He must wear them several days at work, sweating under the day's sun as he walked the steel beams of the skyscrapers he builds. Only now he had me down at his feet, chewing that sweating raunch out of those funky socks he wore.

I groveled at his feet like a sub-human, sock-chewin', perverted, low-life scum and fuckin', raunch-eatin' fag-slave. And so willingly, too. I must have chewed, tugged, and pulled at his socks for 20 minutes to get them off his feet with my mouth.

First, I had licked his boots until he allowed me to have an even more thrilling joy at his socks. Now, having enjoyed the socks, I was granted an even greater thrill—to be down to his raw-exposed, naked, hot, sweaty feet. I touched them with hands and face, and inhaled them. It was an erotic pleasure I had never had before, and I was engrossed by their beauty, strength, dominance and aroma. I was enslaved and captivated by them. Feet—they are sexual, and I kissed them.

He laughed at me aloud. He was amused by my perversive willingness to worship his feet. I kissed his toes, one by one. I kissed all up and down his wet, naked feet with exciting admiration and hungry lust.

"Damn, man! You're a sleazy bastard! I never thought you'd lick boot and chew sock . . . or kiss and lick my dirty, sweatin' feet with your mouth like that. But I like it! Yeah, asshole, wash those big, stinky feet of mine with your mouth. And don't forget my toes while you're slurpin' all over my feet," he said, and laughed. "Maaan, I found me somebody who's gross. And I'm gonna take advantage of your sleaze-lovin' talents, asshole. You're gonna clean my whole body with that mouth of yours. And you know why?" he asked me. Ohhhh, I loved sucking his toes, licking his meaty soles and heels. I loved inhaling and tasting his feet. I liked the way he teased, enticed, and made demands of me.

"Why?" I moaned, licking his feet.

"Because I got it all! You hear me, fag? I got it!"

"I got it!" Steve said. "And you want it," he added as he stood before me displaying his hot cock.

"Ahhh, Steve, it's beautiful. I want it. I really do. I'll suck it for you," I told him.

"Would you kiss it?" he asked.

"Ohhhh, yes. Yes!" I answered.

"Would you lick all over it?" he asked.

"Yes, yes," I answered.

"Would ya drink my piss?" he questioned.

"Yes, yes!" I answered.

"Would you swallow my sperm down your fuckin' throat?" he asked.

"Every drop of it," I answered.

"Would ya lick my feet and suck my toes?" he asked.

"Oh, god, no!" I answered.

"Then you don't suck on this cock of mine," he told me.

I went down on the floor and kissed his feet. I licked them, and I sucked on his toes. I only did it because I wanted to suck his cock. Only thing is, when I got to licking those tasty feet of his, I forgot why I was doing it.

SNEAKER SCENE!

*W*ow! I thought as I jogged into the locker room after my work-out. *The whole fucking basketball team must've just left! Sure as hell smells like it—but I missed 'em!* Glancing down the aisles between the metal lockers as I headed for my own at the far end, I saw that I was alone. The distant trickle of water from the bathroom urinals which never stopped and the soft, rubbery thud of my gym sneakers on the hard floor as I trotted along were the only sounds. The locker room was empty all right—but the heavy male smell in the air told of the recent presence of dozens of sweaty young jocks. The familiar fragrance of used jockstraps, T-shirts, and gym shorts, moistened by hard male activity, and sweaty sneakers and tennis shoes, dirty athletic socks, and hot, muscular bodies all mixed together was never really absent, but sometimes it was stronger, fresher, heavier—like then . . .

Shit! I thought, *How I hate Thursdays!* On Thursdays I had classes all morning and into the afternoon, and never made it to the gym until well after three. It was now a little after five, and as usual the locker room was deserted. On every other day of the week I could make it at a time when the shower room would be full of groóvy young studs soaping up their hard, athletic bods, their fascinating cocks and balls swinging free in the wet air. And the locker room would ring with their male voices and loud laughter as they ran around in various mind-boggling states of undress. By three they were already out, swimming, running, playing basketball or handball or tennis, working out in the weight room, etc., and by five the last guy had usually pulled on his snug jeans and left—except me, on Thursdays! At least on Thursdays I could get in and out of the locker room in record time—after all, there was nothing to hold me there . . .

I plopped down on the bench in front of my locker, feeling the sweat running down the groove of my spine. Tugging lightly at the shoulder of the sweat-soaked T-shirt clinging wetly to my skin, I wondered why the hell they didn't air-condition this joint. *They have enough money at this fucking university*, I thought. *But then again*, it occurred to me, *if they did, it might get rid of this great smell!* It was a hot day in the early spring of my Freshman year, and. . . .

I nearly jumped out of my sneakers in shock at the sudden sound of that deep, mocking male voice! Snatching the raunchy strap I had been sniffing down out of the way, I saw a young guy, no older than me, standing in the aisle and grinning at me, his head slightly cocked to one side and thrown back in wry amusement. Well over six feet tall, he stood there like a colossus, with his massive muscle-bound legs spread apart and his hands planted firmly on his narrow hips, his crotch hidden by white gym shorts. Though he was wearing heavy athletic socks with sneakers just like mine, he was naked from the waist up. Glistening wetly in the harsh light, tiny rivers of sweat wound a tortuous way among the ridges and valleys of bulging muscles on their long journey from the broad shoulders down his strong, solid torso. At any other time such a vision of masculinity would have made my cock jump erect in salute, but now I felt it wither in embarrassment. Below a tangled, wind-blown mass of dark blond hair I saw bright blue eyes set in a handsome young face glide down my body and come to rest on my jocked crotch. I knew the distended pouch of my jockstrap was contracting visibly with my quickly fading passion.

Struck dumb and unable to move, I waited as his eyes resumed wandering over my nearly naked body. *How long*, I wondered, *has he been standing there watching me? Shit! I bet he heard me opening the lockers!*

As if he read my thoughts, he spoke again: "What'd you do? Find it left in a locker?" His eyes had come to rest again, this time on my feet. But he glanced at my crotch again, continuing, "You've still got yours on, so I bet you found somebody else's—right?"

"Well, actually, I . . ." I managed, but he interrupted me.

"Don't lie—I heard you going through the lockers back here. I didn't think there was anybody else here right now."

He spoke meditatively, the mocking smile now gone. I saw he was staring at my sneakers, the Jack Purcells, identical to his though smaller in size.

"I heard you come in," I said, "and I was just checking to see if anyone had left anything . . ."

"Shit, man, I saw what you were doing!" Looking up at my face, the wry, mocking expression again spreading across his own, he started tugging at his shorts, pulling them down around his thick thighs and exposing his stuffed and bulging Bike Jock. "And I dig it too, man! I groove on guys and their sexy gear as much as you do!"

I grinned at him in relief, feeling my cock start to stiffen again at the thought of making it with this groovy stud. Leaving his white shorts stretched tightly between his thighs, his hands went back to his slim waist as he thrust his crotch out toward me and said, "How'd you like to smell a *really* smelly jock? I've been wearing this one all week, and it's really hot and sweaty right now—I just got back from jogging five miles!"

"Shit, yeah!" I said, "I'd love it!" With my eyes riveted to that over-stuffed, moist jock of his I went over and knelt down in front of him. The sweaty smell of his hot young crotch assailed me, overwhelming me with a sense of strong, athletic masculinity! I leaned close to the rounded elastic mesh, pulsing and throbbing before my eyes, and sniffed the heavy, virile scent of it good!

"Go on, man!" I heard him say, urging me on, "Lick that sweaty strap of mine! Suck up some of that good male juice! Get a taste of a real jock's crotch!" I needed no urging; eagerly my tongue sought the warm, rank material, stroking and licking up the moisture clinging to it, pushing against his heavy nuts and feeling the hardness of his dick through the tight, confining strap. It was like tasting a whole fucking locker room full of sweaty, sexy young guys!

Wow! I thought, as I licked and sucked and smelled that rank, smelly crotch. *Why the fuck haven't I ever done this before—I've had the chance, damn it!* My hands gripped his thighs as I started to rub my face around on the giant, rounded pouch, smearing his gamy crotch-sweat all over me.

"Oh, shit, man!" he said, suddenly backing away. "Let's take a break. I'm so fucking turned on! I've been getting harder and harder ever since I saw you sniffing that dirty jockstrap!" He reached down and pulled his gym shorts off completely. "Hey, where is it anyway?"

"Right here," I answered, picking it up and handing it to him, "where I dropped it."

"Wow, it's still wet!"

"I know—that's why I was smelling it. I've never done that before—I was curious . . . boy, did *yours* smell great though!"

"Fuck! You don't know what you've been missing! I love to get my nose into sweaty, smelly athletic gear!" He proved his point right then by pressing that raunchy jock to his face and inhaling deeply. "Ahhhhh . . ." he sighed, "Now *this* strap came off a real funky stud! What a randy smell, real sexy and strong! By the way, what's your name? Mine's Steve."

"Doug," I replied.

"How'd you like to smell my sneakers, Doug? They're pretty sweaty right now too!"

"Well, I don't know about that . . . Your crotch is one thing; I really dug that, but . . ."

"Don't you think athletic sneakers are sexy?"

"Oh, yeah, sure!" I answered, "To look at and wear, anyway. But I never tried smelling 'em . . ."

"Man, you don't know what you're missing!" said Steve. "We're both wearing Purcells, too—they're the sexiest ones!"

"I'll tell you what I'd really like to do," I said. "I'd like to suck you off—I know I dig that!"

"O.K.—provided you let me suck you off too!'

"Sure thing! I dig it both ways!"

Steve stepped up to me and, spreading his legs, began rubbing his bulging jock against mine. I started feeling his broad, sweaty chest, grooving on the feeling of his crotch pressed against mine. Then he spoke: "Boy, am I ever hot!" he cried, "I hope you can take the load I'm gonna lay on you! Am I ever gonna pump it!"

"Hah!" I laughed, "That's what they all say! I'll believe it when I taste it!"

"Oh, you don't believe me? Then I'm gonna make you jack me off—I've got a good idea, and besides that way you'll *see* how much spunk I can pump!"

I suddenly regretted having laughed at him, because I really wanted to feel that big, sweaty tool of his unloading in my mouth. "All right, then—but I just *gotta* get your cock in my mouth first, O.K.?"

"O.K., Doug!" he said smiling as he stopped rubbing our jocked crotches together and started feeling me. But he stopped and looked around and said, "Let's hit the john and get into one of the stalls—it'll be safer there."

I agreed, and we set off down the aisle of the locker room, following the sound of those ever-running urinals.

The john at the Indoor Athletic Building was long and narrow. The urinals were against one wall, and opposite them ran the row of toilet stalls, about twelve in all. One of the narrow ends opened to the shower and locker rooms; the other being a dead end. The stalls were unusual in that their sides were actual extensions of the wall itself, extending down to the floor but not to the ceiling. The doors, however, retained the usual gap between door and floor; still, those stalls afforded an unusual degree of privacy, especially the ones at the end, so far from the entrance and little used.

Steve and I went automatically to the last stall, against the dead-end wall, opened the door and went into the small cubicle. As

Steve locked the door, I said, "You told me you really groove on a guy's sweaty gear, but you haven't smelled *my* jock yet!"

"Shit, Doug, I'm gonna smell your whole fucking sexy bod!" he replied, turning and grabbing me. He kissed me passionately, and I felt his tongue probing deeply in my mouth. We squirmed against each other, rubbing our hard, sweaty young bods, dressed only in jocks, sneakers, and socks, roughly together, two muscular young athletes grooving on each other! Our mounded crotches pressed together, I could feel his hard prick against mine, separated only by two moist, sweaty jockstraps. My tongue forced its way into his mouth, and I began tongue-fucking him, sliding it quickly in and out past his lips and preparing his mouth for my raunchy tool!

Finally we broke, panting. Steve lifted one of my arms and buried his nose in my armpit. "Mmmmmm . . ." he moaned, "What a funky smell—I love it! You really worked up a sweat, didn't you . . ."

"Get your nose in my crotch if you want to find out!" I answered, pushing him down to his knees. His face was only inches from my hot strap, and I tensed my crotch again and again, stiffening my prick and making the taut elastic pouch pulse and stretch before his eyes. He sniffed it good all right—even started rubbing his handsome face around on it like I had done to him. Then I saw that he had started licking the foul, wet jock, getting a taste of my heavy male crotch!

Then he rose and sat down on the toilet, the bloated bag of his jockstrap dangling between his muscular legs, and said, "Lemme smell those sexy sneakers of yours! They really turn me on, especially on a stud like you!" I raised a foot and he grabbed it, studying the gym shoe closely. He stroked the warm, moist canvas and ran his hands over the laces and rubber sole before shoving his face down against my sweaty sneaker. I could hear him moaning and sighing in ecstasy as he sniffed and smelled the heavy athletic reek of my tennis shoe. "Oh, shit! What a . . . what a smell! . . . your fucking sneaker . . . really smells . . . so fucking sexy! . . . Shit! Ohhhh . . ."

Finally I said, "Hey, man, get up! I just gotta get into that heavy jock of yours—I'm so fucking hot!"

"You sure as hell are!" he replied, "I can tell by the smell!" But he stood up and I took his place on the stool, as he spread his legs

43

and straddled me, leaning forward with his hands on the wall behind me. That rounded mound hung right in front of my face, as hot and juicy as ever! I felt it good, kneading the lumps of his big balls and sliding my hand under his crotch to where the straps spread out over his ass, fingering his warm, moist crack. He was so hard his cock was pushing the rank pouch out away from his groin, the big cock head caught tightly in the stretched elastic. Unable to wait any longer I yanked the jock to one side, and a massive beam of hard meat, a little longer than my seven inches but a lot thicker, bounced out before me! A strong, sharp odor, fresh and pungent, filled me and I realized how sexy a smell can be! My mind spinning over that heavy, rank male scent, I opened my mouth to taste that tool, but Steve pulled away. "Are you hot enough to want to smell *my* sneakers now?" he asked.

"Well, really, I just don't think that's my scene, Steve. I'm afraid I wouldn't like it—but I sure love the smell of your hot crotch!"

"O.K., that gives me an idea. Lemme get these sneakers off." He untied his moist, sweaty tennis shoes and pulled them off. Leaving one on the floor, he took the other one in his hand and stood facing me. "This is something I really like to do anyway," he said.

With the heel toward his crotch, he lifted the canvas tongue of the sneaker and stuck his long, thick dick, still hard as a rock, up inside! The big balls nestled comfortably into the heel, and then he said: "All right—if you dig the smell of my fucking cock, go ahead and smell it!"

That scene got me really turned on! I did think that Jack Purcell sneakers really *looked* sexy, and the sight of that stud's big cock and balls stuffed into his sexy sneaker nearly drove me wild! With no hesitation I leaned forward and sniffed the giant shaft of male meat disappearing under the canvas. The heavy male odor of his raunchy sneaker mingled with that of his hot, sweaty joint and I found I loved the smell of sneaker and cock! I started licking the hard cock-flesh, grooving on the taste of it and feeling its warmth and firmness. My mouth went around the broad rod as my tongue buried itself in his moist, sweaty pubic hair, licking and tasting the gamy athletic juices! Steve was squirming and moaning, massaging his crotch with the dirty sneaker, which of course also sent waves of rank odors into my face and up my nose . . .

He started pulling the sneaker slowly forward, exposing more and more beefy sausage for me to lick and suck. The strong, virile taste and smell had me so madly turned on I thought I would pass out when he got to the end and the monstrous cock-head jumped up, finally free of the sweaty canvas. Sucking hard, my hungry mouth enveloped it quickly. I felt gobs of sticky, slimy pre-cum juice lubricating my mouth, but Steve pulled back.

"All right, man, now jack me off! Beat that mean meat of mine good, and I'll show you how much spunk I can pump!"

He turned sideways, between my legs where I sat on the toilet and leaned back against the wall of the stall. The full length of his fat cock stuck up and out from his randy crotch, and my right hand went up to it, stroking and feeling the hot flesh. *Shit!* I thought, *if he wants a good hand job, I'll give it to him all right! I'll milk those big fucking balls of his dry! What a sexy jock! And then I'll fuck his mouth good . . .*

I began stroking Steve's big cock slowly, sliding the sweaty sheath of flesh back and forth over the hard rod, watching in fascination as the skin bunched up in the groove just behind the giant head, swelling till it overflowed and spread quickly down over the moist dome, slimy with jockstrap juice and clear sex-fluid. My encircling fingers barely failed to meet my thumb around that fat, hard column. I squeezed tightly, attempting to make thumb touch finger, and Steve groaned sensually, and said, "Yes, man, squeeze it! Ohhh . . . that feels so fucking good! Rub it, Doug, pound it hard and fast! My crotch is full of hot juice just waiting to spurt out! Ohhhh . . . yes! Faster, man, faster! Beat my meat, shit, yeah! Jack me off!" He raised the sneaker he had fucked, which was still in his hand, to his face and started sniffing the heavy odor of the rank, sweaty shoe!

The giant shaft of hard male meat I was gripping tightly and roughly rubbing felt hot and alive in my hand. It pulsed frequently, suddenly growing even more rigid and stiffening, and I could feel the thick tube along the underside swell with each throb. The big, helmet-like head would visibly expand and redden before my eyes as more clear fluid oozed out of the slimy slit, glistening like crystal dew against the shiny red cock-flesh. That hunky young jock obviously had a super-sensitive joint—his huge prick was so highly responsive to the erotic friction of my pounding fist, stiffening and throbbing in frantic passion! *Shit!* I thought.

What a live-wire tool this stud's got! I bet it does spout cum like a fucking geyser! Wish I could get his creamy spunk in my mouth—maybe he'll let me lick off the end after he cums . . .

I was really grooving like mad on that monstrous staff of wild, virile maleness. I licked my lips, remembering the randy jock-taste I had savored and wishing he had let me suck him off so I could taste and swallow his lusty young juice. I could see he really grooved on a good hand job though—his whole bod was as responsive to a jack-off as his dick, squirming and twisting his arched torso, tensing and thrusting under my tight, rapid strokes.

The smells in that close stall were getting heavier by the second —two athletic male bods sweating freely in the warm air, two well-used jockstraps sending out their heavy crotch-reek, the randy cock-odor of two hard pricks, Steve's wet, sweaty sneakers adding their raunchy athletic aroma to mine, still on my feet, the faint odors of piss and sweat lingering in the john from the dozens of sexy young studs there so recently—all combined to send my mind reeling and spinning! My free hand went to his heavy crotch and began pawing and kneading the big, smelly nuts in their tight sac, feeling the wet pouch of his strap nestled to one side, tracing the elastic straps of his jock from where they spread out from his crotch-mound across his firm, rounded ass, running one finger lightly down the crack of that muscular young ass and then poking it deeply into his hot, moist asshole . . .

I could tell that my exploration, added to the pounding friction of my fist, was driving Steve wild with pleasure! I glanced up and saw that he now had his mouth and nose shoved inside his sneaker, and as he twisted and nuzzled the sweaty gym shoe I glimpsed his tongue flicking and darting, licking the rank, randy inside. I thought of the raunchy, masculine, athletic smell filling his nostrils, and my stiff rod throbbed between my legs as I at last turned on to the idea! I released my maleness from the confining strap and, without a break in my pounding rhythm, reached down and grabbed Steve's other sneaker off the floor, eager to inhale its heavy locker-room scent! I remembered the pungent male odor of his tennis shoes when I licked his big cock stuffed inside, and now I couldn't wait to really bury my nose inside!

But I missed my chance then, for just as I was bringing the sexy sneaker to my face Steve gasped and jerked up, and I felt a savage jolt in the big hunk of meat I was rubbing. His hand roughly squeezed my neck, kneading and massaging, and I looked back at his thick, long sex-tool. His whole bod had gone rigid as a rock and his breath came quickly in short, deep gasps. Another pulse followed and the massive red cock-head, slimy and moist and hot, swelled like a balloon as I tightly squeezed the bony beam and quickened my hard strokes.

Suddenly Steve thrust the sneaker he had been licking and smelling directly in front of his enormous throbbing dick, with the rubber toe up and away from it so that the thick shaft was aimed directly inside! I was now rubbing his other sweaty sneaker in my hot crotch, around, over, and under my stiff cock and big balls, and I saw Steve was watching his frantic dong closely. His muscular young bod fiercely jerked like an electric shock had racked it just as the stony column exploded in my hand—and I saw a thick, white stream burst out of the big slit and jet straight into the sneaker with a splash! I stopped rubbing it and began kneading and squeezing the hard, beefy sausage as another fat jet of milky juice shot out. I couldn't believe what I was seeing! This super jock-stud wasn't just spitting out wads of cum; his giant young cock was pumping and spurting it out like a fucking firehose! Thick columns of slimy pale sperm spurted out with each jolt and shot through the heavy air to disappear inside the dirty white sneaker! I could clearly hear each forceful jet strike the moist sole inside his tennis shoe and splash around with a juicy, wet sound.

Gradually the jets of hot white juice grew thinner as I continued to squeeze and milk Steve's big male tool, until only heavy floods of creamy fluid gushed out and fell into the sneaker, instead of being sprayed straight in, and finally the throbbing, jerking rod oozed big blobs of cum which just dropped heavily in the sexy shoe which Steve now held directly under the end. A slimy white rope column led from cock into sneaker as the last of his rich, virile spunk seeped out. At last he broke the sticky rope of cum by wiping the canvas side of the gym shoe against his swollen cock-head.

Then he tipped his cum-filled sneaker a little towards me so I could look inside, saying, ''Look at all that slimy cream, Doug! I told you I could pump a mean load! Go on, smell it too!''

I saw a large pool of heavy pale-white fluid nestled in the heel of the raunchy sneaker, and nearly came off right then! I stuck a finger in the slimy, viscous liquid and felt it—it was thick and dense, and quite warm. The sharp male smell of his hot cum mingled with the sweaty, locker room odor of his sneaker drove me wild with excitement! I couldn't get over the sight and smell of this groovy jock-athlete's heavy white spunk sloshing around inside his funky sneaker!

Steve, still holding the sneaker in front of my face, cried, "C'mon, man! Lemme see you *drink* my fresh hot fuck-juice right out of my fuckin' sneaker! I'm gonna pour my slimy, smelly cum in your mouth and you're gonna *swallow* every fuckin' drop! And lick out my sweaty sneaker till it's clean too! C'mon, open your fuckin' mouth and get ready for my heavy load!"

The strong male smells of sneaker and cum had me so turned on I eagerly replied, "Shit, yeah! Pour it in my mouth, you sexy jock! Pour it *all* in, shit, yeah! I wanna *taste* and *swallow* your hot slimy cum!"

I opened my mouth for the raunchy load as Steve tilted his smelly sneaker over it. I saw the thick, slimy juice spill out of the heel and felt it slowly fill my mouth, still warm from his hot crotch! The funky male taste of young cum overwhelmed me as Steve cried, "That's it, Doug! Taste my creamy juice and swallow it! Oh, *shit*, what a sight! Now lick out my sneaker; get it *all!* Don't miss a drop!" He shoved his athletic sneaker in my face as I gulped down the smelly white slime, and I started licking the moist, sticky inside of the sexy canvas madly, eager to taste more of this groovy young jock's sexy juices!

Sweat and cum mingled in my mouth and rank athletic odors filled my nose as I buried my face inside Steve's warm, wet sneaker, licking and sucking up the heavy mixed fluids of his hot young bod. Wild with excitement I chewed madly on the wet, sweaty canvas and nuzzled that funky sneaker of his as my own cock, stiff and hard as a crowbar, pulsed and bobbed up and down all by itself—if I had so much as touched it I would have blasted white juice all over that fucking stall! Steve was rubbing it around on my face hard, saying, "I told you there's nothing like the smell of a fresh, hot sneaker! I knew you'd dig that heavy athletic aroma just like me! That's it—smell it good and lick it clean!"

"Gimme your hot sweaty crotch, man!" I cried, pushing the sneaker, now sucked nearly dry, out of the way and grabbing his lean muscular hips. I pulled him to me, my mouth instantly swallowing his big, half-hard sausage all the way down to the root, its length sliding comfortably right down into my throat! My arms went around his firm ass, hugging him tightly to me as my lips ground against his firm, tight groin and his curly crotch-hair scratched my nose and eyes. I could feel the elastic pouch of his jock, warm and moist, against one side of my mouth as he grabbed my head, dropping the sneaker. We squirmed against each other for what seemed like an eternity, but it couldn't have been, because I was unable to breathe with that giant hunk of fuckmeat hanging down my throat, swelling up and starting to stiffen again! Finally, nearly choking from lack of air, I managed to force myself back against those strong, gripping hands and gasped again and again, inhaling the raunchy male aroma of that sexy stud-crotch. I sucked hard on the big, plum-like cock-head, feeling the last of his heavy, wet cum ooze out of the slimy slit into my thirsty mouth!

Only when no more juice seemed forthcoming did I release that thick, meaty sextool of his, only to lunge down on those big smelly bull-balls of his hanging under the bony beam of the rod, licking, smelling, sucking like mad! My mouth found the moist jockpouch nestled alongside all that heavy male equipment, and I ate it into my mouth, chewing on it and gnawing out the randy athletic juices to taste and swallow. I was quite literally out of my mind over the strong male tastes and smells of that hunky athletic stud! My face buried in his hot juicy crotch, I licked and sucked and ate like a madman, till Steve pushed me away, saying, "Hey, Doug, take it easy! I want you to blow your wad down my throat, not all over my legs! Look at that cock of yours jerking like it's about to juice. . . . C'mon, man—it's time for you to fuck my face!" he finished, grinning down at me.

"Shit, yeah!" I cried, "I can't wait to pump it to you! I've never been this hot and horny before!" But before standing up, I grabbed the straps of his jock and pulled it down over his now-hard dick, saying, "But gimme this jock of yours to chew on while I'm gettin' my rocks off!" Stepping out of his jockstrap, he knelt in front of me as I grabbed his other sneaker, the "uncleaned" one, with one hand while stuffing the ripe, gamy jockpouch into my mouth with the other, and stood up. And to think that only a short time before I had hesitantly, tentatively, gingerly . . . *sniffed* a fresh ripe jock—but that was before I met Steve! Now I was practically *eating* one—and not just any old used jock, but a raunchy, rank, gamy, strong, funky athletic strap fresh and hot off a sweaty jock-stud's juicy crotch! Before I met Steve, the idea of getting even a whiff of a guy's smelly sneakers would have turned me off—now I had my nose buried deep inside one of Steve's warm, moist sneakers (the one he didn't "use" before), grooving on that unique athletic aroma, strong and pungent!

The straps of Steve's jock dangling obscenely from my working mouth, I took his sneaker from my face for a moment and glanced down at the big hunk of muscular masculinity kneeling in front of my throbbing crotch, and saw that Steve was busily untying the laces of the Jack Purcells I was wearing. I knew what he wanted, and lifted one foot so he could get my sneaker off. As though afraid some of the randy fumes might escape him, he quickly slapped the moist canvas shoe over his mouth and nose while with his free hand he yanked the lace from the holes, pulling up the tongue so he could get his handsome jock-face more deeply inside my funky sneak! He gasped and moaned as the muscles across the broad, tanned shoulders, wet and shiny with sweat, rippled below me. Then he removed my other sneaker and worked on both, going from one to the other, licking and sniffing, groaning and grooving like mad!

Taking his jockstrap from my mouth, I said, "Hey, man! Let's have that hot suckin' mouth of yours! My crotch is so full of cum it's gonna explode any second!"

Dropping one sneaker, he slipped the other all the way down on his stiff prick and stared at the hot pulsing meat jutting out from my hairy, sweaty crotch straight toward his face. The whole circumcised head was wet with pre-cum slime and a big clear droplet swelled at the slit on the end. His tongue darted out quickly, licking it up, and in between the quick, rapid strokes of his tongue on my massive, slimy cockhead that followed, he muttered, "Oh, yeah, man . . . screw my face . . . fuck my mouth good . . . shit, what a great cock . . . oh, yeah . . . ram that hot meat down my throat . . . spew that hot slimy sperm . . .yeah, down my throat . . .shoot your load down my gullet . . . fill me up with thick hot spunk, man . . . oh, shit, I want it!"

Steve's jock was back in my mouth, and suddenly my cock was deep in his mouth! I gasped at the warm, moist pressure on my throbbing tool and began driving it in deeper. I felt a resistance as my cockhead hit the back of his mouth, but kept pushing as Steve squirmed below me, till suddenly I slipped in all the way, my cock sliding right down into his throat! I began pumping my hips, driving my big hard fuckmeat in and out of his mouth, slamming my crotch hard against his sexy face again and again with each savage thrust. Steve was now fucking my sneaker, sliding it up and down on his dick while his free hand slipped up between my legs to stroke my thrusting, pumping ass, urging me on faster and faster. Still chewing and sucking on his raunchy jockstrap, I shut my eyes, lifted his funky sneaker to my nose once again, and leaned forward with one hand on the john door supporting me. Nobody had ever deep-throated me before, and it felt great! The hard-driving, fast-fucking action continued until suddenly a vicious spasm seized my crotch and I rammed into him harder than ever, feeling a hot wetness rushing down the massive, rigid length of my cock to explode out the end in a massive burst of thick hot slime spurting fiercely straight down his throat! Giant wads of heavy, creamy fluid gushed out my madly jerking, pulsing cock as it swelled and pumped, swelled and pumped, swelled and pumped! Steve pulled back to take some of the juicy wet gobs in his mouth while my whole rigid bod jerked with each wild contraction in my tight, hard crotch, my sexy dick spitting thick jets of white slime into him again and again. . . .

To make a long story short, he drained my fucking balls dry! Swallowed it all—every fucking drop of my thick spermy semen streaming down his thirsty throat! I thought I'd never get him off my already softening cock—he kept sucking and sucking. And then I found that my sneaker—the one he had been fucking while I balled his mouth—was full of warm, slimy juice! Needless to say, I had him lick it out for me after removing the laces completely—eating his own hot cum out of *my* funky sneaker!

After a good bit more heavy kissing and clutching of each other's hard, sweaty bods, we finally left that stall, our jockstraps once again cupping our heavy athletic crotches (his now clean!) and wearing nothing else but white sweatsox. Our sexy sneakers, having been very well used in *every* way that day, dangled from our hands as we raced back to the locker room.

I bet that for days afterwards, strange, strong odors continued to assail anyone who happened to make use of that last stall in the locker room john!

* * *

This scene happened in the spring of my Freshman year. It's completely true, just as I have written it down. I remember everything that happened in detail, since it was one of the wildest, most fantastic scenes I ever got into, and it opened me to a whole new turn-on, a whole new dimension of possibilities in sex! Ever since Steve flipped me out on his big "trip," I've known it's also one of mine—among many!

Unfortunately, Steve was a senior, and graduated the next June. He went to grad school on the west coast, and I only got to see him a couple of times after that. At present I haven't seen him in nearly four years, though we still keep in touch. He's a lawyer in San Francisco now, and if anything, wilder than ever. He's gotten into piss in a big way the last few years, really digs fist-fucking a lot—both ways—and still grooves like mad on sneakers, of course!

Needless to say, we made it several times more that spring, before he graduated, though not again in the locker room, though we were often there together. Usually we made it in his room—as a senior, he had a single—and a couple of times in mine. I remember a lot from those scenes, but not as clearly as that first one we had, and sometimes the details blur together so I'm not sure what happened when. We got into some *wild* scenes together —centering around athletic gear, and especially sneakers, of course! He used to say that while he had been able to get some other guys into the scene some, he had never found anybody who was as wild about it as I was.

I remember one day we decided to really go all out. After a long, hard workout at the gym and a run, we didn't shower or change, but went straight to his room. I had already brought over all my gear, and we got all of his out—sweaty, smelly athletic T-shirts, sweatshirts, gymshorts, jockstraps, and of course, sneakers. He had eleven pairs, including a couple of hi-top Converse basketball sneaks, deck shoes and several tennies, and a couple of football shoes, as well as three pairs of the Jack Purcells, his—and at the time, my—favorites. One was brand new, one pair really old and beat-up, and the third medium—the pair he had been wearing the day we met. In comparison, I had only six pairs—football cleats, a pair of white Keds, two hi-top basketball sneaks (one white Converse), and two pairs of Jack Purcells—all of which I still have. (Steve says he still has all of his too—and that he now has over sixty pairs, more than twice as many as me!)

Anyway, we spread out all our combined gear, and purposely we hadn't cum off in days. Shit, we were at it for hours! We got high on grass and beer, and did everything we had ever done, and everything we would ever do together! I remember that I came four times, and his big stud-cock blasted out five big loads of hot jock-spunk! I know I sucked him off the first time, because I wanted that first and biggest load to spurt in my mouth. Later he jacked off with my jock-strap over my open mouth and shot the juice into it, and another load went up my ass; he came all over several sneakers and then watched as I licked 'em all clean, sucking up every fucking blob, and I think it was his second load that he shot into one of my Jack Purcells as I did the same, and we took turns drinking out our mingled cum! (Another time when we were together we made a point of filling up a sneaker with our spunk—a total of seven loads from both of us—man, was *that* sneaker ever a sexy sight when we got through with it!) I fucked both his mouth and his ass that day, and also had him eat my cum out of a jockstrap I shot it into. After our initial scene, we kept changing sneakers and gear (unfortunately Steve couldn't wear my sneaks, and his were too big for me), grooving like mad on each other and all that funky athletic stuff.

One of our favorite things was fucking—either way—with the fucker licking and smelling the sneaks on the guy he was screwing, while the fuckee, covered with smelly jocks and surrounded by funky sneakers, sniffed the fucker's sneakers, still warm and moist from his feet, and licked 'em out! Sometimes the fuckee would cum all over a sneaker, or into his jockstrap if he had it on, while being fucked, and then the fucker had the additional pleasure of eating the other's warm, slimy fuckspunk out of jock or sneak!

We usually arranged to make it together after a workout, so we'd be hot and sweaty, and the gear we had been wearing would be fresh, warm, and moist. Then we'd finish by taking a shower together—easy, since Harvard provided students with private baths—always a great deal of fun, even though we had already managed to pretty much clean up each other's bods . . . with our tongues! But our gear rarely got washed—especially our jocks, which always got washed out pretty good in each other's mouths!

Even though neither of us was as heavy into sweatsox as some other stuff, I do remember once that we took one of Steve's fresh, moist socks and had some fun with it. First I slipped it down over his big thick jock-cock like a rubber, and jacked him off into it. Then I took it off and put it on my dick—the toe was pretty wet, but there was still a lot of liquid cum inside—and Steve beat *me* off into it, mixing *my* hot creamy spunk with *his* in his funky, sweaty athletic sock! Then we took turns sucking on that raunchy, cum-laden sock, while the other cleaned up the sucker's cock with his mouth, back and forth, until both cocks and the sweatsock were clean and dry! I really got off on that scene, and that's one I've never been able to make again with anyone. . . .

Of course, no matter what we were doing, we always had a pair of sexy sneakers on. Once, I remember, we even took a shower together still wearing our sneaks! Another time, when we slept together, we kept our sneakers on all night. And going down on each other's sneakered feet 69-style was always a big favorite. We often traded sneakers for a while, so we could groove on each other's sexy athletic shoes in hot jack-off sessions between scenes, and the same went for jocks, T-shirts, etc.

All in all, we had a great time that spring! While I've gotten into ''sneaker scenes'' many times since with other studs, I've never again run into anyone quite like Steve—a guy who was both (1) completely wild and uninhibited, versatile and capable of going at it for hours, cumming again and again, and (2) super-handsome and sexy, hunky and muscular, and hung with a prize-winning hunk of male meat with two big jockpouch-filling bull-balls that churn out lots of rich, tasty male spunk! Sure, there have been some who came up to Steve in one way, and some who matched him in the other—but never both. That spring we were two wild, horny jock-studs, a couple of cumpumpin', cocksuckin', ass-fuckin', jocksniffin', crotchlickin', sneakersmellin', sweatdrinkin', bodylickin' sneakerfreaks!!

TOE-JOB

I'm just a country boy, and live in the backwoods of Arkansas. Y'all call it the Ozarks, but to me, it's home. I live in a cabin, and do my bathin' in a tub out back.

The guys hereabouts know me best for my love for sweatin' male body and hard cock. Fact is, I'm a pig when it comes to raunchy, hot country boys who are horny. There's the Dodson twins, Kip and Henry from across the creek, Jason, Carl and Zeb from Seven Fountains . . . and my favorite buddy, Larry, who I just can't get enough of.

Anyway, ol' Larry always seems to show up when least expected . . . and always hot, horny, and raunchy.

Understand me now . . . ain't none of these guys *queer* like me. But they do love gettin' blowed, and fuckin' my young ass.

Ol' Larry knows me best, though. He came walkin' outta the woods in his longjohns and barefooted . . . with one of those mornin' hard-ons . . . and expectin' ta be taken care of, ya know? He walked right up to me in my bathtub and told me ta give him some suck. Well, there ain't no cock in the country that I love in my mouth better'n Larry's. And y'all know I sucked onta his bone like there ain't no tomorrow.

Damned if he ain't got the best, raw-raunchiest piece of meat I ever sucked on. Now, if y'all have ever sucked dick, ya know where I'm comin' from . . . havin' a guy's cock in yer mouth who you really like. Well, ol' Larry puts me right there!

"You cocksuckin' pig," he says. "I gotta piss!" he tells me.

"Mmmm . . ." I moan, slurpin' on his raw-sweaty, delicious manmeat. I think of Larry and his hot cock in my mouth. I think of the warm, wet piss I want to drink that is his. And as easily as is told me, his dick erupts inside my suckin' mouth.

"Drink it, you fuckin' fag!" he tells me. And I'm there, swallowin' Larry's hot-sexy stud-piss into me.

He pulls from my mouth, piss all a squirtin' all over my face and down my body. His yellow jetstream pisses into my bathwater.

"Ahhhh," I shrill in ecstasy. "Piss on me, Larry," I beg him. Layin' back in my tub, he pisses all over me, and I love it.

Larry knows me. I'm a queer he pisses on. I'm a filthy, raunchy, sub-human fag to him. To piss on me is to humiliate and degrade me as a low-life. But to be pissed on by Larry is an honor to me.

Again, he pissed on my face, grabbed me by the head, and pulled me to him and shoved his stiff pisser back in my mouth.

"Drink it, toilet mouth!" he demanded, sendin' the last of his piss down my guzzlin' throat. "Now blow me!" he ordered, and again I was suckin' on his fuckmeat.

"Ahhhh . . . you love my dick," he told me as he fucked into my suckin' mouth. I fondled his balls, and inhaled his sweaty-smellin', raw, hot crotch odor as my mouth slid wetly back and forth on his stiff, round, meaty dick.

"Ohhh, yeah . . . taste that fucker! That's *meat*, man!" Larry teased and enticed. "My meat in yer mouth. Blow it, fag! Gimme *suck* . . . lots and lots of *suck*," he wooed sexually. "Ohhh, I love that wet-suckin' fag mouth of yers on my dick," he told me. "Just keep doin' that, homey. It feels real good gettin' sucked off by a dick-hungry, queer-pig like you," he said.

Ohhhh, how I liked the way Larry talked to me. I have always loved Larry's hot meat, and as he stood there beside my tub in his longjohns, watchin' and feelin' my mouth wetly slidin' on his cock, Larry's body was sweatin' in the late morning sun. I could smell his body aroma as I tasted his cock. His sweat soaked his longjohns as he felt wet trickles of sweat roll down his flesh from his armpits and ass. He was a raw, sweat-raunchy lean-built, muscled, B.O.-reekin' stud in heat . . . gettin' himself some *head*.

His cock was swelled so thick and round in my mouth as I loudly sucked my squish-smackin', wet-strokes along its length. The wild, raw taste of his meaty cock kept my own cock stiffly excited deep in the pissy bathwater I sat in.

We were two raunchy country boys gettin' it on.

Larry's body was beginnin' to flex with every muscle to the rhythmic joy of my mouth on his cock. His load boiled and rumbled deep inside him. I sensed his approachin' climax, and sucked greedily on his stiff bone. Larry was always a good hoser. He was that lean-bodied stud with heavy balls with a big load.

"Ahhhh . . . eat me, you cocksucker!" he commanded, shovin' into my mouth and eruptin' into my gulpin' throat. Blasts of his thick, creamy cum began fillin' my mouth. Instant excitement flushed my whole body as my own hands splashed beneath the water to grip my own eruptin' cock.

I am so addicted to the raw-starchy taste of Larry's cum. I swallowed his tasty sperm into me as he pumped blast after blast of the stud-slime into me. His cock throbbed with sensation as he fucked his load into my meat-hungry mouth. The loud squish-smackin' sucks of mouth on slippery, cum-coated, stiff throbber gave added joy to his ego as he fed me his slimy fuck.

My own sperm erupted into my bathwater in equally excitin' blasts. I swallowed him all into me till he ended his climax. Then I spent those glorious minutes rubbin' my face all over his beautiful, flaccid, swingin' meat . . . a lickin' and a cleanin' it off for him.

When I finished lickin' his manmeat clean, Larry stripped off his sweat-soaked longjohns. He stood handsome in all his naked glory before me. His upper body was hairless, and it glistened in a sheen of his sweat. He stood lanky and lean, and well-muscled.

"Man, it's hot!" he said. Then, he sat at one end of the tub opposite me, swung his legs up till his feet rested atop each of my shoulders, then lowered himself into my tub with his arms. He now sat across from me—restin' his arms atop the sides—facin' me. He grinned as he stared into my eyes.

"That was good *head*," he told me as he brought one of his feet down off my shoulder to rest flat against my pec below it, and rested the side of his bent leg against the side of the tub. "Did y'all like that cum of mine, homey?" he asked.

"Ohhhh, man, did I?" I told him. "I love blowin' you, Larry. I can't get enough of yer fuck in me," I said. He beamed with pride and grinned again.

"Water feels good. I was sweatin' heavy in them longjohns," he told me.

"Oh, I know . . . but I sure liked the smell of you while suckin' you off," I said to him. He grinned again.

"Y'all like sweat-raunchy guys, dontcha?" he asked.

"You, I do," I answered. Again, he grinned. I was servin' his ego and he liked it.

Call it ESP, if you will, but I suddenly sensed what Larry was thinkin'. Surely it was the sight he was seein' before him. That of one of his big, dirty feet restin' on one of my shoulders and one on my chest. Then there's that straight image and ego he liked havin' served.

I reached up out of the water and gripped the ankle of the foot on my chest. He grinned again.

"Speakin' of y'all likin' my raunchy body," he spoke ornery-like. "Can't be a part of me more sweaty, smelly and raunchy as my feet right now. Ya like my feet, do ya?" he asked, grinnin' at me. He slid the foot on my shoulder up onto my face, pressin' the dirty, meaty bottom to it. "Kiss it, homey! Kiss my dirty, stinkin' foot for me," he said.

"Ohhhh, Larry, Larry," I moaned, at the feel and raw smell of it. I brought my other hand out of the water and gripped its ankle. I began kissin' the dirty, meaty sole of his foot. The whole thing was so erotic, so sexual.

"Maaan, ya never cease to amaze me," he said with a disgusted tone in his voice. "You are a *pervert*, man! Yer a pig!" he jeered at me. He moved his foot, slidin' his spread toes over my nose, forcin' it between them.

"Smell, you fucker! Get fuckin' *high* on my stinkin', sweaty feet, you pig!" he demanded.

I had never smelled or kissed, or ever tasted another guy's feet. But I *was* high on 'em. I was inhalin' his raw-sweaty foot aroma, and loved it.

The thought of this whole raunch scene was a turn-on to me. I mean, here was Larry and me sittin' in a tub of bathwater that he's pissed in and I cummed in, and I'm smellin' and kissin' all over his dirty, stinkin', raw-sweaty foot. This was truly hillbilly heaven for me! And I hope it never stops!

"Lick it, ya foot-freak," Larry ordered me. I began lickin' and felt my cock gettin' excited again underwater. I also felt a warm rush in the water and realized Larry was pissin' again. I couldn't help myself and allowed my own growin' cock to join in by pissin' underwater, too, as I tasted his delicious wild foot. I lapped dirt and tangy, salty sweat into my mouth. The taste seemed to ignite more hunger in me. This was a whole new experience for me.

Larry's feet were sexual, and I was gettin' into lickin' 'em.

We were both hosin' in the tub water with our warm piss that passed through our excited, hard cocks with a tinglin' sensation, like it always does after you'd just cummed a little bit earlier. And Larry felt a different sensation all over the bottom of his foot at the same time—my wet, lickin' tongue against his meaty-fleshed sole.

"Ahhhh . . . gobble on my feet, you queer turkey!" he teased at me. As I licked at his foot, slidin' over my face, I felt Larry's other foot slide down me into the pissy bathwater. And slowly, he began bringin' his wet, drippin' foot up out of the water and spreadin' the wetness over my chest.

I had both my hands around the ankle of the foot on my face, and as I licked, tasted, and smelled at his stinkin', wet, sweaty foot, he kept dippin' his other foot into that pissy water and rubbin' it all over my upper body.

"Hey, you cocksuckin' piss freak . . . I wanna toe job!" Larry demanded, jerkin' his foot free of my grip and off my face. "Suck on my toes like ya did on my dick," he told me as he splashed the foot off my face into the bathwater. Pissy water sprayed all over both of us. His other foot rested on its heel at the top of my stomach at the waterline, his toes drippin' wetly before my face. I sucked down onto the big toe, instantly tastin' the raunchy, pissy flesh.

"Mmmm . . ." I moaned down its length. The toe was salty-tastin', hard, and meaty. I flushed its length with my spit, and sucked the juiciness down my throat. His sweat and piss was raunch-tangy tastin' as I swallowed it with my spit. I found it erotic and sexually excitin' to suck on. His feet were beautiful to look at so closely as I sucked toe. I stroked its hugeness, feelin' its strength and masculine shape.

He was so right. I am a pig. I suddenly realized I'm into suckin' toes and lickin' feet.

"Ohhh, god . . . I love feet," I moaned excitedly as I pop-sucked off his toe and kissed it. I sucked back down on it.

"Them's stud feet, baby! Mine! Queer 'em, ya raunch-lovin' faggot!" he abused and enticed me. I bobbed up and down on it, goin' for the crusty deposits of sweat encaked around its toenail. One piece broke out and was inhaled down my throat and swallowed into me. My cock ached with excitement.

Why had I never discovered this hunger for feet before? The more I sucked and tasted one toe, the more I wanted the others. And Larry, too, was enjoyin' this new-found experience. He pressed the other foot against my cock, pinnin' its hardness between the heel and sole of his foot and my stomach beneath the water.

"Hard again over me. Yer really gettin' excited over my feet, aintcha, baby?" he asked as I lapped between his toes, then sucked onto another. My hips moved up against the pressure of his other foot . . . tryin' to get a rhythmic fuckin' excitement for my throbbin' cock.

"I'm sure glad I discovered y'all bein' a fag-ass queer, ya know?" he said. "I mean, there ain't no country woman in these parts that is a filthy, raunch-lovin' low-life when it comes to sex with a guy the way you are. Fact is, I couldn't find myself treatin' a woman the way I do you," he talked as I sucked his wild toes. My body was on fire as I established a rhythmic grindin' fuck against his big, sexy, meaty foot in the water.

"Ahhhh, Larry," I moaned, grabbin' the other huge foot I was toe-suckin', and lifted it to my face. I kissed at the fleshy meat of its sole. "I worship you!" I told him excitedly. "Yer the man, the stud . . . the greatest body I've ever had," I moaned, and licked at his one foot while I fucked against the other. The warm water splashed about us as I lusted greedily at his feet.

"Do it, man!" Larry demanded, realizin' I was lost to his feet. "Suck and fuck my dirty feet," he demanded enticingly. "Them's big, raunchy, *man's* feet!" he told me, grindin' them into my face and cock.

"Ahhhh . . . Larry . . ." I groaned ecstatically. The excitement was wild sensations totally over his feet.

"Feel 'em . . . taste 'em . . . you bitch-fuckin', feet-lovin', faggot-assed queer!" he abused sexily.

"Ohhhh . . ." I gasped as my cock exploded at his foot beneath the water, the water burnin' my cock slit as cum oozed out in long, ropey strands floatin' in the water.

Wildly, I licked at his foot. Never have I ever yielded to the sexual dominance and beauty of any man's feet before. Big, strong, sexy feet.

"Ahhhh," I sighed as the last of my heavy load spurted into the murky bathwater. I began kissin' at his foot with uncontrollable passion and appreciation. "Ohhhh, I love yer feet!" I moaned passionately.

"I know, fucker," he said calmly. "There ain't nothin' ya don't like about my body," he said, grinnin'.

"GET YER FAG-ASS DOWN THERE AND LICK MY FEET"

It was a hot, humid summer afternoon, and I lay on the river bank, watching the boats speed by, and other people swimming.

It was the place where I could watch the guys, and fantasize over their sweat-glistening, muscular bodies without suspect of my homosexuality. It was also the place where all of them were barefoot.

You see, I have this thing about guys' feet . . . a sexual fetish, you know? I mean, it really turns me on to stare, and fantasize goin' down on some of these hunky guys' big, strong, meaty feet I see here at the river. I guess you wouldn't understand it unless you were queer, and had the fetish. Unfortunately, I have met no one in my small hometown who does.

I am 19, and I have never had another guy sexually. For five years now, I have masturbated my way through many fantasies, and had just about every good-looking guy in this town . . . mentally.

Right now, I'm probably the most frustrated gay in the whole world. What's worse is I lie here on my stomach, atop my towel, with my chin resting atop my folded arms. And just thirty feet away from me stands Marc.

Marc is home from college for the summer. He got a scholarship at State when he became all-state quarterback in high school last year. Marc has one of the most perfect bodies I've ever seen in my life.

As he talked to some other hunk, I was starin' at two pairs of the sexiest feet on the river. My cock was hard as a rock, aching inside my swim trunks as I lay atop it. A bead of sweat trickled down my forehead as my mind registered sexual attraction to the beauty of Marc's big feet.

Ohhhh, how I wanted to crawl that thirty feet to them. I wanted to touch them . . . feel them with my face and hands. My cock ached so hard, I had to reach under me to tug open the top of my trunks. As I raised my ass slightly, I let my cock pop out, free of its captivity. I lay back down on it, pinning it against my stomach and towel.

I had taken my eyes off Marc's feet for the moment, and when

I looked again, there—just two feet away—were those big, beautiful feet.

"Whattya say, Craig? I ain't seen ya since I got back home," Marc said as he sat down, leaving those feet of his crossed, one atop the other, not far from me.

I stared at them, my mind spinning in a thousand thoughts. I was mesmerized . . . no, *entranced* by his feet.

"Craig, you OK?"

His voice brought me back to reality.

"Marc," I responded, finally looking up at him, into that handsome face and sexy, blue eyes. "I'm sorry, I was lost in thought. Welcome home," I said, then asked how college was.

Marc sat, telling me about college, and many times my eyes gazed upon those feet of his as he talked. About ten minutes passed by while he talked, when suddenly one of his feet came sliding toward me, and he rested his toes on my arm.

"Craig . . ." he said, "if I didn't know better, I'd swear you haven't heard a word I've said. You just keep starin' at my feet. You got something for feet, man?"

With my other hand, I touched his foot as I stared at it.

"Heyyy, maaan, what the fuck ya doin'?" he asked, pulling his foot away. "Ahh . . . Craig," he said, looking around to see if anybody saw what I did. He looked into my eyes. "Not you, buddy. You're not . . . ahhhh, man," he sighed in a tone of realization that meant he knew. "Fuck, say something, will ya?" he said, seeing the hurt in my expression.

"I'm scared, Marc. I've been fighting it some, but right now I'm the most frustrated teenager in the world. I've had no one to talk to about it. I shouldn't have touched you, Marc. I'm goin' crazy. I want a guy so bad . . . and if this town found out about me . . . well . . . I don't know . . . probably they'd beat the hell outta me," I said.

"Damn, buddy," he said, staring deep into my eyes, "don't panic, and give me a couple minutes here, OK? You just laid one heavy trip on me, ya know? Does anybody know?"

Tears filled my eyes, but I fought them. I shook my head "no."

"C'mon, let's go somewhere and talk," he suggested.

"I can't move," I told him.

"Why? I mean . . . ohhhh . . ." he caught on suddenly. "You're excited! You're lying on a hard!" he guessed.

"Yes," I said.

"And I caused it!" he said. "Ohhh, maaan! Look, eh . . . why don't I meet you at my car. I'm parked by the bridge. When 'it' goes down, we'll take a ride," he said, standing up.

"Look, Craig, if it's any consolation at all, there's someone in this town who's just like you. I know 'cause he's been down on me. I promised him I'd never tell anybody, and I haven't. I can call him for you," he said, shocking me.

"Who is he?" I asked.

"Hey, you wouldn't want me tellin' on you, would ya?" he asked.

"No," I answered.

"Tell ya what . . . we'll talk first," he winked, and walked away. My heart pounded, and I pondered if Marc was going to let me go down on him.

"Damn!" I cussed. How in the hell was my cock going to go down thinking about it?

It was almost a half hour before I made it to Marc's car. I climbed in, beside him, and my cock grew instantly hard at the sight of him.

Marc slowly maneuvered the car through the narrow dirt road of the old strip mines, and parked among the trees.

"Nobody gonna bother us here, Craig. What say we take a blanket with us to a clearing over there, and lay out for some rays while we talk," he said, climbing out of the car, not waiting for an answer. Once the blanket was down, Marc stripped off his swim trunks, and stood before me.

"There ain't much we're going to be able to talk about until you let out all that emotion you got pent up inside you, Craig. I ain't queer, like you, but I ain't beyond lettin' a guy turn me on, ya know?" he told me as he sat down on the blanket. I removed my trunks and stood, staring down at his beautiful, naked body.

The difference in our sexuality was obvious. I had a stiff, excited hard-on, and he laid himself out on the blanket with his thick six inches of flaccid, limp cock lying atop his thigh. He rested his head atop his folded arms, posing his hard, muscular, athletic physique to me. Then he raised one leg, and pressed his big, meaty foot against my throbbing cock, pinning it against my groin.

Ohhhh, I closed my eyes, and stroked at his foot with both my hands.

"Ahhhh, Marc . . ." I moaned.

"Yeah, Craig. I hear ya, buddy. You got something for feet, dontcha? You couldn't take yer eyes off 'em back at the river," he said as he dug his strong toes into the flesh of my cock.

"Ohhhh, with very little effort, I could cum all over your foot right now," I warned him as I held it against my cock and groin, fucking against its meaty bottom.

"Maaan . . . I ain't ever had this experience before, but I'm game for it. Of course, you understand, Craig, that if you cum all over that foot of mine, I'd expect you to clean it off afterwards," he said.

"Ohhhh, I will Marc. I'll get down and lick your feet for hours . . . I'll worship them!" I told him.

"Damn, Craig, I've had me lots of ladies, and even a couple of guys sexually, but all of 'em wanted my body and my cock. Ain't nobody ever wanted my feet, man. And, maaan, them feet of mine gotta be dirty and all raunch-smellin' sweaty, ya know?" he told me.

"Ohhhh . . . Marc, Marc . . . you hot . . . fuckin' stud!" I squealed as my cock erupted all up my belly, and on the bottom of his foot and toes. "Ohhhhh . . ." I moaned in sheer, wild ecstasy as my warm, thick cum poured out of me, and flowed all over my groin, cock, and Marc's wild sexy foot.

"Ahhhh, fuck!" Marc said, surprised. He shoved his foot up my cock and wiggled his toes as my cum squish-smacked loudly between his foot and me.

Cum oozed between his toes, and down the top of his foot, and onto my hands. He was smearing it all over me and his foot, as I unloaded even more of it with my biggest load ever.

There was a certain raunchy eroticism about it that fed into Marc's ego as he slid his foot up and down my slippery, slimy cock, and feeling the warm, thick jism oozing all over the sole and between his toes. I was rubbing the sperm that dripped onto my hands all up and down the top of his foot.

"Ahhh, maaan, you are *wild* . . . different . . . crazy . . . a sleazy, fuckin' pervert!" he told me, jerking his foot away.

He brought his leg down, and crossed the cum-dripping, glistening foot atop his other one. He propped himself up on his elbows and stared at his sperm-coated foot as he wiggled his toes, and listened to my cum squish between them.

I was staring down at the chiseled, hairless, flexing muscles of his beautiful body. He never looked up at me.

"I don't know about you, Craig," he said with a tone of suspect. "Get yer fag-ass down there and lick my feet, you bastard. I wanna see you eat yer own cum, and that dirt and sweat of mine. Now!" he demanded, with a total change of character. His tough talk really turned me on.

"Yes, sir!" I answered like a slave, sinking to my knees, then lying down at his feet. I pressed my face to his big, sexy feet, thrusting my nose between two of his toes.

"Ohhhhh . . ." I moaned in sheer ecstasy as the raw smells of cum, sweat, and B.O. filled my nostrils. I wasted no time slurping at the taste of them all.

"You're a sleaze, Craig. You ain't just queer for guys, you're queer for raunchy guys, ain't ya?" he said.

"Ahhhh, Marc . . . yes, and you're the first man I've ever had. I'm so turned on to you and your body, and to your feet," I told him as I slurped my tongue between his toes.

"Yeah? You're queer for me, and like me raunchy? You worship me dirty, dontcha?" he pursued, liking my tonguing on his toes.

"Ohhhh . . . I'm slave to you, Marc," I moaned, and slurped between two more of his toes.

"Yeah, it makes sense, and I think I'm gonna enjoy this, Craig," he said as he lay, watching and feeling me queer at his feet.

I was feeding his ego by feasting on his feet. Here was an ol' high school chum, lying at his feet in the hot sun, licking the raunchy sweat from between his toes. The guy was really perverted and queer for him. The whole experience was nasty and wrong, yet exciting and different. Marc's cock was stiff, and his body glistened with sweat.

"I'm gettin' excited by this, Craig. I'm raunchy, and I like my feet bein' smelled and licked like that. C'mon, you queer-assed faggot, suck on ol' Marc's toes and show me how much you really appreciate what I'm doin' for you," he demanded.

"Ohhhh . . . yes . . . yes," I moaned, and sucked onto his rugged big toe. "Mmmm . . ." What taste . . . what wild, erotic, exciting joy it was.

"Yeah, that's it, baby . . . suck on that fucker and taste the man you like. That's 'jock feet' you're suckin' on, Craig. *My* feet, baby," he enticed me as I blew on his toe.

Ohhh, his talk had me so turned on. His feet-smell, too. I whirled my tongue around it, inside my mouth, while I sucked its hard, rugged length. Ohhhh, how many times I dreamed and fantasized sucking, kissing, and licking Marc's feet and toes. And now I was *really* doing it.

"You're a foot-freak, Craig!" he told me. "C'mon . . . suck my toes, man! All ten of 'em, one by one, baby. Eat what ya smell down there," he teased and encouraged me.

I guess my fetish really was odd and different to Marc. It was also interesting in a sorta dirty, sexually erotic, ego-serving way that made him feel superior to me. Marc is an athlete, a jock with all that pride and ego over his body, and sexual power that women wanted.

I sucked off his big toe, and sucked onto the next one. I had cleaned one, and now the second had all that raw, tasty, sweating flesh to suck off all over again. It was a taste of B.O., distinctly only of a man, just like its aroma was. I licked and sucked its length wet and hard, and I never felt so excited and hungry as I did right now.

Marc felt the wetness, the suck, the tongue sliding along the sensitive sides of his toe. "Damn, it felt good getting a toe job. But how could Craig be so queer perverted for feet like that, when everybody I've ever had was always after my cock first," Marc wondered. "But then again," Marc thought, "here Craig was coming out of his closet by getting me. And at the right time, too, for the sleaze he was. He was queerin' the best jock in town, and it made sense that it be by worship at my feet first."

"You sleazy, fuckin' low-life," Marc called me as I sucked onto his third tasty toe to eat more of his raw sweat. "Worship me like a slave at my feet, Craig. Get nasty fuckin' mouthy on them big, sweaty fuckers. You *love* my feet, Craig . . . you're queer for 'em because they're the best 'jock feet' in town! C'mon, you hungry, raunch-lovin', toe-suckin' foot-freak . . . suck them sweaty toes of mine," he intimidated me. "There's somethin' about all this, Craig. Somethin' that's makin' me feel wicked about you," he said.

Ohhhh, I sucked onto his fourth toe, slurping its tangy man-taste into me. My cock had never gone soft after I had cummed onto his foot. Marc excited me that much.

His handsome face . . . his smooth, hard, all-muscle, athlete's body . . . his big, sexy feet . . . and his raw, sweating, wild-tasting B.O. dominated me. His dirty verbal abuse was exciting, and just as dominating as his feet.

I was inferior to him, I was queer for him, I wanted to be the low-life slave I've always fantasized being to such a jock.

Mmmm, I slurped onto his smallest toe, and lapped the tasty raunch into me, swallowing it forever.

Marc recrossed his feet, and I went right to work, sucking onto his other big toe. I tongued all under the huge pad of it as I felt the hard nail and knuckle of his toe slide along the roof of my mouth. Marc watched, and felt my queer mouth wetly suck on it. My toe job was having its effect on him as his huge cock throbbed in full-hard heat against his rippled, flat stomach.

I closed my eyes to all that male beauty that excited me even more. I wanted to lick, smell, and make love to every inch of his hot, sexy feet before he began tempting me to the rest of his body.

Again, I cleaned another big toe, and went onto the second. Now I was thinking of rubbing my face all over the sweaty, meaty bottoms of them, whiffing the smell and licking his B.O. from them. I sucked off the second, and onto the third toe, and swallowed more tasty raunch.

The sun beat down on our naked bodies, and sweat poured from our pores. Marc still lay propped up on his elbows, pondering Craig's perversion for his feet. He watched, awed by the whole experience.

"Damn, Craig, you make me want to be dirty, man! You doin' this makes me wanna degrade and humiliate you, and make you my fuckin' queer slave," he told me with a jeering tone in his voice.

The comment was positively intriguing and exciting to me. I sucked both his smallest toes into my mouth, driving my tongue between them inside my mouth.

"Ohhh, yeahhh, you like the idea, dontcha, toe-sucker? Look up here, Craig," he said. "Look at this hard, sweaty fuckin' body, baby! Whatta ya see, buddy fag of mine?" he teased down at me, looking up his body, into his eyes.

"Ohhhh, Marc . . ." I moaned lustfully as I kissed the bottom of his top-most foot, just below the toes, gazing over the top of it. "I've beat my meat hundreds of times at the thought of you. I wanna lick your dirty feet, worship you any way you wanna make me. Oh, god, I want to be a dirty, low-life pervert," I moaned, pressing my face against the meaty bottoms of both his feet. "Ohhh, Marc, Marc!" I groaned at the wild, raw feet-stink that filled my nostrils and made my head spin with wild sexual greed I couldn't control. My mouth drooled wet spittle onto his already wet, sweaty, fleshy, meaty sole and heel. My face was actually smacking loudly on his wet feet. I was licking them like a greedy pig. It was all my dreams and fantasies come true.

"Ahhh . . . yeahhh, it feels weird, man, but I like it. I never knew I was that sensitive on the bottoms of my feet," Marc said. "Hey, Craig. Who's got the best fuckin' feet in town, man?" he asked me, shoving his feet hard on my face.

"Ohhhh . . . they're on my face . . . Marc. I *love* your feet. I'll lick them for hours for you," I spoke with my mouth squashed against his wild, sexy, wet, smelly, tasty feet.

"You fucker! I'm fuckin' horny from all this toe-suck and feet-lickin'. Get yer ass up here, man, and suck on my dick!" he demanded. He spread his legs, and I crawled my way up between them. "Ahhhh . . . get it in yer mouth . . . hurry," he said.

Ohhh, his cock was big, thick, long, round, and hard . . . and I wanted it! I grabbed it, and sucked onto it, hungrily and greedily.

"Ahhhh, yeahhh . . . yeahhh . . . suck me, Craig! Ohhhh . . . you're a natural, buddy. You *need* that fucker," he moaned as I slowly tasted, and slid up and down with cautious, loving mouth. I didn't want to scrape his hot, tasty meat with my teeth.

Ohhhh, sucking cock was more than I ever imagined. The smell of crotch was beyond anything I had ever imagined. I ran one hand up his rippling waves of stomach muscles. Everything about him was hard, B.O.ed, wet, and so masculinely dominating.

I lay on my side, and relaxed against his leg. I wanted to suck Marc as slow and long as I could, hoping to give him the best cock-suck he ever had. Marc calmed down from what came close to becoming a quick climax. But now, the slow suck he was getting, with my hand rubbing on his stomach, calmed him to the time-less joy of *head*. He realized he had a virgin queer mouth on his cock. A friend he never knew was queer.

Man, what was all this? Craig was worshipping him, doing wild pleasing things to his feet and cock. Marc watched the guy who helped him through high school suck on his dick. And it felt good, too. Marc wiggled his toes. The thought of Craig having sucked them and licked all over them for him; and now, rubbing on his belly and sucking his cock with nothing, but true honest, sexual affection to please him as a queer.

"Ohhh, Craig, I do love gettin' sucked, man. And you're doin' fine, baby. You got me thinkin' some wild things about all this. I ain't had many queers, man, but I got me this feeling of not sharin' you with anybody. Ohhhh . . ." his speech was interrupted by my mouth somehow tantilizing a nerve . . . a sensitive spot on his cock. "You fucker, you're askin' for a load, suckin' like that!" The subject had changed.

I wanted his load now. His body, his voice, his wild-smelling crotch and big, throbbing cock had me turned on. I picked up the pace, stroking and sucking me a stud's cock.

"Alrighhtt! Go for it, baby! Suck!" he cried out.

Ohhhh, what hot, raw meat-cock he had. I was going to be a good cocksucker . . . I really loved it. He lifted one of his big feet up, and rested it atop my ass. The thought and feel of it drove me insane to suck on his dick.

"Ahhhhh, you . . . cock . . . suckin', fuckin' . . . queer. Take my load!" Marc moaned as he grabbed me hard behind my head with his strong hand, and held me down on him while he exploded into my throat.

Ohhhh, no . . . I swallowed and gulped Marc's starchy-tasting, thick, creamy sperm into me. More and more, he shot into me my first load of another man's cum. Ahhhh . . . this was the ultimate gift of being what I was.

BUTT-LICKIN' ASSHOLE!

Closer . . . it moved toward me . . . he was going to sit on my face!

"Ohhhh . . ." I moaned at the sight of his round, firm buns. Closer he came towards me, and I could smell the raw, masculine sweat of its flesh. He's a hunk with a tight, firm butt.

"Eat my ass!" he commands, sitting on my face.

So many hot male asses I've breathed into me, smelling their natural-raw, sweating man-raunch. My nose and mouth were buried in the crack of his ass.

It excites me to kiss a guy's ass . . . and tongue the length of his crack . . . tasting him.

He loves the feel of wet tongue licking the sensitive flesh of his hole, and presses against my face, wanting more of the sensations I bring him. I spread his firm cheeks with my hands, and lap wildly at his hot hole. "Ahhhh . . . lick it, you butt-lickin' asshole!" he moans in ecstasy. His hole is so flesh-sweaty tasting, and I lap his manly raunch into my mouth. "Ohhhh, you bitch! Suck it out! Eat my hole . . ." He moans at my wet, probing, hot tongue. "Don't stop . . . don't ever stop," he tells me. I don't want to stop!

I can't get enough of his smooth, slimy hole that yields me so much raw, fleshy sweat. His aroma is so sexually *male* and erotic, so intoxicating that it drives me wild with hunger. His hand wraps around his now stiff, excited cock. Stroking it only adds to the joy I bring to him at his super-sensitive hole. He realizes my passion for ass . . . my hunger . . . my need.

"Ohhhh, yeahhh . . . lick that fuckin' hole, you faggot! Ya like my butt, do ya? Pig out on it . . . suck it!" he began to entice and dominate me. My fingers gripped the firm, fleshy mounds of his buttocks, squeezing and spreading them apart. The crevice between them was warm against my face as I lapped the beads of sweat that clung to the hair and delicious raw flesh. My wet tongue awakened the flesh and ignited every sensitive sexual hot-spot a man's hole has. His flesh and ass muscles flexed and quivered, the joy of my oral worship upon them.

I closed my eyes and got so into licking and sucking on that smooth, sensitive orifice of his all-man ass. Greedily wanting more and more of the sensation of tongue and suck, he sat harder, smotheringly at my mouth. When I tongued a super-sensitive spot, his body would jerk away, then return for more in one quick motion.

"Ohhh, you fucker!" he'd gasp at such a moment. "Eat butt!" he'd demand, shoving back on me. "Clean my hole good. Smell it, and taste it!" he'd instruct as he fisted his cock with intense stroking. "Get that fag tongue inside me, ya butt-suckin' bastard," he told me. I pressed at his manly hole with all the strength of my tongue. He was tight for a moment, then relaxed it to my loving mouth.

"Ahhhhh, yeahh . . ." he moaned at my tongue's entry into his asshole. I went into the opening a half inch, and his whole butt quivered and tightened around it. "Ahhhh . . ." he shrilled with wild ecstasy. He relaxed again, and shoved back for more.

Another quarter inch of my wet tongue entered him. He could feel my warm breath against his flesh and hole. I pressed into him another quarter inch, now having an inch of wet, warm tongue up his ass. The sexual, erotic ecstasy of my action brought a sensual, light dizziness to his head.

His cock throbbed to his erratically jacking hand, and his whole ass quivered in sensations he found too much to control. His cock erupted with wild, turbulent forces that began sending long, ropey strands of his wild, spunky load into the air, which came splashing down onto my stomach. Warm, slimy splashes of his sperm wetting my abdomen.

"Ohhhhh . . . ohhh . . . ohhhhh," he moaned out each of his eruptions of manly stud-cum onto my lower body.

When his climax subsided, he knelt up, pulling from my face and popping his ass off my tongue. He then stood up rather slowly and spent.

"Ah, man," he said in a disgusted tone as he turned around and stood straddling over my body at my hips.

Ken was a hunk of a man, and stood in all his naked 6'2" tall, solid-hard, 185 pounds of beautiful male body above me. His huge, half-hard cock hung out from his muscular body, dripping with his glistening, thick cum.

"Now look what you made me go and do with yer perverted rimming and reaming," he said to me, with his hands resting on his narrow hips, as he stared down at me on my back on the floor. "Ain't no fag-ass queer gonna make me waste my sperm like that. You hear me, bitch?" he asked as he lifted one of his big feet and stepped it on my cum-coated stomach.

"Yes, sir," I answered him as I felt the foot sliding through his own slimy cum on my belly. The flesh-meaty foot squish-smacked loudly as he slid over the lumpy abdominal muscles of my stomach.

"You got a nice, hard belly there, homey," he told me. "A little slimy-wet, though," he said, grinning down at me with an ornery look in his eyes. Instantly, my cock began to rise with excitement at the thought that he was going to step on my face with his cum-coated foot.

"Ohh, Ken," is all I could say with premature anticipation.

"You know you gotta eat my load, dontcha?" he asked and informed me . . . without the grin.

"I want to," I said, breathing somewhat erratically. I have a sexual fetish for strong, male feet. And Ken had such feet. They were big feet that were strong and meaty . . . veined on top . . . with big, strong toes with toenails that seemed to be pressed into the flesh at the tips of them. Ken knew of my fetish, and he knew he had the man-feet that turned me on.

He also knew how to tease and aggravate me with them to a point of begging him to have them.

"Did ya like my butt?" he asked, grinning again. He continued sliding his foot on my belly.

"Ohhh, you know I did," I answered. I closed my eyes and gripped his foot around the ankle with both my hands as it stroked my stomach.

"Ya know," he said, "any guy who would kiss, and lick, and suck on another guy's sweaty butt has gotta be a real *raunch-lovin'*, *low-life faggot*. You a raunch-lovin' faggot, are ya?" he asked teasingly.

"Ahhh, Ken," I sighed excitedly, "when it comes to you, I am." I envisioned his feet in my mind, as he raised his foot and stepped on my throbbing cock, pinning it to my stomach. "Ohhh," I shrilled in a high, sighing pitch. The cum was becoming dried on my belly and his foot. "Ohhh, please, Ken," I began to beg. "I want your *feet!*" I yelled the last word loudly.

"I know," he said calmly as he foot-jacked my cock against my belly. "Yer a real pervert, man!" he abused down at me. "You stick yer fag-ass tongue in my asshole one minute, and you wanna lick my fuckin' feet the next. Just what the fuck are you anyway?" he jeered at me.

"Oh, god, I'm a pig! I'm a homo . . . a fag . . . a fuckin' queer who worships you," I answered with wild excitement. "Please . . . please, I'm beggin' ya for your feet!" I pleaded. I was hot and horny, and losing all control to him. But still, he wouldn't bring it up to my face. He sat down in a Lazy-Boy recliner chair and shoved back on it till his feet hung out over its foot rest about 2½ feet from the floor.

"Get up here and sit at my feet," he told me. I sat up at the foot of the recliner, and reached for his beautiful feet before me.

"Don't touch my feet, asshole! Just look at 'em close," he demanded. If I was to get his feet, I knew I had to obey. Ken was being ornery and was going to rape at my mind by teasing and enticing me with these big, beautiful man-feet . . . just inches away from my face. He wiggled his toes purposely, and grinned enjoyingly at the wanting, excited expression on my face as I stared at his feet.

"You willing to be slave to me for my feet, baby?" he asked sexily.

"Ahhh, yes, yes, Ken," I agreed. "I'll do anything you ask," I told him. He smiled, knowing I would.

"Good, you little foot-sissy," he teased, "kiss each foot once, and go get me a few beers outta the icebox. If yer gonna service my feet, then I'll need some beer to drink while you work."

I kissed each of his feet on its sole, and quickly went to fetch the beer. The aroma of his feet floated inside my nostrils and kept me excited for those hot, sexy feet of his. My cock bobbed hard as I walked back from the kitchen with a cold six-pack for him.

He took the beer, and he slid his feet back, his leg rising, bent at the knee, and rested the foot flat atop the foot of the recliner. It exposed the strong, veined top and his toes to me as I sat back down on the floor. His other foot remained extended over the edge, its bottom of toes, sole, and heel facing me. I stared at the beauty of his feet before me as I fondled at my excited, hard meat in my lap.

"Look at 'em, man!" he told me as he popped open the hissing top of a beer.

"It's hot in here, ya know? And my feet gotta be sweatin' as bad as I am right now," he said. He raised one of his arms and turned his face toward his own armpit to take a purposeful whiff to make his point. "Whew-eee!" he exclaimed. "I'm gettin' raunch-smelly in here," he said, looking down at me as he lowered his arm. He grinned ornerily again at me. "Can you smell my feet from there?" he asked.

"Yes, and I love it," I answered him. He laughed aloud.

"Fuck! A pig-ass, foot-freak faggot would," he said. He spread his toes wide on the foot closest to my face. I could see the muscle flex at his calf as he did so. Ken had powerful, strong, long,

73

sinewy legs. "Stick yer nose in between those toes and get yerself a closer whiff," he told me.

I leaned forward and slid my nose deep between two of his toes, and inhaled deeply. The scent was unbelievably intoxicating and erotic. He relaxed the foot and let his toes squeeze my nose tightly between them. His raw-masculine, sweaty foot odor filled my nostrils.

"Whiff it, you sissy! Smell that raw-raunchy body odor. That's feet-stink, man! Yer smellin' the stink off my dirty, sweatin', cumcrusted, raw-naked foot, baby. You like my feet-stink, do ya?" he asked, lifting his beer to his mouth. My heart was pounding, and my cock throbbed excitedly in my stroking fist. With my nose pinched between his toes, I sounded like someone with a deviated septum.

"Ohhhh," I moaned with *lightened intoxication* in my whole head. "You smell like a man," I told him. He lowered his beer and stared at me whiffing the aroma from between his toes.

"Yeah . . . and you eat smell. Yer filth, man! Kiss my feet like the low-life foot slave you are, bitch," he demanded.

I took his foot in my free hand and stroked at it as I passionately began kissing all over its meaty shape. I pulled my nose from between his toes and kissed down his smelly, cum-crusted, meaty sole. As I kissed at his foot, Ken picked up the phone and dialed it. I loved kissing and smelling his big, sexy foot.

"Hey, buddy, how ya doin'?" he spoke into the phone. I kissed slowly across the bottom of his toes. I then leaned towards his other foot and kissed along the tops of its toes. "Just sittin' around drinkin' a beer and gettin' my feet kissed by a fag," he told the party on the other end of the line. I licked up the strong veins along the top of his huge, athletic foot, and around the side onto his ankle.

"Yeah, he's a cute little jock, well-built and hard. But a real pervert, ya know?" he said into the phone, then drank his beer. I lost all control and began licking at the ankle and top of his foot. The smelly-raw flesh yielded a wild, sweat-salty taste that was every bit as delicious to me as his smell.

"Fuck, no. He's a pig for raunch. He's so *high* on my B.O. now, he's lickin' the dirt and sweat and stink off one of my feet like a dog doin' it to a bone!" he told his buddy, as I swallowed a huge gob of my own saliva mixed with the sweat and grime off his manfoot.

"Oh, no . . . this asshole does it all," he conversed. "He's a body-licker who lingers a lot longer at my armpits, asshole, my balls and my dick, and at my feet," he laughed to his friend on the phone. Ken slid his foot forward till the toes hung out over the recliner's edge. I sucked onto two of his toes and began slushing at them with wet, swirling tongue.

"Ohhh . . . that feels good. He just began givin' me a toe job. The guy's really sissy for other guy's feet," he told his friend.

The conversation between Ken and his friend went on for a half hour about other things that didn't pertain to me. But during that time, both of his big, hunky feet became my personal possessions. I inhaled and kissed, licked and sucked, massaged and rubbed them in sexual homage. All while he drank his beers and talked to his friend on the telephone.

Ken was a stud in whom dominance, arrogance, ego, manipulation, and self-pride were all natural traits of character. My role in his lifestyle was that of exactly what I was to him—a queer that was good-looking and built well enough to be acceptable to service him and his body. And even then, I was accepted because of my lustful, bizarre, homosexual perversions he didn't get physically from his female companions. Our relationship is a simple one—I am a secret queer in his life he uses when he wants the perversions.

His friend on the phone will never know me. He said his "goodbye" and hung up the phone. His feet glistened in my wet spit. The dirt and grime, sweat and dried cum were gone. I had licked and sucked his man-raunchy feet clean. All of it was inside me.

"Well, asshole, have ya had enough of my feet for awhile?" he asked. I licked off the meaty bottom of one of his feet.

"Ohhh, I could lick your feet forever," I told him, rubbing both his feet, now crossed one atop the other. He grinned down at me, our eyes staring into each other's.

"Okay, homo! What the hell. I got a few more calls to make," he told me. I began licking his feet.

* * *

I cannot get yesterday out of my mind. Nor can I think of anything else, other than Danny and the sex we had. What happened to me? Why did I do it? Am I queer?

All I know is that I want to do it again.

I remember how I was working on my bike in the garage, which is separate from our house, and on the alley behind our property. He said, "Hello," and startled me. He was 18, same age as me, but I never seen him before. He wore a T-shirt, Levi cutoffs, and sneakers. I was wearing my school athletic shorts and sneakers. "My name's Danny, what's yours?" he asked, smiling.

"Todd," I answered, standing up and wiping my hands on a rag.

"I was just walking up your alley and couldn't help admiring your bike. And you," he added.

"Me?! Why?" I asked him. He smiled at me.

"Well, you're hardly an ugly guy," he explained. "You ever had sex with a guy?" he asked. A thousand thoughts and feelings went through my mind, and one reaction was a hard-on.

And before I knew what was happening, Danny was on his knees before me, had my shorts down, and was sucking my cock. And in a few wild, glorious minutes in his mouth, I was cumming down his throat like I've never cummed before.

Minutes after my climax, and under Danny's influence, I was on my knees in front of him. His cutoffs no longer on him, I remember him guiding me onto his throbbing, hard cock with his hand on my head. The smell and first taste of a male's cock in my mouth was as exciting to me as when his mouth was on mine.

Sucking it seemed to come natural to me, and I enjoyed what I was doing. My hands explored his thighs, hips, and firm ass, and up under the front of his T-shirt to caress his flat stomach. I sucked slowly, at first, enjoying the roundness and length of his cock as I tasted it. I knew I liked his cock in my mouth.

After a while of sucking him, I wanted his cum like he took mine. I began wetly stroking his cock with the rhythm of my mouth and hand at a faster pace.

Soon it happened! And Danny introduced me to a male's load of cum in such a way that I could enjoy its eroticism. He splashed into my throat to swallow, pulled back and splashed my mouth, splashed my teeth and gums, then finished by splashing my face with his warm, thick, tasty cum. He held his stiff, cum-dripping dick at my face to lick his delicious, tasty sperm off it. I really went wild cleaning him off, and eating his sperm.

We closed the garage door, and got naked. We kissed and explored each other's body with stroking hands.

Then he had me sit on my bike and got down on his knees on the garage floor below me. He began biting at my ass, then kissing and licking it. I laid back, and fisting my cock, enjoyed the wild sensations he was bringing to my whole butt.

I've had sex with maybe two girls since I reached puberty. And I thought it was good. But now, what Danny has done to me, has brought me sex that was a hundred times better! Ohhh, nobody has ever licked my butt like Danny was doing for the first time for me. My ass was so sensitive and sensitized. My cock throbbed with excitement. Danny was teaching me sensations I never knew before. He began licking up my crack, and I went wild. His warm breath and licking, wet tongue . . . his nipping bites on my fleshy butt felt so unexpectedly good to me.

I slid forward into his face, wanting more of his butt-licking joy on my virgin ass. I spread my legs wider, and his tongue found my quivering, excited hole.

Ohhh, how I begged him not to stop. Danny wasn't about to. He really turned-on to tonguing my asshole. It must be the queer equivalent to eating pussy on a girl because I now know what was on his mind as he lovingly tongued my hole. I moaned at his wet attack on my ass. I couldn't take much more of the sensational ecstasy he was giving me. I jacked at my cock and told him I was going to cum. That only made him lap at my hole more.

When his tongue entered my hole, that was it! I cummed my second hot load all over my chest and stomach. And when it was over, he was up between my legs, licking up and swallowing my cum off my chest, stomach, and stiff cock.

Danny really loved eating my cum, and went wild licking my second load off my body. As he sucked my cum clean off my cock, I felt his finger slide wetly into my ass. It stung for a moment as it entered, but felt good after that.

He later stood up in all his naked beauty with one wild hard-on. He instructed me to lie on my stomach atop my bike, helping me get comfortable.

"I gotta fuck that beautiful, hot ass of yours," he told me as he straddled the bike behind me. He spit on his cock several times till I could hear it squish-smacking wetly in his jacking hand.

"Relax your body," he told me. And talked me slowly through

the pain of the first cock to ever enter my ass. There wasn't that much pain because I relaxed every time he instructed me to.

Soon, he was deep inside, bent over, kissing my neck.

"I'm gonna fuck you, Todd!" he told me as his sweating body pressed against my back. The whole garage smelled of naked, sweating bodies. Our male bodies. I like the raw smell of us and the sex.

"Ohhh . . . do it!" I remember moaning to him. I can still feel that cock of his in me today from when he fucked me yesterday . . .

I wish his cock was back in me now, like yesterday. If felt so good feeling his round, stiff cock sliding back and forth inside my ass. I liked it when he told me how I had a fine, tight, beautiful ass he loved fucking. How he told me that guys were better sex to him than girls. He told me to feel his meat inside me . . . the joy of it filling me and rubbing my insides.

His hands stroked my sides and hips as his own hips thrusted and pounded his fucking meat back and forth inside me. It was a wild feeling of sensation that enlightened me to the joy of Danny, himself. I liked him and his masculine body, naked against me. I liked his cock, having sucked it, and now being fucked by it in my quivering ass.

I loved it when he cummed inside me, and pumped his creamy jism into every void in my ass with squish-smacking strokes and moans of ecstasy over it.

Oh, Danny, where are you? I want to do it all again today. You're better than girls, Danny. I'm like you are, Danny. I want you, your body, your loving cock.

I'm here in my garage again. I'm naked, and lying on my bike, just for you. Where are you, Danny?

"I GOTTA PISS, BABY"

"My name is Spence, but my friends call me 'Butch.' That's all ya gotta know about me, except that I'm a horny guy who likes gettin' naked and bein' sleazy, dirty, raw, and dominating to low-life, scum-faggot, assholes like you. In my stuffy, hot garage with my bike is where I play. I like bein' sweaty and stinky with body odor that a sleazeball, suckin' faggot like you best appreciates,'' he explained.

''Get yer fuckin' clothes off, asshole! Tonight you're *my* scuz-worshippin' wimp-fag,'' he told me.

My name is John. Looking at a photo of Butch, you could understand why I'm here, getting naked for him. Butch is straight trade who answered an underground newspaper ad that I placed seeking straights for raunchy sex. My ad told more of what I wanted, and Butch is that rare answer to my fantasy.

''Get yer ass *down*, pervert, and crawl that dirty cement floor to me,'' he commanded. I obeyed, and crawled to his smelly, sweatin' foot planted firmly on the floor.

''Kiss it, *fag*!'' he demanded. I obeyed. ''Smell it!'' he ordered. Again, I obeyed. ''You're the lowest form of human being on the face of the earth, asshole. You smell my dirty, sweatin' foot, do ya?'' he asked.

''Yes. And I love its raw man-odor,'' I said, inhaling it into my nostrils. He spit on my back.

''You're scum!'' he jeered. ''Lick what ya smell, like a dog,'' he grinned. ''Lick that foot, you queer fuckin' dog!'' he demanded.

I licked at the top of his foot, and savored the tasty sweat of its flesh. His foot was rank and smelly, and I really turned on to it. I was licking this cocky, straight biker's feet as he abused me. I liked his dominance and raunchiness, and couldn't control my lust for his foot.

I rolled over on my back, and he stepped on my face. I grabbed him around the ankle with both hands, and licked at its meaty, wet, smelly bottom. I *wanted* to be scum at his feet. I sucked onto his toes.

''Go, homo . . . do it to me! Suck on my feet like the dirty, fuckin' faggot you really are. You're gettin' me horny feelin' that wet, suckin' fag mouth on my toes. I'm gettin' hot ta get real raunchy with yer ass! Feel, and lick yer way up my leg, you pig!'' he demanded.

I stroked and licked up his shin, and around, over to his calf, forcing my head between his leg and bike. His leg was strong and firm, and I was crawling up it . . . kissing, licking, and rubbing its muscularity with my arms . . . like a queer slave climbing his master.

His legs were wet and slippery with sweat. I made it to my

knees, straddling his foot, and pressing my cock to his shin. I stroked and licked his muscled, hard thigh . . . tasting his salty, deliciously raw sweat. He fisted my hair, and jerked my head back, and slapped my face with his cock as he spit on me.

"I gotta piss, baby! Right through my hard-on. And you're gonna drink it all down that faggot throat of yours. Wrap yer mouth around my dick!" he demanded, jerking my head down, and stuffing his dick in my mouth.

There was a pause . . . then he blasted my mouth, and I immediately began gulping down his warm stud-piss.

"Ahhh . . . drink! Gulp my fuckin' piss, you queer shit-faced bastard. You're my fuckin' human toilet-faggot, you asshole! Drink me!" he abused.

I gulped the straight master's piss because I wanted to suck on the cock already in my mouth. I emptied his bladder like a champ, and he liked that. He had him one wild raunch pervert . . . and he knew it!

When his pissing ended, I shoved full-bolt onto his hard meat, burying my nose into his wet, sweaty, pubic patch. His pisser tasted sweaty-raw in my mouth as his crotch smell filled up my nose.

"Ohhh, yeaahh! Bury that bone in yer mouth. Taste a *man's* meat, you faggot! Gimme a blow job, cocksucker!" he coaxed me, stroking my head.

He talked slow and sexy, with tease directed at my homosexuality. And I liked it to serve my mental masochistic need to be put down by a straight. It also served Butch's ego.

I began romancing his cock. Slowly making love to it, I appreciate its beauty, thickness, and length . . . its smell and taste . . . and most of all, its sex. I sucked up and down its length, worshipping it. He leaned back—atop his cycle—a young, handsome, beautiful, hard-bodied male. He glistened in sweat, and smelled raw and savage . . . a sexual man.

He felt and watched his cock appear and disappear with every full-stroking suck of my mouth. He liked being appreciated and blown. He liked the bizarre, raunchy, sexually perverted pleasures he received from a queer.

"Ahhhh . . . yeahhh . . . you love suckin' *my* cock!" he teased. I slowly moved my hand up his hard stomach, rubbing the taut, wet flesh.

He was so rank and sexy. I knew that later he would have me lick his wet, sweating body from neck to toes. And the thought of it excited me more. I quickened my pace on his beautiful, hot meat.

"Ohhhhh . . ." he moaned. "I wanna cum!" he said. My hand moved up his chest, and I kneaded a nipple with my fingers. I sucked faster on his meat.

"Ahhhh . . . you fucker!" he moaned, sitting up quickly and forcing my head down on his cock.

"Eat me! Eat . . . meeeee!" he commanded, filling my throat with warm spunk.

Damn, how I love it when he makes me swallow his load like this!

"Ohhh . . . you cum-suckin' bitch . . . eat my 'fuck'!" he demanded. And I swallowed him into me.

"KISS MY REEBOK
LIKE YOU'D KISS YOUR GIRLFRIEND"

Mark and I were studying in one of the study rooms at the library before final spring exams. Mark was preparing an outline I desperately needed. I had goofed off all semester either ditching class or not taking notes (when I did go). Mark started mouthing off, as he usually did. . . . I had said something gramatically incorrect and Mark told me to learn how to talk. I smart mouthed him back, telling him he should take notice of the one who was ranked in the top 10% of the class (me), and that he'd better tend to his own problems and learn how to write. I never dreamed Mark would react the way he did. He spent the ride home sulking and wouldn't speak to me. When he got out of the car the only thing he said was, "Don't bother picking me up in the morning. . . . And you can kiss off ever seeing my fucking outline."

I didn't sleep at all that night. I finally got up at six in the morning and called Mark's house. His girlfriend answered. She told me she was catching a plane out of town and that Mark hadn't found a ride to class. She told me to come on by and pick him up. I got to Mark's about an hour ahead of schedule at 8:30. I knew I had to talk to him and I was desperate to get it over with. . . . I had to get ahold of his outline if I was going to pass and I figured I'd have to eat a little "crow" and grovel a little in order to get it. I could see Mark sitting on the sofa through the window. I knocked on the door. No answer. I knocked again and there was still no answer. Mark just continued sitting there reading the morning newspaper. I remember thinking, "Oh shit, this is going to be harder than I thought." I used my key, opened the door and walked in. I stood there for what seemed like about 10 minutes while Mark just kept on reading. Finally he looked up and with a straight face asked me, "You need something, faggot?" I started apologizing for what I had said the day before. "I'm sorry man, I really am. I didn't mean anything by it. I'm really sorry." "Saying you're sorry ain't gonna get it. You're gonna have to *show* me how sorry you are or you can forget it," Mark said.

"What do you want me to do?" I asked nervously.

"You can start by stripping, you cunt!" Mark ordered.

"Wait a minute . . ." I said, not liking the way this was going.

"No, *you* wait a minute, cunt-face, I told you not to pick me up today. I didn't invite you in here. You want that outline bad enough to do exactly what I tell you. If I'm wrong about that, you can get the fuck out!" Mark was definitely pissed off. He was red in the face. I immediately started stripping. I knew he was right. I *had* to have that outline. What can he do, I thought, paddle me, make me streak? Whatever it was, it would be worth it in order to get ahold of his outline. I was in competition with Kent Marshall for the "Outstanding Scholastic Achievement Award." The student to win the award was offered a management position and the decision about who was going to be the recipient was being made at the end of the semester. Mark knew I would kill to get that outline ahead of Kent. Right at the moment it seemed that my entire plan for getting in ahead of Kent was fading fast. Mark was aware of how I had slacked off, counting heavily on his outline to carry the day. If Kent got that damned award he'd end up being my boss, and I couldn't let that happen.

I stood there bare-assed naked in front of Mark. He let me stand there in silence until he finished with the part of the paper he was reading. Finally Mark got up and went to the pantry. He came back to where I was standing and ordered me to put my hands behind my back. He tied them together so fucking tight I couldn't

82

have gotten loose if I tried. As soon as he had my hands tied, he walked around me, tripping me as he passed. I fell to the floor at his feet right in front of the couch. "Clumsy bastard," he said with a sneer. Then he went through my pants. He got my car keys and wallet. He then put all my clothes in his trunk and locked them up.

Mark returned to his place on the sofa. He sat directly in front of where I lay prostrate on the floor. I could see his once-white Reeboks and his pushed-down white gym socks.

Mark picked up his newspaper and started reading again. Just as I began thinking that he'd forgotten about me he shoved his dirty Reebok in my face. "Kiss it," he ordered, not looking up from his sports section. "Kiss it like you'd kiss your girlfriend, kiss it like you know I'm your fucking superior and that you realize what a fuckin' honor it is to touch my fuckin' foot!"

Well, here we go, I thought. This is what he's going to put me through in order to get that outline. . . . he's going to make me kiss his feet. It could be worse, I thought. I shrugged (as best I could with my hands tied), and pressed my lips firmly against the dirty tennis shoe on Mark's sweating foot. After a couple minutes of my lip-kissing the top of his shoe, Mark drew his foot back and kicked me in the mouth. "I told you to kiss it like it was your fucking girlfriend, not your grandmother, you fucking faggot. Since you don't seem to be able to follow orders, roll over on your back, dog boy!" It took a few tries, but I got on my back, lying very uncomfortably on top of my tied hands. As soon as I got in position, Mark stomped his foot down on top of my face. "Now you can lick the dirt and scum off the bottom of my shoe, you asswipe!" What the fuck, this is more than I bargained for, I thought. But I was so stunned from getting kicked in the mouth and from having my "best friend" step on my face with a dirty sneaker on his foot, that I found my tongue stretching out of my upturned mouth and drawing across the filthy sole of Mark's firmly placed Reebok. "Come on, faggot, I wanna *feel* that tongue of yours sliding across the bottom of my foot! Lick harder and faster, asshole!" Mark ordered from his comfortable, seated position above me. I did as I was told, pushing my tongue hard against Mark's shoe sole and pulling it back into my open mouth as quickly as I could. I had licked Mark's shoe sole from heel to toe when he finally lifted it from my face. "Okay," I thought, I guess he's finished fucking with me. . . . the thought hadn't finished passing through my mind when I opened my eyes to a view of his "other" foot coming down to rest atop my face.

"Okay, bitch. It's time you do a little groveling while you're lickin' the dirt off my shoe. I wanna hear you tell me what a fuckin' low life you are and how you're gonna beg tonight for the honor of lickin' my superior, rich sweaty socks." I said it all and Mark loved it. He was starting to get real "hot" and was about to get on to more serious humiliation when he looked at his watch and said, "Shit, I gotta get to the review class. You're not going, pussy. Your entire chance of passing is going to be kissing my ass so long and so diligently that out of the goodness of my heart I decide to give you the outline."

Mark got up and tied my legs to the coffee table and each arm to the legs of the sofa. He left me tied spread-eagled on his living room floor. He went to the closet and got his golf clubs out. "Kent and I are gonna play a little golf after class so I'll be a little late getting home." He then pulled forty bucks out of my wallet. "You don't mind paying for our green fees do you?" he said with a laughing sneer. "No fuckin' way," I screamed. "You can't take my money, I agreed to a little humiliation to get that outline, but if money's what you're after you can forget it. I can *buy* a fucking outline for forty bucks. . . . untie me, the deal's off. I'll go to the review and take my own notes. There's no way I'm gonna pay for that bastard's golf game while I lie here naked letting you use me as your fuckin' doormat!" Mark just looked down at me and laughed. "You know what your problem is, you talk too much." I heard him go to the bathroom and open the clothes hamper. He came back in the room holding a pair of dirty sweat socks in one hand and a pair of dirty, streaked underwear in the other. He ordered me to open my mouth "nice and wide." When I obeyed he shoved both of his filthy, sweat stiffened socks into my helplessly waiting mouth. "This oughta keep you quiet while I'm gone," he said as he wrapped duct tape over my mouth and around the back of my head. He drew his foot back and kicked me hard in the ribs. . . . he laughed at my groan and muffled scream. He had no mercy, he just kicked me again, a little harder. "Yeah, those good tastin' dirty socks will keep you quiet enough. With that he placed his dirty underwear over my head, making sure the right part was placed right over my nose.

''Okay faggot boy, I'm gone. Have a really nice time while I'm gone. Oh, I'm taking your new car, and Kent's gonna be driving.'' With that and a laugh, he was gone.

I lay there butt-ass naked. I could taste nothing but his foul foot sweat and I could smell nothing but his dirty underwear. I wasn't able to do anything except lie there and wonder what was going to happen to me when Mark got back home.

It was about three in the afternoon when I heard my car pull up in front of the house. It had been unusually hot for springtime and Mark had cut the air conditioning off completely. So I lay there all day sweating in that stuffy, sun-exposed living room. It had been even hotter out on the golf course. Mark and Kent were dripping with sweat when they walked in. At first I didn't realize Mark had anyone with him. I heard them bring several bags into the room and put some things up in the refrigerator. Then I heard some whispering. My heart sank. Surely Mark wouldn't be such a lowlife as to bring someone else in here with me spread out like this. Then my heart fell through to my toes. I recognized Kent's voice.

I didn't have too long after that realization to ponder the situation. All of a sudden I felt steel spikes touching my exposed ball sac. Mark pulled the underwear off my face and ripped the tape from my mouth. I was lying on my back so the first thing I saw was Kent's face smiling down at me. It was his golf shoe I felt bearing down on my balls. ''Give me a good reason not to squash your pathetic little nuts with my golf spikes . . .'' Kent said. ''Sir?'' I said instinctively (and instantly hated myself for having said it). ''That's a start, bitch,'' Kent said in that superior voice of his. He sure was one overconfident cocky son of a bitch. ''At least you know your place. . . . now tell me why I shouldn't smash your little jewel bag,'' he said as he began applying pressure to my nuts. The steel cleats were coming close to breaking the skin. Mark's dirty socks were still shoved tightly in my mouth and Kent laughed at my efforts to beg him for mercy. ''Well, these golf shoes are pretty dirty and scuffed up. I guess I could see how good you are at cleaning and shining shoes. Yeah, that sounds like a good fuckin' idea,'' he said as he took his foot off my balls and moved around to sit in the same spot Mark had sat in to make me lick his Reeboks earlier.

With the top of my head pointing toward the sofa, I could see

Kent's brown golf shoes at either side of my head. He was dressed in pleated, khaki pants, so I could barely see about three inches of the dark brown cotton socks he was wearing. He placed his right foot on my shoulder, and then the left one came down on the other shoulder. I felt the spikes digging into my bare skin as Kent leaned forward and jerked Mark's sweat socks from my mouth. Kent was really enjoying my humiliation and was getting off even more on the fact that I was helpless to defend myself. I was tied and at his complete disposal.

"Yeah, I want you to lick these golf cleats clean, pussy. That's about what you're qualified to be . . . my fucking shoeshine boy. Maybe that's the job I'll let you have when I win the Scholastic award. You can think about that while you're licking the mud from the spikes of this shoe." He lifted his right foot from my shoulder, leaving small, surface puncture wounds where he'd pushed his cleats into my flesh. He brought his foot down hard on top of my face. "Eat my fuckin' shoe mud, faggot!" Kent commanded as he pushed the toe of his shoe onto my mouth.

I started licking between the steel spikes. I could feel Kent's toes moving inside the shoe. It was about then that I heard Mark start clicking off Polaroid photos. Mark got some great shots of me lying before Kent, licking the mud off the bottom of his golf shoe. After I had cleaned the soles and spikes to Kent's satisfaction, he decided he wanted to carry this humiliation a step further. Kent told Mark to bring in his shoeshine kit while I got re-tied. Kent got me in position on my knees, my hands behind my back and my face looking down directly at the tops of his shoes. The brown, wing-tip/tassel golf shoe was covered with dust and dirt. Kent ordered me to "get to it" and of course, I knew exactly what that meant.

God, I hated this. Here I was kneeling before the person who I had (only yesterday) planned to make my flunky at a new job. All semester, although I was goofing off, I had envisioned Kent as my employee with whom I could do anything I pleased. Now the tables had turned and I found myself touching my tongue to the dirt and leather of Kent's fucking golf shoe! As if that wasn't enough, Kent made me put my nose in the brown shoe polish and apply the polish to his shoes with the tip of my nose. I was then ordered to put my sock on my dick and "hump" his golf shoes "until they shine like mirrors!"

When I had finished getting his shoes perfect, Kent shoved his foot in my face and said, "Okay, get my shoes untied with your teeth, and take 'em off my feet the best way you can, using your face." "You're outta your fuckin' mind," I exclaimed. This was it, "either I get the fuckin' outline or I'm outta here, I ain't kissing nobody's fuckin' feet for no stinkin' outline," I asserted, knowing I had already kissed Mark's. But that was different from touching my lips against Kent's sweaty brown things. There was no way I would allow Mark to make me be this clown's "foot servant." Kent raised his eyebrows as if to signal Mark. Mark got up and walked to the dining room table and got something out of one of the bags they had brought in. Mark said, "Here we go, let me see if I can give this fuckin' pussy asshole a little incentive . . ." and with that he began paddling me with a stiff leather, studded strap. Mark had a very strong arm and soon my bare ass was throbbing with pain and I found myself having no trouble at all doing exactly what Kent had ordered.

I finally managed to get those brown, newly shined shoes off Kent's hot sweaty feet. The aroma of Kent's sweat-filled, brown socks hit my nostrils immediately. He'd obviously been wearing them without washing. Kent placed one foot on my shoulder and the other one he pushed firmly against my face. I could hear Mark busily snapping photos. "Alright, since it looks like you wanna be my fuckin' permanent pussy slave, get those socks cleaned up. I want all the foot sweat sucked right out of 'em." Kent said. I felt his toes curl as he pushed his foot harder against my face. He had the ball of his foot positioned right over my nose, so the arch was pushed right up against my mouth.

I thought again about resisting, but one glance at the scowl on Mark's face and that strap in his hand was all it took. I opened my mouth and slowly slid my tongue down between my chin and Kent's foot. I found myself licking and sucking away at my arch rival's stinking sock. The feel and taste of his sweating foot was nauseating. Each time I gave any hesitation to take a breath, Kent would grind his foot harder into my nose. When he had slid his sweaty, smelly sock all over my face and had seen to it that every inch of the bottom of his sock had been licked he pulled his foot away from my face. Before I could even close my mouth he had that foot shoved inside, with the dirty sock still on. They (Mark and Kent) laughed hard when Mark took a good shot of me with

Kent's socked foot sticking out of my mouth. "Come on, faggot, let me feel you suck on it like the fuckin' bitch you are," Kent commanded. He continued taunting me, "Yeah, I expect there will be many a day that my shoes will get shined by your little slut tongue. I'm gonna love makin' you get down on your knees under my desk to give me a blow job while I look over your day's work. And you'll do it too cause if you don't fuckin' make love to my nuts like they're your fuckin' wife, I'm gonna give you more work, dock your pay and make you sit out in the office in front of everyone with my dirty sock hanging out of your mouth."

With that, Kent and Mark laughed and Kent pulled his meaty foot from my sore, open mouth. He now had both feet propped up against each of my shoulders. He took one foot and put it under my chin, lifting my face up until I was looking directly into his eyes. He replaced the foot on my shoulder. "Now it's time for me to hear you grovel. I wanna hear you tell me that you want to work as my fuckin' personal shoeshine boy, foot massager and sock laundry. I wanna hear you say that I'm your superior and admit that compared to me you're a piece of dog shit, nothing but a personal slave for me to order around." I started groveling, saying everything Kent wanted to hear, and Mark was getting it all on cassette tape. I knew I was never going to get back on top at this point. They had me. I was a slave. I belonged to Kent now. He would control what was left of my life. I would submit to him and his humiliation as long as he found it amusing. And I got the impression it would be to my advantage to make certain that he was continually amused!

CUMMIN' OUT AT AGE EIGHTEEN

I was born an only child. My parents were illiterates, and I, too, grew up working and lacking in schoolin'. I didn't make friends too easy because I was shy and sometimes kids made fun of me because I wasn't very smart and slow about things. The mountain forests around the mining and lumber town was where I played. And I never had any close friends my own age.

After my Ma died, when I had just turned eighteen, my Pa sorta went crazy. He drank a lot, and beat on me from time to time whenever he got drunk. And things got worse between us, then better. I was well built for my age and I started fightin' him back when he started beating on me. But Pa was older and stronger from workin' all his life, and always beat me, and throwed me out of the house. And I began to sleep by myself in the woods. It was at this time I met Josh and Clement.

They were a couple of lumbermen who come home with my Pa one Friday night. They had all been drinking in town, and my Pa was acting strange with them. I sneaked outta the house and hid at the edge of the woods to watch them. It was summer and all three of them hung around outside at the stoop. The two men with Pa were shirtless. They were both well-built muscular men in their late twenties or early thirties. My Pa was drunk and was being teased by the two men. I watched as they ripped open their flys and pulled out their huge cocks and teased my Pa with them. And then my Pa put one of them cocks in his mouth and was suckin' back and forth on it. He'd do it to one man awhile, then to the other. He'd do it to one man as he stood, and back to the other who sat on the stoop. They called him "faggot" and "cock-sucker" and a queer. They would tease him, and order him to suck their cocks.

It was my first time to see sex between men. I was intrigued by both of the men's cocks. They were rugged, goodlookin', hard-bodied men who had control over my Pa with their cocks. As time passed, they all three ended up naked.

I watched as they made my Pa kiss their butts and lick at their assholes. I watched them sit side by side on the stoop drinkin' and laughin' at Pa as they made him lick their big feet, and suck on their toes.

My own cock was hard with excitement, and I had to pull it out of my jeans to relieve the ache. It felt sensitive and so alive in my hand. . . .

I stroked at it as I watched Pa lick all over one of the guy's feet. The men's feet seemed sexy and attractive to me, just like their cocks were. I even began wishing I were Pa, and lickin' those feet myself. There was something so sexually erotic about their feet. And Pa being down on them like some slave.

Then one man got up, as the man sittin' made Pa suck on his cock again. The other man moved behind Pa, spit in his hand, and rubbed it over Pa's asshole. Within minutes, and with some movin' around by everyone, there was Pa on all fours like a dog, suckin' one guy's cock, as the other was fuckin' Pa's ass. The man fuckin' ass was exciting to watch. His whole body was defined muscles, as his hips and legs and firm butt moved rhythmically back and forth, shoving and pullin' that beautiful hard cock in and out of Pa's ass.

The other man was excitingly beautiful as well, his powerful legs extended one on each side of my Pa, sittin' on one step with his arms restin' atop the step above. His head was thrown back, his eyes closed to feel the action, and his big adam's apple moving up and down with pleasure in his throat. His chest was hard, and his body tapered down to a flat muscular stomach. I stared at my Pa's mouth suckin' up and down the round, beautiful cock.

Their bodies all sparkled with a sheen of sweat. Moans of ecstasy, the flesh squish-smackin' together reached my ears from where I sat. Pa's mouth and ass were filled with man-cock. As much as I'd hated him these past months, for some reason I couldn't figure I was envyin' him right then.

Later, they all passed out from sex and booze. One of them slept in the back of the pick-up truck they came in. My Pa passed out in the house. The second stranger lay naked on the stoop. I sneaked quietly from the woods to the truck, and stood in silence just feet away from the sleeping man. I studied his naked body, from his messed hair and handsome face all the way to his big muscular feet. I stopped along the way to look over his limp cock, as it lay across his powerful thigh.

Quietly I undressed and stood naked beneath the bright moon and stars. Our two-room old unkept house was tucked away off a gravel road a mile out of town, near the river's edge. It was surrounded by woods and could not be seen from the road. I went to the stoop and watched the second man sleep. He, too, excited me with the beauty of his body. He was blond-haired (the other man's was brown) and both had hairless, hard, pleasing upper bodies. The blond's legs were longer, and blond haired. His feet were exceptionally strong and meaty. Those long legs and feet were so erotic to me.

I moved quietly around the stoop to get closer to his feet, and silently stared at 'em. They were tanned, and veined along the top of them, and accented by a few blond hairs. The nails of his sexy round-strong toes looked as if they indented perfectly on them with flesh at all sides. His feet seemed physically magnetic to me. Closer, my face moved toward it as my eyes admired the beauty of his naked foot. Then, I smelled the scent of it as my nose was within an inch of his toes. The smell made me hungry, and I found myself lickin' lightly up the length of the bottom of his toes, stroking the foot lovingly with my hands.

Suddenly, the guy looked up and saw me watchin', and I took off, running into the woods and toward the river. I heard the man running behind me, but I made it to the river bed and increased my speed. Seconds later, his whole body crashed me from behind. We wrestled, but he was strong. He rolled me onto my back, and pinned me down with the weight of his body full length atop me.

"Don't fight me, ya little bastard! Or I'm gonna smack you good. Now calm down and relax!" he demanded, starin' into my eyes. I relaxed, and felt his powerful arm slip under my back, makin' me arch my back and press against him to allow his arm under me. There was a silence, and I realized he had to feel my excited cock pressed hard between us. He was so big, and muscular, and the feel of his body excited me more.

"Ya want a man, boy? Relaxxxxxx!" he told me, and pressed his lips against mine. As he kissed into me, he rolled over on his back, bringing me on top of him. Arms and legs wrapped around each other, and our cocks grinded hard against each other, between us. His cock was much bigger than mine, and I liked the feel of it on my belly.

"This yer first time with a man, boy?" he asked, as his hands slid down my back and gripped my butt firmly.

"Yes," I answered and kissed him again on his lips. He drove his tongue into my mouth and I sucked on it. My hands were everywhere on him I could reach. He was so hard and muscular, everywhere. And he smelled so raw hot-sweaty. I loved the feel of his flesh as I now licked at his neck and shoulder.

"Why were you lickin' my feet, boy? Do you like my feet?" he asked.

"Oohhh, yes . . . you have sexy feet. I couldn't help myself when I got so close to them. You were such a beautiful man lyin' there sleepin'. I just had to get close to your feet. And when I smelled them, I just had to lick and taste them. Will you teach me sex between men?"

"Yer barely a man," he said grinning. "And yer the youngest faggot I've ever been with. Ya see, kid . . . yer queer, and I ain't. I only take advantage of a queer when I'm horny, and there ain't no woman around. A queer is a guy who sexually likes guys only. Here, let me show ya," he said, as he got up and straddled me. His two powerful blond-haired legs were folded against my sides, as he lay on my stomach. His cock was hard and very big as it jutted from his long haired blond crotch, into the air for me to see. I reached over his thighs and took it in my hands, as my arms rested atop his legs.

"That's it, feel it, boy! Because this is why you're queer!"

* * *

Months later, when I was more experienced, I fantasized about the guy's inner thoughts at the time:

"My cock was aching and his hands all over it was edgin' me to a climax. I ain't a queer, yet the boy had me turned onto him. He was a handsome and tight-bodied boy. His muscular definition was ample enough for anyone to know he would grow to be a hunk of a man. He was the first guy I ever kissed. I hated any queer I ever got sucked by or fucked. But this guy was innocent, lovable and curious; he was sparkin' some interest inside me that was sexual, curious and caring. He had to be *mine*, perhaps something secret and lasting awhile. He already admired me. I had to baptize him, make him want me more . . . Explore sex with each other. *I want this little fucker to myself!* I must control him, make him dependent on me sexually . . . Damn, my own secret sex boy to love me as his man."

* * *

The feel of this mature man's cock in my hands, the feel of his hairy legs against my arms, the beauty of his hard, rippling muscled upper body, and the feel of his ass pressin' against my cock excited me.

"Ya like it, do ya?" he asked, reaching down and graspin' my head behind my neck, and pullin' my face toward it. The head of his cock touched my face between my mouth and nose. With his free hand, he fisted his cock and began guiding it across my lips, chin, cheeks and nose. The aroma of his big cock and crotch smelled sweaty and exciting to me.

"Ya wanna kiss it, boy? Go on, let yourself go and kiss all over it. You do want me to know you care for it, don'cha? Yeeaahhhh, kid, that's it . . . love my dick!"

And I was kissin' all over his hot big dick. As I kissed, his body raised slightly, his foot beside my head, which he had laid back on the ground. He was kneeling on his other knee to balance himself. I could see his hangin' balls and beautiful ass from below him. I turned my head sideways and kissed his ankle. He stood up and placed his other foot at the other side of my face, and now my head was vised between his feet. I was lookin' up his long powerful sinewy legs at his juttin' cock, hands on his hips, and he was lookin' down at me. The moon outlined his body, accenting the ridged muscles.

"Ya feel my big feet, boy? You like them, don'cha? Now listen to me good! I'm gonna walk over there. And I want ya to come over there and go down on my feet all you want. And finish the job you began back at the old man's house. When you've had all ya want, we'll lie together and kiss, and explore each other's bodies. Come on!" he said, and walked away.

He sat down at the foot of the tree. His legs were extended and his feet were crossed. I lay down at his feet on the soft river bed, and brushed the sand from the bottoms of his feet. And I then began licking the massive sweaty bottom of one foot. It was instant euphoria to me. His feet flesh was tasty sweat, and the meaty bottoms and sides instantly satisfied my hungry lusts for them. They were sexual, and unbelievably erotic and exciting to me. I could not control myself from licking and feeling all over them. I'd lick off one right onto the other, folded together the way they were. There was something so powerfully sexual about them that was exciting inside me when I saw my Pa doing it, and the way the men looked down on him as he did. It was like my Pa was serving them like a slave or somethin'. Like I was doin' now, lickin' his feet for him as he watched. A handsome, naked, beautiful man I wanted to please, yet enjoy. If I could just satisfy this guy so much, maybe he'd like me enough to want me lots of times.

"Hey, kid—you like them big sexy feet of mine, do ya?" he asked.

"Ooohhh, yesss, you have hot feet, powerful feet, mmmmmm,

93

(slurp) beautiful tasty feet!'' I moaned as I licked at his meaty round toes.

"Suck my toes for me," he told me and I sucked onto his big toe first, and began suckin' it.

"Oooooooohhhh . . . Yeeaaaaahhhhhh, that feels good, boy. Yer a good faggot for my feet. Suck! That's what queer boys do real good, is suck. You love a man's toes in yer mouth. And suckin' up and down 'em, just like ya would a cock. I like your sucks, kid! Yer a good foot licker and a good toe sucker. And I got good feet that you like ta lick and suck.

"But, a boy shouldn't have too much of a good thing all at once. Not his first time. So why don'cha crawl up here into my arms and kiss me," he said, and pulled his feet from my clutches, and face.

I crawled up and sat beside him. He put his arm around me and pulled me to him. My body was sandy and felt rough against our skin where we pressed against each other. Just before we kissed, I saw his jutting hard cock, and reached to fist it in my hand. I turned my face into his, and our lips melted into each other. My whole body felt tingling sensations as his hand fisted my cock.

"Mmmmmmmmhh!" I moaned as we kissed, to the stroking of his fist on my cock. I began doing to his cock everything he was doing to mine. The feelings to my own cock were intensely sensitive. The sensations made my whole body shudder with wild pleasures. We broke from our kiss with sucking inhalations of excitement, and I cradled my head on his shoulder, at his hard, wide neck.

"Ahhhh, that feels good," I moaned, as I kissed and licked at his strong neck.

"You wanna get off, kid?" he asked.

"I think so," I answered.

His hand was now pumpin' my cock faster and faster. It was so exciting, I had stopped pumping his and slid off his shoulder and to the ground on my back. I threw my arms over my head and my legs stretched out and began to shake.

"Ooooooo, I think I'm gonna cum!!!" I moaned. His hand intensified with fast rhythmic pumps and the sperm jetted from my hot cock into the air, and came splashing down on my face, neck and chest, and again on my quivering flat-muscled stomach.

"Ooohhhh, I love it! You made me cum!" I moaned happily.

"Taste yerself, kid. Lick it off my hand and swallow it. Taste how good yer own spunk is. Then I'll feed ya lots of mine right down yer throat."

I licked it all off his hand, sucking his fingers. Then, he was up and standing, bracing and balancing himself with arms extended and his hands on the tree. He lifted his leg, and stepped down atop my stomach, and began sliding his naked foot up my belly and chest firmly.

I reached and stroked his long, muscular calf and shin, as I felt and heard the squish-smackin' sound of his foot sliding through my slimy cum. I looked down my chest to see his foot moving toward me. I watched the sperm oozing between his toes, filling the voids, and spilling out the top. Cum was coating the tops of his toes and foot. It slid down my neck, my chin, and toes filled my open, waiting mouth. The cum was abundant and I sucked its delicious thickness down my throat.

My own slimy sperm was strangely tasty, and licking it off the bottom of his feet as he slid it over my face was exciting.

"Yeah, kid, do it! Eat yer own fuck, yer creamy thick cum, off my big foot. Mmmm, cum-coated toes and feet of mine all over yer face. Eat my feet, ya hungry boy-faggot of mine," he demanded. For ten minutes he rubbed his feet all over my face as I licked at them, every now and then shoving the toes into my mouth to suck clean.

Then he sat back down, resting his back against the tree. I sat up and crossed my legs, facing him.

"Did you mean what you said?"

"What's that, kid?"

"That I'm your boy faggot."

He raised his arm, summoning me.

"Come here!" he said, and I crawled beside him with my back to the tree. He wrapped his arm around the back of my neck and hung to my chest, his fingers lightly massaging my nipple. I rested my hand on his hairless stomach and massaged it.

He explained to me about my being queer, what it is, and how it's now accepted by many people as right. He explained the law of consent at age eighteen, my then age. And I told him about my Ma dying and Pa goin' to drinking and the beatings he gave me. How I was shy and had no friends til now, that I could talk to.

"I wanna be your boy-faggot. I need somebody like you to teach me sex. I need somebody I can talk to. Everything can be our secret. Yer so handsome, and strong. Even if yer not a queer, you got to like me some." I bent down and kissed his chest, then raised to meet his lips. We kissed, and my hand found his cock.

As I fondled the cockmeat, he explained to me about his job, and dates with women, and other things. And how he wouldn't be seein' me but maybe one day a week secretly. That I had to accept that and make no demand on him whatsoever. He laid the whole relationship between us on the line, and I agreed.

"Okay, then, you can be my friend . . . and my boy-faggot. So why don't you replace that hand of yours on my cock, with yer mouth?" he grinned.

"I've never sucked a cock before, and I want to suck yours good for you," I declared.

"Relax, kid, suckin' will come natural to ya. You like my cock, don'cha?"

"Yes," I answered.

"Then let's begin by me teachin' ya positions. Look at it, kid," he said as he turned and stood towards me.

"First, suck my cock on yer knees. Get up on yer knees, boy. Look at that cock, baby! It's big, and hard, and round, and mine. I'm gonna shove my hot dick in yer mouth, kid. My cock, my big cock, in yer mouth. You *do* want my cock, my sexy sweet hot meat in your mouth, don'cha, kid? Suck it for me!" he said, stepping up to me kneeling.

I sucked onto its huge roundness, and slowly ran my hand up his hot thighs. Sweaty cock meat filled my mouth, and euphoria exploded all through my body. Its taste, the smell of his crotch, the beauty of his rippling muscles erotically ignited lusts never felt before.

"Yeaahhh! That's doin' it! Slow and easy, boy-sucker. Get used to my cock in yer mouth. Don't bite it, just suck on it slowly at first. Aahhh, yeah, yer a natural. That's me kid! Me in yer mouth. Mmmmm! Cock must taste good to you. And yer mouth feels real good to me," he said, then pulled away from me, poppin' his cock from my mouth.

"You like it, kid?"

"Yes, yes, I want more!"

"Sure, kid. But sit down, first. There at the tree." As I sat down, he knelt down, straddling my hips with his long, beautiful legs and again pressed his cock to my lips. I sucked onto it as I ran my hands up the front of his hard man body.

"What yer doin' is called suckin' cock, or givin' 'head,' or givin' me a blow job. And yer doin' real good at it. Now what ya wanna do is not tire yerself tryin' to race hard to get a cock off. Ya start slow and enjoy tastin' it, gettin' the feel of it, makin' it grow in yer mouth. It ain't how much of the cock you suck into your mouth, it's the head of the cock that's most sensitive and reacts to your sucking.

"Ahhh, yeah, ya listen to me. That's good, kid. You enjoy my cock. It's your first, and I want you to remember it forever. Just enjoy suckin' it and listen to me as we go," he explained.

I was enjoying him. And listening to him too. He was so sexy, and it excited me to suck him. I now had the cheeks of his ass in each of my hands as I sucked slowly on his cock. They felt firm and powerful, round and erotically exciting to me. I *liked* guy sex. This man was so much more sexually exciting to me than any woman or girl I've ever known. I liked his muscles, and raw smell, and long legs, and manly feet. I loved his cock and sucking it. Every part of him turned me on, and on.

Again, he pulled his cock from my mouth. "Come on, kid, turn sideways here, and lie on yer back," he instructed me, and I obeyed. Again, I watched the moves of his body, as he positioned himself over me. Then, extending himself over my head as if he were going to do a push-up, his cock once more entered my mouth. Only this time, he slowly fucked my mouth as I sucked. He was firmly stretched above me, propped up by his muscular arms. Above me was the exciting beauty of his stretched muscular body to see. His hairless hard chest and stomach accented by lined muscles. He had one of those tiny hard navels like mine that made me take a mental note to kiss and lick at sometimes. His narrow hips moved up and down slowly, his meat rising and falling in my mouth. I fisted my hard cock, my always hard cock since I met this man.

"Oooh, oohhhhh yeah, love yer fuckin' mouth! Especially if it's yers. Feel the rhythm of my cock, and how it's the same as when you sucked it? That's the key, kid. The whole secret to suckin' cock. First, it's slow, then little by little you go faster. It's progressive rhythm, boy! Feel it?" he questioned, as his hips fucked a bit faster and his cock pumped my mouth.

I was beginning to understand. Start suckin' cock slow for growth and taste, to excite and explore the cock. Then the progressive rhythm, just like his hand did on my cock earlier when he jacked me.

Again, he pulled from my mouth and changed position. This time he sat up against the tree, with his hard, wet, shiny cock in his hand. He stroked it.

"Look at it, kid! So big, and hot and fuckin' horny from that wet faggot mouth. Look at these balls of mine! All tight and swollen and ready to pop a big load of cum in yer mouth. Come here, and lick all over my balls. That'll really get me hot for the wild blow-job yer gonna give me."

I crawled between his legs. I licked all over his swollen-sweaty tasting balls as he stroked his hot cock over my face.

"One more thing, kid! When yer suckin' me off, fist my cock and stroke the head of my cock with mouth and hand with that same building rhythm. Pace yerself faster and faster till ya get what ya really want: my hot fuckin' cum. And yer gonna get a lot of it, kid. So swallow as many times as you can. It'll be the most exciting tastiest load of man juice you'll never forget. It'll be mine. Ooohhh, that feels good . . .

"Scoot yerself down some, while I lie all out for ya. Yeah, that's it, kid! Now get comfortable any way you want and give me your first blow-job," he said. I knelt at his spread legs, looking down at him lying there with his head resting in his folded arms. I lay on my side between his beautiful legs.

I extended my arm over one thigh, blanketing it with my arm-pit. I rested my elbow at the ground next to his hip, and let the forearm edge up onto his stomach, my hand resting atop his navel and abdominal muscles. I fisted his gorgeous huge thick round cock, and bent to kiss its swelled head. I let my saliva drip onto it and stroked it with my hand, getting the palm and fingers lubricated with the shaft of his cock.

"Ooohhhh, maaaan!" he moaned, watching and feeling me. "Am I in heaven? Is this really happening to me?" he questioned, as I went down on his cock.

A breeze blew through the trees, and small waves smacked against the riverbed. The moon shone full and bathed our bodies. And mouth plus hand violated huge majestic cock, as boy sucked onto man. It was naked male sexuality in a ceremony of the flesh.

It was a sexual baptism of experienced man to the inhibitions of an adolescent.

We both relaxed, both enjoying the throes of passion. Both heads dancing with the wild euphoria of mind-shattering orgasm. Sensuality joined emotion, sensation welded to sensitivity. Bodies emitting intoxicating masculine aroma . . . hearts pounding, the rush of physical excitement . . . moans of approval, joy, ecstasy . . .

BORN TO SERVE

The dominant/submissive relationship with my older brother began innocuously with Patrick (my brother) ordering me to get up and change the channel on the TV, go to the kitchen and bring him a soda . . . (etc.). It didn't take long for him to begin adding a snap of his fingers to each command. That small gesture was an effective display of his power and a powerful means of humiliating me in front of other people.

As I look back on the experiences, it fascinates me to see the swift yet seemingly calculated (on Patrick's part) progress. It seems as though each new day brought a new confidence for Patrick. Of course, he knew (as did everyone) that he was older and physically much stronger than I . . . but after starting with the relatively innocent demands for personal service, it took less than a month for him to start forcing me to demonstrate my subservience in more profound ways.

Patrick and I attended a small private (Catholic) school which made it convenient, if not "right-down" easy, for Patrick to use his newly discovered unlimited power over his younger brother.

It was at school that Patrick first decided he wanted to see me on my knees at his feet, for no other purpose—serving no other function than to amuse him by obeying his humiliating order. In the weeks prior, nearly everyone had at one time or another witnessed Patrick ordering me to perform some task. This time was a bit different. We were in the boys' restroom during recess. Patrick was sitting on one of the counters talking to three or four of his classmates. I was just about to leave when I heard him say, "Hey Allen, John wants to see you kiss my feet. Get over here and down on your knees." He snapped his fingers and I knew I wasn't going to be able to get out of it.

I remember my face flushed hot with embarrassment as I slowly got down on my knees and drew my face in close to the toes of Patrick's dirty, brown penny loafer. I could hear my brother and his friends laughing at me. I just knelt there, staring at Patrick's foot. I knew that if I refused to obey him he wouldn't think twice about "punching me out" . . . He moved his foot forward, closer to my lips and told me very firmly that I was to kiss his foot. By this time there were several other kids gathered around to watch me prove my total submission to my brother, Patrick. I lowered my face about an inch (or two) and pressed my lips against the top of his shoe. Everyone was laughing and snickered and in various ways expressed their disbelief that I would actually get down on my knees and put my mouth on Patrick's penny loafer. When I tried to pull back after kissing his foot what I thought was sufficiently, his friend John put his foot on the back of my head, forcing my face down to the toe of Patrick's other shoe. The entire ordeal lasted only a couple of minutes . . . but the effect(s) have lasted a lifetime.

Of course, things progressed from that point in the five years before my brother left home. Lately I've done some progressing of my own. In the course of events (recently) I have found that I very much enjoy being dominant. I actually like watching someone get on their knees to lick my shoes clean before I make them shine 'em. I like the feeling of power as I shove my sweaty, socked foot in an adoring, worshipful face! My feet tend to sweat a lot, so by the end of the day my socks are more than just moist . . . they're wet, and smell like whatever foot gear they're taken out of. So, it gives me particular pleasure to order a foot massage (with a face).

Since talking to you last night I thought this might be a good time to elaborate a little on the kinds of relationships I've had.

In spite of my unremarkable physical appearance, I have been somehow fortunate in being involved with very attractive men. As I mentioned in our conversation last evening, the two relationships I've had have included a slave/master scenario. Something I failed to mention is that both "masters" were *younger* than I, (which is something I find interesting).

The first relationship was with Michael. I was a Junior in college and Michael was a Freshman (he was 20 to my 23). We started out as "just roommates," but it didn't take long for me to start doing things for him that were over and above the call of duty for any roommate. . . .

I started doing his laundry for him, using the excuse that I had the time (which I really didn't) to do it and he didn't. In a few weeks Michael was not only *comfortable* with me going into his room and picking up his dirty clothes, but he *expected* it and would let me know about certain things he wanted done, like, "Hey Allen, I need my 501's and my white socks washed tonight. You can get 'em out of my bedroom. And don't forget to iron my blue pin-striped shirt, I want to wear it tomorrow!" It was really pretty easy to get him into a frame of mind where he would like the idea of not being responsible for his own laundry. And of course, I loved the arrogance he displayed . . . the way he would sit and watch television or talk with some of his friends while I was working on cleaning his bedroom or washing his dirty laundry. Keeping his shoes and boots cleaned and shined was the next natural "step" (no pun intended).

Now, keep in mind that Michael was a normal college Freshman (outside of the fact that he was gay). He had a natural arrogance, mostly because of his outstanding physical attractiveness. . . . he was goodlooking and he was, shall we say, "aware of it." He had no real intention of using me as a servant. At least not to begin with. I, on the other hand, was quite calculated about how and when I did things in order to coax him along in the necessary evolution toward becoming my Master.

It was a simple thing to reach the point where Michael expected me to perform the menial tasks of his day-to-day life. And given his natural arrogance, it took only a little more for him to evolve into ordering me to do specific things, and to take complete advantage of my submissive and servile attitude toward him. All he had to do was suggest that he wanted something or that he wanted me to do something and I would do it, immediately.

I had created someone to take the place of my sadistic, cruel older brother . . . and I loved it!

When people talk about being "born to serve," I oftentimes get the impression they don't have any idea what they're talking about. They imagine, or fantasize about being completely and totally controlled, but if it happened to them, the joy of the fantasy would quickly fade. For me, I have *lived* it most of my life. It's not "just" a fantasy. Although I cherish it as a fantasy, it's actually more difficult to live without someone to worship and obey than it is to live under that person's power. Complete with all of its humiliations.

After sometime had passed living with Michael, we made an agreement. Michael was planning to move, and I was not wanting that to happen. He had found a situation where he wouldn't have to pay rent or buy food, etc. . . . so, the agreement we made was that I would pay all of the rent, buy all of the food, and (you guessed it) I would serve as his personal, full-time servant. Michael loved it! It was as though he was born to fit his role as much as I was born to fit mine.

Michael was the one to set up certain specific rules for me to abide by. Because I worked full-time while going to school, a person would think that I would have a very limited amount of time to spend fawning over someone else.

Well, where Michael was concerned, I was willing to do anything he told me to do. Since he was by this time very comfortable with being waited on and catered to (as a matter of fact, he was beginning to get cruel with it), Michael decided he would test my limits when we made this agreement. I had to turn my paycheck over to him each week without complaint, and he was allowed to do whatever he pleased with it . . . his feet began playing a greater role in my show of submission to him and his show of superiority to me. It's difficult to understand why a person might want to treat another person so sadistically. It's (even) more difficult to understand why someone would want to be the virtual slave of another. In this case it's fairly easy to explain Michael's position. For over six months I had been jumping whenever he spoke. . . . now, his power and authority were confirmed by bringing it out into the open and verbally agreeing that I would do whatever I was told to do, whenever I was told to do it. This agreement gave him a free hand and Michael wasn't afraid to use his complete power (to his complete advantage).

Until the day we made the agreement which allowed Michael to continue living with me, the only contact I had had with his feet was touching and smelling his dirty socks when I did his laundry and touching his shoes and boots when I shined them for him. The same day that the agreement was made, he ordered me to get down on my knees, bow down to him and kiss his feet as a sign of my willingness to obey him. I was nervous, excited and humiliated all at the same time. But, as I pressed my lips against the rounded toe of his Frey boot, I heard him give an additional order, "lick it, boy" . . . I knew then, without a doubt that I was where I belonged. It wasn't until I had cleaned both boots with my tongue that he placed the toe of his boot under my chin and raised it up until I was looking into his eyes. I saw him smile broadly and then I heard him laugh as he said "you are truly *my* slave, I own you, slave boy!" I knew for certain Michael was my Master and he knew how to treat his property!

"DOWN ON HIS BIG, SEXY FEET"

I'm the quiet type who sits at the bar in "Wally's Place," and observes the games and antics played among the other gay patrons for sex. And since I have been a regular at "Wally's Place" for a year, I have tricked with only three men.

All three men being that special breed of straight, married, heterosexual male with the guts to enter homosexual territory, but approaching a sexual difference with caution.

They were easy to pick out because of their uneasiness in strange surroundings . . . their machismo . . . and sometimes the "moment of truth" when they realize they don't fit in, change their minds, and are about to leave. That's when I move in.

A friendly voice, masculine good looks, and a firm muscular body all make them feel a little more comfortable with me. Almost as if I was straight, compared to the other patrons who were openly gay, making him feel at ease.

The "confessions" came over the next few drinks together. How they were straight, married, and looking for a discreet affair with a guy without having to reciprocate.

Carl was the first such straight. He is a hunk, a construction worker, 29 years old, with a wife and two kids.

"If you'd be interested," I told him, "I'd like to make it with you. Fact is, I really need a straight guy who will dominate the action, and use me like I was his private 'queer.' " The way I said it all made him feel comfortable, made him smile, and served his ego. Like most straights, Carl's interpretation of a faggot was a guy who liked to suck cock and be fucked in the ass.

I invited him to my place, and assured him that I'd bring him far more pleasures . . . plus.

When Carl revealed his whole body to me that first time, I became enslaved to it!

"Ya like muscled, hard men, do ya?" he asked, with pride on his face, and confidence in his voice.

"You're a god!" I told him. "I want to worship you," I said, getting down on my knees, naked before him where he stood.

I placed my hands on his knees, and ran them slowly upwards, feeling his powerful thighs.

"I want to feel, smell, and lick your whole body for you, Carl," I told him as I raised myself higher to stroke his hips, his hard stomach, and over his chest.

I was excited over the beauty of his hard muscles. I reached out and stroked his biceps as I pressed my face to his abdomen, and tongued into his navel.

"Ohhhh . . ." I sighed, getting turned on by his fabulous, hunky body. I circled his waist with my arms around him, and hugged him tightly, kissing and licking at his hard belly. "You're one hot number," I moaned as I rubbed my face against his flesh.

"I'm a horny number," he replied, putting his hands atop my shoulders, and shoving me lower to his groin until my face was in his pubic bush.

The hair was wet and pungent with sweat, and I inhaled the warmness of his crotch. His heavy, thick, half-hard cock pressed against my chin and neck. He then gripped me behind my neck with one hand, and grabbing his meat with the other, he pressed his cock to my face, shoving my head back.

"My ol' lady never gives me head, man. I ain't had a good blow job since I got married," he told me as he rubbed his growing dick all over my face. "I had to find me somebody who can appreciate my cock. I need me a good cocksucker. I finally decided to brave that 'queer bar,' wantin' somebody like you. You like my cock, fag?" he asked down at me.

My arms had slid down his body, and were now around his thighs, as I fondled his buns in my hands while his cock traced over my face.

"Ohhhhh . . ." again, I moaned my excitement of him, his

body, and hot fucking cock. "Yes!" I answered, "I like everything about you. I wanna give you mouth . . . suck you . . . blow you . . . and turn you on!" His cock found my mouth, and he shoved into me.

"Ahhhhh . . . yeahhh!" came his instant response to a wet, warm mouth, sliding onto his hard, throbbing cockmeat. "Give me lots of suck, buddy! Blow me!" he coaxed and demanded as those first instants of hot flashes from a warm, wet suck flushed his hot, stiff cock.

He had another man on his knees before him, queering him at his cock. A fag who worshipped his muscled body, and was down on him, sucking on his dick. Carl sensed the power and dominance he and his body had over me. I could feel his muscular thighs flex against my arms, and see his hard stomach contract into massive mounds of abdominal muscle.

His cock was hard, round, raw-tasty, meaty-delicious flesh in my mouth. To suck on it was sheer exciting joy for me. The thought of blowing this straight hunk of a man only added to my excitement.

There was no role-playing, no games in what was happening now. Carl was a heterosexual, and he made me feel queer to him. I was into queering him, and being what I really am. I enjoyed sliding his long, thick, round shaft with my mouth. He was a man, and I was sucking his meat!

I was into him, and sucking wildly. The thought of taking his load came to mind. I wanted his sperm . . . wanted to swallow him into me. And Carl was there, too. He liked being sucked by a queer, and wanted to cum down his faggot-ass throat. The truth came through in his voice.

"Ahhhh, you cocksucker! You mouthy, fuckin' asshole! Suck me! Ahh . . . do it . . . do it!" he demanded as my wet mouth smacked loudly on his super-sensitive cock-meat.

"Mmmmm . . ." I moaned as I hummed on his hot dick.

"Ah!" he grunted as his body flexed.

He grabbed my head in his hands, and thrust his hips forward. He hosed into me like the stud he was, filling my throat and mouth with his thick, slimy sperm.

"Ahhhh! Eat me, baby! Eat my cum!" he demanded, as he held my head in place, while he pumped the thick wads of his creamy "fuck" into my mouth.

I gulped and swallowed the pungent, spunky-tasting, slimy cock-cream down my throat. His stud cock filled my mouth, flooding it with more cum. His "fuck" flushed my teeth and gums, and oozed out my lips, down my chin.

"Ahhhh . . ." he sighed his last jismic shot of cum into me. He slid his hands down behind my neck. "Suck it!" he commanded, jerking my neck to make his point.

Obediently, I resumed sucking his sensitive, creamy, cum-coated, slimy, round, stiff, meaty cock.

"Ahhhh . . . yeah . . . suck my dick clean, you faggot. Don't stop till ya got every drop of me inside you," he said as he stood more relaxed, and majestically, over me.

I sucked slowly, savoring the last tastes of his spunk.

"Maaan . . . I ain't had head for a long time, but I gotta admit that was the best blow job I've ever had. You queers can suck!" he said. I sucked off his half-flaccid cock, leaving it clean and shining wet.

"Ohhhh," I moaned as I ran my hands up his thighs, onto his hard upper body. "You're a man to be sucked. I was meant to worship you totally . . . to bring you lots of pleasures only a pervert can give," I told him. I knelt straight up with my arms around his waist, and licked his stomach.

"I really turn you on, don't I?" he asked. I looked up at him, into those sexy eyes.

"Ohhh, man," I moaned my pleasure of holding him. "Men don't come any better than you. Please spit on my face, and make me get you a beer!" I begged him. He grinned down at me, feeling that power over me. He spit in my face.

When I returned to Carl with his beer, I found him sitting relaxed in one of the living room chairs. He looked like a Greek god reigning from a throne. I handed him the beer, and sat on the floor at his feet, between his out-spread legs. I bent and kissed his limp cock in homage. I fondled at his knee, and slowly ran my hand down his lower leg, and onto his strong muscular foot, stroking the top of it.

"You got sexy feet," I told him, rubbing its flesh gently with my fingertips.

"Yeah? You into guy's feet, are ya?" he asked.

"It's one of my perversions, meant for a man like you to take advantage of," I told him.

"Damn, man, you're somethin' else! I ain't had nobody ever want to go down on my feet before. What is it that turns ya on to 'em?" he asked, curiously.

"Lots of things," I said, looking down at his foot as I rubbed its huge shape. "One reason is—they're yours. They're as dominating as your body and cock are to me. And you, for that matter. There's something about being inferior and queer to a straight stud like you. It's sorta like being masochistic. I *like* being treated like a low-life fag by you. I wanna be a slave queer you can use and abuse for your own pleasures. You came to the bar for a queer to give you sex your wife doesn't give you. What you got is a queer who will service you any time or any way you secretly want. Your whole body is a turn-on to me," I explained.

"You wanna be my own personal fag?" he asked.

"Yes!" I answered.

"OK, fag! You go get me another beer, and shove that footstool over here, and we'll see just how perverted you are for my feet," he commanded.

I was up and dutifully obeying his command, and finally found myself at his two huge, beautiful man-feet, which were resting atop the soft, stuffed footstool. I reached up and stroked them with my hands.

"Ya gonna smell 'em?" he asked.

"Ah, yes! I wanna smell 'em and kiss 'em, and lick the sweat off 'em for you," I told him as I leaned forward and pressed my face to the meaty bottom of one foot. I wedged my nose between two of his toes, and inhaled the rawness while I kissed the sole.

"Maan, you are low-life. It's raunch ya like, ain't it?" he asked.

"Ahhhh . . ." I sighed my excitement for his raw, sweating, smelly foot. "Yes . . . yes . . . I love to smell and lick your B.O. You're all-man!" I praised him.

"Hey, man, do it! Lick those fuckers and let me feel that tongue of yers on 'em," he coaxed me on.

I had sucked this straight Adonis' cock, and had swallowed his cum into me. And now, I was down on his big, sexy feet. They were beautiful, masculine, attractive, erotic, dominating, and symbolic to me.

"Ahhhh . . . feet!" I moaned my love for them, and licked at the sole wildly.

"Ahhh, yeah . . . you love that fucker. Lick it, you faggot! Ya like raunch, I'll give ya plenty of stinkin' feet ta lick. It feels good havin' my feet queered. Worship 'em, slave!" he commanded.

Ohhh, his dominance was coming out, and I loved it. He was the master factor I wanted and needed so much that was real. "Ahhh, yes, yes," silently I answered his demand in my mind as I obediently swashed his meaty-fleshed, sexy foot with my tongue.

Carl watched, and felt my hand and mouth on his feet while he sat, drinking his beer. He, too, thought in silence. He ran a hand down the front of his body to his cock. His thoughts drifted into the past, and the workouts he'd had to possess the hard-muscled body he now has. He remembered his tough days in high school —the sports he played . . . the fights to prove his manhood . . . and the girls who swooned over his muscles. He remembered he'd fucked lots of girls and women before he got married. Even those first couple years of marriage, his wife couldn't get enough of him. Then came the kids, and less sex. He still loved his wife, and the kids.

He thought of today, and how he sought something different. He had missed the swooning over his body and muscles . . . missed getting head . . . and missed the power and control over another. He thought of earlier today, when he was just horny and wanted a blow job. He had passed the gay bar, and remembered thinking how easy it is to get a fag to satisfy him.

"And now," he thought, "here I am in a beautiful apartment, naked, and getting hard in the cock a second time while this good-lookin', straight-appearing queer is lickin' my feet, and being my slave. A guy who couldn't get enough of suckin' on my joint, n' really dug eatin' my cum."

Carl thought how no one in his past had ever kissed, licked, or smelled his feet sexually. He liked the feeling of his mouth and hands on them.

"This whole thing of having a queer . . . me bein' naked with another guy as he sexually woos me a lot different than most chicks have all sorta serves me somehow. The fag digs hunks, and I can use him, abuse him, and make him do anything I want for pleasure. He's a pervert, into my flesh, muscles and sweat. The fucker's kinky into me. He wants to be my slave queer. Fine!" Carl thought, then spoke.

"You're mine, faggot. You know that, dontcha?" he asked.

"Ohhhh, yes, yes, yes!" I moaned excitedly as I lapped up his big toe, and sucked down wetly on it.

"You toe-suckin' bastard, you better get used to them sweaty fuckers 'cause I'm gettin' to like havin' my feet serviced. Do it, asshole!" he demanded, teasingly.

Ohhhh, I needed no coaxing to enjoy such delicious-tasting, sexy feet. I sucked at his toe, getting it wet and loosening the hard build-up of dried grit encased between the nail and flesh. Soon, the particles began to come out of the crevices, into my mouth.

"Mmmm . . ." I moaned, swallowing the tasty, dirty, sweated grit. I loved eating the B.O. off his feet.

I moved onto the next toe to eat more of his gamy nail-grit.

Ohhhh, how I liked being a low-life, sleazy, bastard fag at his feet.

Carl could never do what I was doing. What I was doing amused him, and made him realize just how much of a low-life, sleaze pervert I really was to him.

His smaller toes I sucked two at a time, swallowing his grimy sweat-grit into me. My wet, sucking mouth was soothing to his toes, and Carl was amazed I was sucking out the scuzzy build-ups of grime from them.

"Ohhh . . . you scuz-eatin', fuckin' slimeball! Suck that slimy, stinkin' toejam off my feet. Lap 'em like a dog, you faggot-assed foot-freak," Carl demanded. I licked off his toes, and onto the meaty-fleshed bottom of his foot.

It always excited me to lick the bottoms of a guy's feet. Especially Carl's big, fleshy ones. I stroked his foot with both my hands as I inhaled and licked the sole of it. I brushed it with my face, kissed it, and made love to it like the foot-freak he labeled me.

Ohhhh . . . his feet smelled so raw . . . were so sexy, dominating . . . and were driving me wild with their aroma and taste. Carl began being active with them, and pressed them onto my face, grinding the meaty soles of both feet over my face.

"Maaan, I don't know how you can do that," he said, "but I got the kind of feet you like, huh?"

"Ohhhh, Carl, they're the best. I worship your feet. You rule me with them. I'll lick 'em for you for hours," I moaned, so happy and contented with such wild feet of such a man. I scrubbed my wet tongue around the hard heel of the foot, tasting its masculine, delicious flesh.

* * *

Carl called me about a month later.

"Hello, asshole!" he said when I answered. "Remember me?" he asked.

"Carl! How could I ever forget? That body, your cock, and those big feet of yours," I answered, excited at hearing from him again.

"You remember me," he said. "Ya miss my feet, do ya?" he teased.

"I haven't been the same since I worshipped you that day I met you. What's up?" I asked jokingly.

"Eh, me and my ol' lady had a fallin'-out this morning before I went to work. I need a place to stay for the night till things cool down at home. Whatta ya say?" he asked.

"Sure, hunk!" I answered, thinking of those big feet and that stud cock of his. I heard him laugh into the phone. "You at work?" I asked.

"Yeah. I got another hour to go," he answered.

"Sounds like you're gonna need a tongue bath after you get off," I joked sexily.

"I don't know . . . I'm pretty funky, man. But then again, you like that raunch, dontcha?" he asked.

"*Yours* I do!" I told him.

"Well, I been sweatin' all day. If you can handle the stinkin' B.O., I'll sure as hell let ya have it," he said.

"I'm hungry already. I'll pick up some beer for when you get off," I told him.

"OK! I'll see ya later, fag!" he said, and hung up. My heart was pounding with anticipation.

When Carl arrived, the sight and aroma of him was so totally erotic to me, I could hardly keep calm. He wore his hard-hat. A dirty, sweat-soaked, sleeveless T-shirt. Faded, dirty Levis. And his worn, old construction boots.

He immediately accepted a beer, peeled off his T-shirt, and suggested I remove his boots and socks while he sat atop the counter that separated the dining room and kitchen. I didn't hesitate to get down on the floor, and unlace his boots.

"I figured you'd wanna get down and check out my dogs right away. They gotta be funky after workin' all day in the sun," Carl spoke, proud of the fact that he had me turned-on the moment he

110

called me.

He drank his beer, and watched as I removed the big dirty boots from his socked feet. The masculine, sweaty-raw stink of his socks and feet filled my nostrils.

"Ohhh, Carl . . ." I could scarcely moan at the wild aroma of them. I stroked at his socked feet.

I stretched out on my stomach, full-length, on the floor. I pressed my face onto one of the big, socked feet as I held it, sniffing its wet pungence. He brought his other socked foot up onto the back of my head, and shoved me into the other.

I opened my mouth, and bit a chunk of sock into my mouth. Ohhhh . . . the wetness of his sweat saturated in the dirty cotton ignited my taste buds as I chewed it into me.

"Ah, you like those funky socks, do ya? I shoulda figured you would," he commented. My fetishes never ceased to amaze Carl.

He slid his foot off the back of my head, and then walked away from me to get another beer, leaving me lying helplessly on the floor. He returned, and I resumed smelling and chewing onto his socks.

"Man, you are somethin' else," Carl began. "Get up and sit down here on the floor," he told me.

I got up and sat before him. He peeled off one of the socks, and held it out, dangling before my face.

"Ya like chewin' on a guy's stinkin', funky, dirty socks. Here, chew on this fucker!" he said.

I opened my mouth, and bit into his raunchy sock. Ohhh, its wetness was wild, its smell unbelievably exciting. Carl let go of the sock, and it fell dangling off my chin as I chewed his feet odor out of it. He sat watching me, amazed at my perversion for his rotten, funky socks.

As I chewed, I reached down with both hands and rubbed his naked foot.

Carl gulped at his beer. He couldn't help but ponder about this second meeting with a queer. For weeks since the first meeting, he knew he wanted more of the perverted worship that this queer had given him. There was something to the raunchiness, the ego, the domination he liked being. Now Carl watched his queer chewing on his dirty, greying, old, fuckin' stinkin' sock as he rubbed Carl's foot.

I was excited chewing Carl's sweat out of his sock, and hungering to go down on his almighty foot which was in my hands.

"Get down on my foot, ya hungry fucker!" Carl told me. "Let me feel that wet homo mouth on it," he said. I spit out his sock, and lay out again on the floor at his foot.

Ohhhh . . . it was big . . . and smelling wildly raw. I kissed all over his toes and rising arch. I licked at his ankle, and back along the round sides.

"Roll over, faggot!" Carl ordered me. "I wanna step on yer face," he grinned down at me.

I rolled over, and he sat high and mighty above me. He stepped hard on my face, purposely, with a touch of sadistic dominance about him. It was his heterosexual ego. I liked it, and grasped his foot with both hands around the ankle.

"Ohhhh . . . Carl, Carl!" I moaned. His foot was *everything* in my face. I kissed the sole of it wildly with lust. It was meat! Raw . . . tasty . . . smelly . . . feet! It was Carl's, and I licked him. I worshipped his foot.

"Lick!" he demanded more.

He even leaned over and began letting long, bubbly strands of spit drip down from his mouth to his foot. The spit splashed and oozed down the sweaty flesh of the top of his foot and toes.

"Maaan, this is gonna be a night you are never gonna forget," Carl told me as he lifted his leg and peeled off his other sock.

He brought the second foot down on my face. I was in Heaven . . . and I lapped wildly at pounds of meaty feet.

"Do it, fucker! Eat feet!" the master demanded.

FOREIGN G.I. TRICKS

THE SWEDE

Steffèn was a Swedish militiaman assigned to the Swedish Consulate in New York. I cruised him at a sidewalk cafe during one summer's Sunday afternoon.

I promised him a sexual experience, with no reciprocation expected, if he would come home with me. An additional promise to have him back at the Swedish Consulate by noon on Monday was also required for him to agree.

Steffèn spoke English well. He was 23 years old and a well-built, stocky, good-looking guy.

Music, wine and cheese, and an hour's time to get relaxed and friendly together at my place, resulted in Steffèn being totally naked . . . except for his unbuttoned uniform shirt . . . lying relaxed, full-length on my living room sofa.

Our predicament was unique in so much as here was a straight Swedish soldier in a super-power nation, like the U.S., with an American queer. A queer that was turned on sexually to a Swedish soldier.

"Do you like my body, queer?" he asked me, smiling.

"Yes, I do," I answered, sitting down on the floor, in front of the couch. I touched his thick, round thigh and gently stroked its flesh. "You are a handsome, sexy Swede soldier I wish to please, and make you feel good," I told him.

"You'll do to me everything I want?" he asked.

"Yes, I am your queer to command," I said, smiling.

"Good! First you will lick my naked feet," he told me.

"Your feet?" I asked, totally surprised by his request.

"You are queer for me, are you not?" he asked.

"Yes," I answered.

"And you said you will do *anything* I want to please me, did you not?" he asked.

"Yes, I did," I said.

"Then queer me at my feet. You will like them," he said.

I moved to his feet, still eyeing that beautiful cock I *thought* he would want sucked first.

"Kiss them, and smell my feet with your nose. You will like the aroma of another man's feet, just like you would my cock," he told me.

I leaned my face close to his stocky, masculine, meaty foot. The aroma of sweating flesh rose warmly to my face, and into my nostrils. I inhaled it, and found myself intrigued by its masculine, raw scent. I reached up and took the foot in my hands, and stroked its shape.

"Ohhh . . . it does smell nice," I said, pressing my lips to the meaty bottom, and kissing along his sole.

"Lick and taste them, and you will love them even more, queer friend," he said.

113

I began licking the meaty heel, and felt the salt-tangy raw sweat and flesh with my tongue and lips. The taste was wild, and licking feet was so sexually erotic!

"It is only proper that a 'fairy man' be made to lick the feet of a real man. You lick my feet good, and I will let you have this hot Swedish cock to put in your mouth. You do want to suck my cock, do you not?" he asked.

"Ohhhh, I do, I do!" I moaned as I licked at his delicious, sweaty, sexy foot.

"Ahhh, you are such a queer man," he teased. "Look at you, down on a Swedish soldier's sweaty feet, licking them like a puppy," he said, amused. "Every soldier should have such a puppy like you to soothe his feet each day. Come, queer, and suck my cock for me."

THE AUSSIE SAILOR

I was vacationing in southern California. I went cruisin' one weekend afternoon to fulfill a fantasy to pick up a sailor. And a sailor, I did!

His name was Darbin. And he wasn't from our Navy, but Australia's! His ship was docked in San Diego, and he was on shore leave.

He had a few drinks, and had been looking for some action, and was at that vulnerable time of desperation, being horny and unable to score with a local chick.

I bought him a drink, and befriended him. Darbin was not naive to port queers, and was soon establishing his control over me . . . before my invitation to a good time.

He accepted only after I agreed to buying more booze, and furnishing meals, and a place, as well as getting him back to base by midnight in two days. I agreed, but reluctantly. I hadn't planned to devote so much time to any *one* sailor . . . especially a straight, dominant one like Darbin.

Once at my hotel suite, Darbin got out of his uniform for the purpose of establishing his worth to me. I forgot all intended time limitations, and any other sailors.

Before me stood a raw-naked, exciting, hugely-hung, tight-bodied, sexy sailor with a buzz-on. His cock was dark and purple-ish, unlike the whiteness of the rest of his body. It was thick and enormous, and evidently that was his pride and joy.

He wasn't hung up on me being naked, and liked my manner of kneeling before him with no need of command. I bent down and kissed his feet in homage. He was glad to see that I knew my place with him. I was but a queer in service to him.

I stroked his feet, and kissed the length—up and down the veined tops of them—as he stood with his hands on his hips, watching me. It served his ego in many ways. An American Yank, inferior to him, was down on the floor, kissing his Aussie feet. His ego swelled at the thought that another man worshipped him sexually . . . enough to even kiss his feet.

"Y'like my feet, queer? Y'worship 'em, eh?" he asked. I stroked one of his calves.

"Yes," I answered with an exhaling sigh, as I caressed his blond-haired lower leg with my face. "I worship you because you are handsome, sexy, and a strong, hard man. I am a slave at your feet, and want to lick them in homage to you. Please let me make your feet feel pleasure," I begged, to feed his ego.

"Later, queer. I'm too randy now! I need y'r mouth on my dong. I need to be sucked off. I'm bloody horny!" he told me. I didn't realize his predicament, and I immediately got up on my knees and grasped his hard, throbbing, big cock.

His dick was a real jawbuster if one didn't go slowly on approaching it. I began by licking it, and really got into its beauty, hugeness, and dominating attraction. It was the hardest cock I ever sucked onto, considering it was so big.

With my jaw stretched to capacity, and aching cheeks, I sucked onto it, I sucked onto it . . . taking the huge head into my mouth. Its feel and taste was so blissfully erotic. I couldn't slide more than two inches past the head onto the widening shaft. I held his meaty whopper, with both my hands at its base, as it seemed to absorb my mouth-watering saliva. Its hugeness pinned my tongue to the bottom of my mouth, rendering it useful only to the bottom side of his phallic beauty as I sucked it.

Just five minutes of jaw-stretching, drooling wet sucks on that delicious, monstrous manmeat, and he unloaded the biggest, most forceful, abundant load of thick, jismic, starchy, pungent man-spunk I have ever tasted. Never have I enjoyed swallowing and eating a man's sperm-slimy load so much.

When it was over, he sat down, forcing me down on his feet after I had lapped his phallus clean. Did I go from one wild experience to another!

With that delicious after-taste of sperm in my mouth, the warm sweaty aroma of his big Aussie feet crept deep into my nostrils.

I gasped, and excitedly began inflicting my lusting greed upon his feet. Like upon his cock, I drooled my wet saliva onto his attractive foot flesh. And again, I found myself greedily licking, lapping, and sucking on him with erotic fervor.

I am as queer for feet as I am for cock. And my Aussie sailor loved sliding and grinding his slippery, wet, sweaty, smelly feet all over my face to be licked and sucked on by his American queer slave.

He drank more whiskey, straight from the bottle, and soon relaxed and passed out, leaving me all the time I wanted for play at his hot-sexy, big, big feet. I rose on my knees, and as I stared at all his slumbering, naked beauty . . . I jacked off. The Aussie excited me, and soon I was milking my sperm all over his feet.

Needless to say, after my climax, I returned to his feet to lap up my cum from them. And began what was two hours of uninterrupted worship of his feet. Until he woke up and wanted more *head*.

It was the beginning of the happiest weekend of my life to date!

BOOT-LICKING A BIKER

It's been awhile, hasn't it? It is Sunday morning, and again, I'm out on the patio with my typewriter under the sun, tanning. I guess I really can't get any more golden than I already am from these past weeks working-out and tanning beneath the rays of the desert sun. I am white only where I wear my gym shorts.

So, how is the boot-lickin', sneaker-sniffin', sock-chewin', feet-lappin' cocksucker? As I say, it's been awhile since hearing from you. Of course, you already know how pervertedly wonderful I am when it comes to being basically graphic in describing sex when writing you. I will send one or two of the mini-series at a time to you. This will assure you're not getting tired of good, dirty pornography I just happen to be good at.

I guess I've seemed to neglect writing you fantasies about your favorites. Well, that's because I just haven't been inspired. Why? Well, probably because I write from looking at undressed photos in gay magazines. And write about certain people that I think are sexy out here. Guys I meet at the bars. Most photos of movie stars are of them dressed, and I can't seem to visualize what they got under those clothes. Someday, I'll come across a good, hot photo and will send it, and a story, along to you.

I have also completed two large photo albums of models and body shots that are a real turn-on for J/O for me. You see, as of late, I've been getting into sucking cock a whole lot. Oh, I manage to sneak down on a trick's feet from time to time, but mostly it's been swallowing some mighty fine loads of stud-cum that's really had me turned on lately. That's not to mention splashing some pretty generous loads down some of their pretty throats, as well.

Lately, since I got those cycle boots, I've really got into the Levis/leather scene. I have been goin' to the bars in Levis, the boots, and black sleeveless T-shirts or tank-tops. The chain tattoo around my left bicep, that is now accented by a dark tan, has stirred the interest in some other patrons, and become an approach for conversation. Later, if I like them, usually resulting in tricking with them that particular night.

Only once these past few weekends have I had to get drunk to trick. But at least I had a good time . . . as I remember it.

Rod was my latest. I scored with him yesterday afternoon, about 2 p.m., at one of the bars. I had laid in the sun all morning, and decided to get dressed without showering, and go to the bar. Nothing like finding someone who could get off to smellin' a raw-tanned, hard body to make it with!

Bein' it was Saturday, and everybody was still out enjoying the good weekend, the bar wasn't all that busy at that time of day. But, there's always the lonely, or horny, or the independents that find the bar peaceful to go to once in awhile, instead of tanning.

Anyway, this Rod was a Levis/leather type who was tall and lean, and accented by four tattoos on his golden, mid-twenties, hot body. He wore one of those body tank-tops that's cut like a tank-top in front, but tapers back into a narrow stretch of material at the center of the back, before it curves around under the armpits. Sort of like a weight-lifting work-out shirt that exposes the shoulder blades more.

Anyway, he had a tattoo on each shoulder blade—both of the Harley-Davidson logos—of which one was the official #1 with the brand name printed behind it, and the other was the spread eagle wings with "Harley-Davidson" printed around it and a helmet. They were both very professional jobs. A tattoo also accented his biceps, and was real professional, as well. Fortunately, he didn't go beyond that with tattoos anywhere else on his body.

Rod was one of those guys who could turn you on with his eyes. Maannn, were they sexy! He was brown-eyed, but it was the way his eyes were shaped that really was beautiful. Full brows, and a sort of slant at the outer corners of his eyes that made him look hot. Not like an Oriental, but just sexy someway. His body was hairless at the upper torso, and legs and crotch were proportionately haired, as one would expect. And his cock—a wild 8½" of sweaty, round, hot meat that was "succulently suckable." (Ohhhhhh . . .)

Our eyes cruised each other, and an invite to the pool table cinched it. I knew I wanted to go home with him. And by 4 p.m., we were writhing, and squirming, and twisting our hot bodies in a sweaty, exploring scene of each other's muscles and flesh. Maannn, did Ron taste good, smell good, and turn out to be one wild, raw animal of a man sexually!

Rod was as tanned as I am. His apartment was old, but clean, and provided very little comfort from the heat. He had only a portable fan that stirred the air about the bed we groped together in. That, of course, is why we both were constantly wringing wet in our own sweat, and enjoyed sliding all about each other's body . . . lickin' and lappin' each other like hungry fags, and enjoying every drop of each other.

We rimmed each other in 69 fashion, as well as sucked each other's cock the same way. But we didn't stop there. We made our way down each other's thighs, knees, and calves to each other's feet. And, mannn . . . *you know the joys I felt!*

Rod had those "hillbilly big feet" that so often are found on tall, lanky, lean types like him. He is originally from Georgia, and I loved that Southern accent of his. But those feet of his, maannn! This guy has size 12 or 13's that were sensitive, meaty, and glistening in a sheen of deliciously tasting hot sweat. I sucked on toes that were at least two inches long, and not one bit bony, but meaty and strong! And smell . . . ohhh, wow! We buried our noses between each other's toes at the same time, and you could hear the snorting-whiffing-inhaling sounds fill the room. We were two greedy, hungry guys into some *real* sniffin', lickin', suckin' and carryin'-on sex with each other.

Our white asses and crotches were accented by the rest of our bodies being tanned, and gave us perfect targets to home-in on for some real bun-bitin', crack-lappin', hole-suckin' sex at each other's butts. Not to mention gettin' into some real ball-suckin' and teasin' before lip-lockin' onto each other's hard meat.

Man, I jacked and sucked, and worshipped at that hillbilly's big fuckin' love-stick for forty minutes, and through two generous loads of his thick, tasty jism! And he was crazy for bein' sucked, and sucked, and jacked like I was giving him. I was surprised that his cock didn't even deflate a fraction of an inch after his first climax . . . which almost drowned me! No, this fucker's cock stayed up, and he encouraged me to keep suckin' till he came off with another hot load . . . which was almost as big and generous as the first. I swear, between the two loads, he had to have fed me at least a pint of cum. Well, at least it sure felt like it.

Anyway, I want him again, and get him I will. Like next Saturday, since we're to meet at the same place, at the same time.

He got me off my second time just about 6 p.m., and I was home about 8 p.m. that night. I went out about 10 p.m. to the bars, after eating, and got home about 3 a.m. I don't even want to talk about the lazy bastard who is still sleeping in my bed this morning. All I can say is that he don't stand a dime to a tray of ice cubes in Hell as far as the man I had yesterday. But he was a good fuck.

So here I am, writing to you about my tricks over the weekend, and not paying the attention you should be getting from me.

Another accomplishment I have made these past weeks is to have acquired a 25' long towing chain. I've cut it into different lengths, and painted it black. I made two 4' lengths. After cutting a pair of handcuffs in half, I attached the remaining link of chain from each cuff to the end of the 4' towing chain. I already bought another set of cuffs, but have not yet made the second 4' "slave restraint."

Anyway, be advised that I'm just experimenting in my neverending exploration of sex between men. First, understand that these two restraints are not for restraining a slave from movement.

In fact, I want a slave to wear the 4' length of restraint clamped to his wrist, and feel the weight of the chain hanging from his wrists in front of him. The restraint is only to serve his mental attitude of being a slave by the feel of the restraint, yet it does not interfere with any movement he makes during sexual scenes.

His hands will still be free to move, as well as his arms, during sex with a master. I dare believe that you could fantasize that being in such restraints is just something "symbolic" to being in captivity, but not as far as movement. The feel of the weight of the chain only serves to emphasize the fact that you are under some restraint.

Anyway, fantasize, if you will, having such a chain on that hangs down before you, weighting your wrists. And then, imagine a well-built, muscled master before you in torn, old, faded Levis . . . cum-stained, old cycle boots . . . studded belt . . . shirtless, and rippling in handsome, muscled beauty. He is dark-haired, blue-eyed, 6', 180 lbs of all-man, with a bulge in his Levis' crotch that indicates you are in for a full-course meal . . . and then some!

Oh, he understands where your head's at, man! I mean, who wouldn't, the way you're always staring at guy's boots, sneakers, and feet the way you do. Most sexy, attractive guys are knowledgeable of the minds of homosexuals, who are weak and cannot resist the temptations of expressing their admiration of footwear and feet, like you do. You know, always gawking and lickin' your chops with very evident expression that smart guys can interpret. Guys like the stud who has you chained before him.

You're not beyond being a little mistreated. I mean, after all, you do bring it on yourself, the way you have this fetish of yours for boots, shoes, sneakers, socks, and—naturally—the feet of other guys. Face it, man, you're an unusual type of pervert with such a fetish. And you certainly can't limit your fetish only to other men who are into the same thing. That's kinda spreading things thin. No, it's very obvious to straights, bi's, and other gay men that you're a foot-freak, and cannot help yourself when it comes to servicing some hot jock's feet, or socks, or—in this fantasy— cum-stained, old, worn, black boots. You're a man who spends a lot of time on the floor, man! Of course, that stands to reason because you're into the part of the body that has close contact with the floor.

This stud, who stands before you, has your number, though. I mean, he's brought you to an abandoned, old, dirty-floored garage where you will not be bothered. He has already put the restraint of chain on your wrists, and has ripped your old T-shirt right off your fuckin' body, as you stood there facing him. He checks out your build above your waist, and observes you're staring at those old, dirty, cum-stained boots of his!

He grins mischievously at you, and already the thoughts of making you slave at his boots interest him. He raises his powerful leg upward, slowly, as you watch. Then, pressing his boot firmly on your stomach, he shoves you back hard, sending you off balance and falling onto an old stuffed wrestling mat laid out on the floor of the garage. You grab to balance yourself, but find the chain does interfere just slightly at helping you get reachable flexibility.

You're flat on your back, a rather familiar position for you, and suddenly see him towering over you, and feeling the heavy weight of his boot slide toe-first under your head at the base of the neck. Then, standing firmly above you, with all his weight on that boot and leg, he raises his other leg and steps down with his heavy boot onto your stomach muscles. You lift your hands, feeling the weight of your chained wrists, and grab the boot in both your hands . . . in one, instinctive motion that you are used to doing. You are a captive of the chains. A stud male above you. A cum-stained, heavy boot grinding into your stomach. You are slave, and your cock is excited over it, swelling and hurting as it fills the crotch of your tight Levis, you "pig."

Your master reaches over, and pulls a heavy crate from the debris that's piled in the corner of the garage. He then sits down on it, and kicking you firmly on the stomach with his boot, he commands you to roll over and lick his boot. Of course, you cannot resist. You don't want to, and you never could, even if you wanted to. That's because you need such a boot of such a man. And taking the chain's weight and pain at your wrists, you maneuver it all over you as you turn. You grab the boot at its ankle in both your hands, and go for it, feeling the weight of his other boot coming down on your ass as you do.

Yeah, you're a "pig" alright. You can't resist tonguing at the rough surface of those heavy boots. You lick and feel the leather all over with your lips and tongue as he grinds the heel of his other boot into the fleshy buns of your ass. His dirty heelprints all over the ass of your Levis—signification of a master's ability to walk over your fuckin' slave ass!

You're already into that euphoric high you get when you're worshipping with hungry affection on another man's boot. Licking and tasting the leather, and anything else that has collected on them. In this case, some cum stains of other boot slaves who have had to climax all over the surface of his boot in proof of their dedication to his superiority. Cum from other slaves who were high and excited at worshipping another man's boots.

Oh, yes, there are such masters in every city of the country, who would have you down and "doin' it" to their boots. Men with the power of arrogance, ego, and dominance that will drive you to the floor at their feet. Men with the sexual attractions that you cannot resist, and lose all control of yourself when with them.

You're licking frantically at his hot, leathered boot, and feeling the hard, grinding massage he gives you with the other. Stomping down on your ass every once in awhile to let you know who's boss. You run your hands over those leather boots, and feel the strength of his big foot, and muscled lower leg and ankles inside it. You can even detect a slight aroma of his flesh and socks as it drifts down out of the opening in the leg of his Levis. You even envision what his feet and legs look like as you lap the surface of his boot, cleaning its every inch like the slave you really are to him. You even hear the chain scrape the surface of the mat, as well as feel the weight and slight pressure of the cuffs at your wrists. Mmmmmmmm . . . lick and smell that boot, you "pig."

The stud who's having his boot licked, and who's grinding the other boot all over your ass . . . and even sometimes bringing it up to press down atop your head to pin your face down on the other . . . well, he just unzipped the fly of his Levis. Spreading the denim back, he releases his big, masterful, round and hard piece of stud-meat, and begins strokin' it into a huge 10½" of majestic, sweaty hard-on. And it feels good to his strong, meaty fist that grips it.

He slides his free boot under your ribs, at the side of you closest to him, and lifts hard. Rolling you over onto your back like a lightweight, bringing the boot you licked and worshipped up to pin the side of your head against the mat, as he stands. He then releases it, and standing above you firmly on the mat, sends a vicious kick with his other boot that digs hard into the cheek of your ass, as you feel the toe dig hard between your ass and the mat.

"Take off my boot, slave!" he demands.

You obey as you roll on your side, and start working the boot off his foot while he sits down. The kick to your ass didn't hurt that much to you. In fact, it had a certain tingling, exciting effect on you, knowing he kicked your ass while commanding you to service. And you remember seeing his gigantic hard cock jerking during the motion high above you. The thought of sucking such a beauty is also exciting you. You work at getting his boot off, and he makes you hand it to him.

"Roll over," he says, and you obey.

Once on your stomach, he slides his sweat-saturated, socked foot between your face and the mat, the aroma of it immediately filling your nose, and driving you wild with excitement. And then, you feel that heavy boot come flying down atop your ass, smacking your butt with a thud.

Ohhhhhh . . . maannn, the thud of the boot at your ass didn't bring pain because it wasn't brought down hard enough to. It struck with surprise and firmness, only meant to bring sexually stimulating significance, and your cock jerked with spasmodic excitement. The aroma of his sweaty socked foot only adding realistic joy to the whole scene, and you were in unbelievable ecstasy, you so often slaved for men of this caliber. Again, he pounded your ass with the boot. And you chewed wildly at the tangy, sweat-saturated cotton of his thick sock . . . tasting its masculine, erotic deliciousness. Your cock throbbing to a point of sheer climax inside the crotch of your Levis. And you feel your cum saturating the denim, and oozing all over your crotch and pubic bush. Another slap of the boot on your ass, and more of your cum oozes into the denim and flesh of your crotch.

"Ohhhhhh . . ." you moan in frantic, unbelievable excitement that shakes the whole insides of your body, and your head jerks with sweaty sock gritted between your teeth, as you try to rip it from his foot. Your eyes shake frantically up into the lids, spastically accenting your ecstasy of climax, and other reactions. Another slam of the boot on your ass, and the last of your generous load fills every void of the crotch inside your Levis. The taste of sweaty sock mixing with the saliva of your mouth, and trickling down the palates of your throat. Mmmmmmm!

Ahhhh, maannn, how come you cummed? You boot-lickin' ass-hole. Now you're *really* gonna have to do some service to your master when he sees those fuckin' cum stains all over the fly of your Levis. You fuckin' ''pig.''

Write soon . . .

LETTERS TO THE FOOT FRATERNITY

Dear Sock Slave:

I have just removed my filthy, smelly worn high top Converse sneakers and have my sweaty raunchy dirty socks ready for you to get down on your knees and crawl on over here and smell. I want to see your slave face really get into these socks and smell 'em real good for me. I want to hear you beg, lying on your back with your nose smacked into my dirty socks and tell me now bad you want to suck the filth out of them for me.

If I give you permission to suck my socks with that slave mouth of yours, you'd better give it your best, fucker. I want to watch you suck those damn socks clean with your mouth while you grovel around on the floor with my sweaty socks in your mouth. I'll probably piss on 'em and give you a little help with suckin' em clean so your mouth won't get too dry.

If you please me, I'll let you clean up my smelly feet. You'll have to get that tongue between each toe and clean out all the toe jam before I let you lick the soles and heels. If you do a good job, I'll let you suck on my stinkin' feet for as long as it pleases me.

In stinkin' socks, I sign off.

Master David

* * *

I just came from the library on campus, where there were hunky guys there studying for finals. There were countless guys in shorts and sandals, Topsiders and Reeboks, who had abandoned their shoes beneath the table. My fantasy has always been to drop a pencil and then lick the toes of a handsome surfer type studying there. I know I'd probably get smacked for it or they wouldn't un-

124

derstand, but it would be worth it.

I also love to toy with others while in the library there, jiggle my foot, watch them jiggle theirs, especially if the shoe or thong is hanging half down their foot. Wait till it falls off. I like to watch their feet as they study, and sometimes have them catch me staring at their feet. It's a real turn on for me to have them know that I'm enjoying just looking at their sweaty feet.

LICKING TONY'S CIRCUS BOOTS

My name is Shawn. I am on my second tour with the circus. We have just loaded the second train in South Dakota, and now we're on our way to Vancouver. I am 19, and my job is working on the wild animal crew. The crew handles the lions and tigers, and the cage and all equipment involved for just one act—Eric's.

Eric *is* the wild animal show. The master of the big cats, and star act of the show. Eric—the shirtless, muscled Adonis who dazzles the crowd in his light tan trainer's pants and knee-high dark brown boots. He snaps the whip, and pokes the wild beasts around the cage in obedience to his commands.

His handsome face and sweat-glistening body in the multicolored spotlights were the envy of every woman in the audience from puberty to sixty. And Eric *knew* it. That's why he's got an ego that soars.

Not one man on his crew likes Eric or his wild animals, with the exception of me. Well, I don't like his animals either, but Eric I worshipped!

After the train got rolling, the crews made it to the dining car for breakfast. Some just headed for bed after working all night. I spotted Tony, one of the trapeze artists, sitting alone.

"Can I join you?" I asked, smiling, holding my tray. He glanced up with those dark brown eyes of his.

"Sit!" he said, and I did.

Tony was 31, and much like Eric, a performer who dazzled the women along with his brother and cousin with their well-exposed physiques half-naked, and wearing tights, flying on the trapeze.

"And how are all the wild animals?" Tony asked.

"I know the caged ones are OK, and how are you?" I asked him.

"You think I am an uncaged wild animal, no?" he asked, grinning.

"I think you are an uncaged wild animal, yes," I grinned back at him.

He wore a tank top, and I eyed his round shoulders and hard, bulging biceps. Under the table, his foot stepped hard atop mine, and I stared into his eyes as he applied even more pressure, bringing pain.

"You wish to train this wild animal like Eric does his cats?" he said, grinning.

"I do not train animals. I only take care of them . . . wild . . . caged . . . or uncaged," I replied.

"Come!" he said, getting up and heading for the cabin car. I followed, and he led me to the privacy of his small cabin.

Once inside, he peeled off his tank top, exposing his lean, fatless, beautiful, muscularly accented, hairless upper body.

"You like this wild animal, queer-boy?" he asked as he posed and flexed his muscles for me to see.

"Ohhh, yes . . ." I gasped an excited breath at his hot body. "You're an untamed beast," I told him.

He unfastened his belt, snapped open his fly, and shoved his pants to his thighs, and sat down on his bed.

"Pull them off over my boots," he instructed.

Tony never wore underwear, and his flaccid, thick cock was so erotically attractive to look at. I tugged and pulled till I got his pants off. Then he ordered me to get naked for him. And I did.

I felt sexy, and was excited for him and his beauty. I stood before him in a pose for him to observe. His cock began to stir as he eyed my youthful body.

"You are a beautiful 'queer-boy.' Come and lick the boots of a man," he demanded. I went to the floor, and hugged loosely at his manly boot. I began licking the shine he kept on them.

Tony's foot and lower legs filled his boots. He had big feet and firm, muscular shins and calves that left very little gap between the boot and leg. They were boots fitted for him, and were high— just four inches below his knees. There were brown, well-polished, genuine leather that reflected his pride in them.

I licked at the top of one boot, wetting its already polished surface with a sheen of spit. I could feel his powerful leg inside the boot with my greedy, lapping, wet tongue.

"You have become the animal, boy. The lowest of all animals. The queer one. The one to be tamed by men. Lick Tony's boot, boy! Clean and shine them good, and I will let you taste my big, sweaty feet. And I know you like to lick and smell feet, Shawn," he talked down at me.

What he says is true. I do want his hot, sexy feet. But now, I'm strokin', smellin', and lickin' at his leather boots.

He stands, and begins his dominance over me. He steps on the back of my neck, and presses my head down harder onto his other boot that I am licking.

"Lick it, you stupid asshole. Spit-shine my boot like a dog. A queer faggot-dog! Pull off my boot, pervert," he demanded, loosening the pressure on my head, and sitting down. I tugged and worked his boot off his foot. He stood up again.

"You like my hot, sweaty body and cock?" he asked as I knelt before him. I placed my hands on the front of his powerful, tanned, muscled thighs.

"Ohhhh, Tony, you know I worship you and your fabulous body. I slave to you. Ahhh, please, let me kiss your fabulous, hot cock," I begged.

"No! Now get back down, and lick my other boot. You're my slave, and you will lick and shine my boot to earn my body. Lick!" he demanded.

And obediently I tongued at the polished leather. As I licked, he stepped on my bare back with his socked foot. He then began jacking at his big dick, it growing in his hand.

Circus performers had such egos, and Tony was no exception. Crowds applauded him, women idolized his agile, hard, muscular body. And now, he had a queer teen-aged boy he made lick his boots in homage to him.

When I had licked his boot shiny clean, he made me pull it off. And on my back, in his cabin, on the floor, Tony began walking my face step-by-step with his dirty, moist, sweaty, smelly socked feet.

"Smell them, queer-boy. I have strong, smelly feet that sweat and stink for you. Feel them on your face, boy. Smell and taste my dirty socks and strong man-feet," he spoke in demeaning tone as he jacked at his cock, and kept rubbing one foot, then the other, all over my face.

The whole scene really turned me on. His feet and socks *did* stink! And the aroma was very erotic and euphoric to me. This beautiful, naked, male Adonis was standing over me, fisting his huge, beautiful meat as he stepped on my face with his strong, pungent, hot-sexy socked feet.

And I was inhaling them . . . licking at them through moist, rancid socks. He was dominating and enticing me to a whole exciting adoration for masculine feet.

"Take off the sock, Shawn. Take off both socks, and adore the rawness of my feet. Smell them, and lick them. Taste the sweat and flesh of them," he coaxed at me. I removed his socks as he sat down on the edge of the cabin bed.

When I removed them, he placed both his big, raw, wild, smelly feet atop my face, pinning my nose between them.

"Ahhhh . . . smell! Inhale my feet, queer-boy. Feel them with your face and hands. Taste them in your mouth. Worship your Tony at his smelly, hot-sexy feet," he encouraged. He spit on his cock and squeezed at its excitement, feeling that rumbling deep inside.

I was totally engrossed by his feet. They *were* raw, stinking, and masculinely delicious.

"Yes, yes . . . lick them, queer-boy! Lick a man's stinky feet. Worship them because they are mine. You are one of so many who want my body," he said with his ego soaring, and his hot cock throbbing heatedly to the action at his feet.

He fisted at it in furious, feverish passion. Its sensual sensitivities running rampant in wild, raw joy.

He leaped off the bed, straddling my head. His body flexed, his legs bent at the knees, and his cock exploded in coaxed joy. He pounded out long, ropey strands of thick, creamy man-spunk all over my chest and stomach. Lots and lots of thick, slimy cum. He knelt above my head, and milked the last of his manly jism load all over my face, tongue, and open mouth.

It was wild, exciting, and all it should be. The straight, wild, hard-bodied, hunky-lean, handsome, daring trapeze artist cumming all over a simple low-life circus queer-boy.

When all subsided, I was made to lick his cum from his feet as he sat above me, sliding over my body with them. When I cleaned them well, he sent me away.

I slept a couple of hours, and was awakened by my crew boss. He told me that Eric wanted me in his car. I got dressed, and made my way through the crew cars, the dining car, and finally to the last car, which was Eric's.

Yes, he had his own railroad car, owned by him. And it was plush, as well. He was the star.

I entered and found Eric in his huge bed with two of the aerialists from the show. The two foxiest chicks of the twenty or so the circus has.

"Ahhh, come in, Shawn . . . join us," he said.

He lay in all his naked beauty, propped up in a mountain of pillows. One of the girls poured his glass full of champagne as he held it out to her. The other girl lay across his bed, sucking on his huge, hard cock.

"Don't be shy. Get naked and join us. Debbie, be a good girl and get Shawn a glass," he instructed.

I began getting undressed. I was feeling quite awkward with the girls being present. And the one chick's head bobbing on Eric's cock was exciting me. He noticed, and grabbed her by the hair, and pulled her off him.

"Enough, bitch! You're exciting Shawn. I mean, he wants his turn on my meat, too! Don't ya, Shawn baby?" he asked, grinning. He was enjoying belittling me in front of them.

"You mean he's a queer? A hot, young body like that?" asked the chick who was giving Eric head.

"Such a waste!" commented Debbie, handing me my glass of champagne.

"Shawn is my queer-boy. Now don't you girls tease him. After all, you three have something in common—you all know a good man when you want him," Eric teased us all.

"I'll bet Debbie and I can make a man out of him. Let us have him," the girl suggested to Eric. Eric just laughed.

"Who do you want, Shawn? Debbie and Linda? Or me?" Eric asked.

I was sitting sideways at the foot of the bed. I saw Eric's feet crossed, one over the other. I gave my answer by leaning toward Eric's feet, leaning on my elbow, and kissing the toes of the topmost foot.

"Does that answer the question, girls?" Eric beamed with ego.

"Fucking faggot!" Debbie jeered.

"You're a real 'sick-o,' Shawn!" added Linda.

Eric's feet were so huge. And when my face had come close to them, I felt that heat of feet for the second time in one day. Their aroma was so frighteningly dominant, masculine, and intoxicating to me. I stared at their beauty and touched them with one hand.

Tony had ignited a new fetish in me. And now, here I was at Eric's feet. I could smell their powerful aroma, and my mouth watered. I leaned forward again, and stroked the massive bottoms of them with my face.

There was silence as all three of them watched me. It was my first time to ever adore Eric's feet, and he sat there feeling my hand and face caressing them.

Eric was raw and sweaty from the sex he had had all night with the girls. And now, his queer-boy was giving his big, stinking feet affectionate kisses and a massage. It was perverted, yet it felt good. Once again, this queer-boy was showing his animal lust for the rawness and raunch of a man.

I began licking Eric's sweaty, stinking feet at the meaty soles. Linda found it repulsive, and again commented that what I was doing was sick. Eric quieted her by shoving her head down into his crotch.

"Shut up, and suck me!" Eric demanded.

He then instructed Debbie to go suck on his queer-boy's cock, and soon her wet mouth was sliding up and down my hard meat. Her warm, wet mouth and playful hands drove me sexually wild for Eric's feet.

I feverishly lusted for every inch of his big, sweat-stinking feet. The more excited I got, the heavier I breathed. The heavier I breathed, the more of his raw-sweaty feet aroma I inhaled. The more of his feet-stink I inhaled, the hungrier I got. The hungrier I got, the more I licked his feet sweat into me to swallow.

Linda's mouth bobbed the length of Eric's big, thick, long cock as my stroking hands, and wet tongue and mouth traveled over his sensitive feet.

A bitch and a boy were worshipping him at his raw, hot cock and his stinking, sweating feet. They all wanted him because he had it all. His ego soared, cock throbbed, and feet tingled with wild sensations.

Debbie's mouth bobbed the raw length of my cock as I sucked onto Eric's big toes. A bitch was sucking me as I worshipped the feet of a man, sucking his long, hard, round, sweaty toes.

"Ohhhh . . ." I moaned as I drove my wet tongue between two sweat-tasty toes, and my cock erupted and filled Debbie's cunt throat with thick, creamy boy-sperm. I filled her mouth, and my cum oozed out its corners and down my shaft, over her fingers.

Eric then blasted one of his gigantic loads into Linda's mouth. He filled her throat and mouth, and thick rivulets of his creamy white and translucent spunk oozed down his shaft, all over her hand.

Both girls hungrily sucked, licked, and swallowed all our ball juice, while I swallowed that tasty-raw feet sweat from between Eric's manly, big toes.

We drank champagne, and Eric dismissed the girls.

"You will sleep with me, queer-boy," he said, and took me in his arms as we lay on our sides, my backside pressed up against the front of him. We fell asleep . . .

*　*　*

I was in the equipment car, working on a broken coupling for a section of the cage.

Skip, a crewman on the rigging crew, came into the car. He said "hello," then began fiddling around with some equipment.

He was in his early 20's and one hot number. He kept glancing over at me, and I smiled back at him several times.

He was hunky built, and wore a Levis vest over his shirtless upper body. And I noticed he sported a huge bulge at the crotch of his Levis.

"Are you Shawn?" he finally spoke.

"Yes, I am. Who are you?" I asked, knowing his name, but pretending not to.

I had seen him many times working, and knew he was a cocky type and heavy into chicks.

"Name's Skip, man. There's word around that you're the guy to see if ya want some head. You a fag?" he asked, rubbing his crotch.

"For a hot number like you, I am," I said. He was sitting on several rolls of rope and rigging.

"Come over here, man. I wanna show ya somethin' real nice," he invited, with an evil grin on his face.

I climbed over equipment to the secluded tuckaway area in the semi-darkness, and noticed he had dropped his Levis to his ankles, and was sitting with spread legs.

I knelt at his feet, and immediately could smell the heavy B.O. that comes from sweating and lack of showering a day or two. His upper body was hairless, hard, and muscled. His arms bulged at the biceps, the left one sported a tattoo.

I focused on his crotch, which was accented with a beautiful hunk of thick, heavy, six inches of flaccid man-meat.

"Ohhh, man, that's nice," I said.

"Yeah, I know. And it's raunchy, too! Come here," he said, grabbing me behind the head, and pulling my face close to his heated, warm-smelling crotch, while groping his meat with the other hand.

"Smell it, man! I like to sweat and smell like a real man, ya know. Just sniff that B.O., and look at my meat. I'm proud of my cock, ya know? I mean, to me, a raw-raunchy hunk of fuck-meat like this, and a queer like you, are meant for each other. Go on, man, rub it with that pretty fag face of yours. And get 'high' whiffin' my hot, sweaty crotch."

He was right. Pressing my face to his crotch brought on unbelievable heights of euphoric pleasures. His cock was beautiful, not only to look at, but something erotic in its flaccid state to enjoy, even in raunchiness. I *was* destined to lick, play, and suck its flaccidness into hardness, but not too quickly. Meat needs to be tenderized before ya wanna get cookin' on it.

"Ohhh . . ." I sighed, inhaling his raw-raunchy crotch.

I rubbed my face all over his balls and floppy meat, smelling and kissing them for him. He stroked the back of my head with one hand, and guided his flaccid, smelly cock over my eyes, nose, cheeks, lips and chin.

"Oh, man, I like a nice face to rub on. Ya like the smell and feel of it, do ya?" he asked.

"Ohhh, yeaahhh . . . don't stop . . . just rub my face with it. You got hot meat I wanna lick and suck for you," I breathed heavily, intoxicated by its raw, masculine aroma.

"Sure, baby, I hear ya . . ." he said.

"I WEDGED MY TONGUE BETWEEN HIS TOES"

It was into the second week of August, and the "Big Apple" was an oven, just like my apartment. All the fans did was rotate the hot air around.

As usual, I was broke and trying to occupy myself, watching my old B&W TV in my jockey underwear shorts, and sucking on the ice cubes left after drinking another glass of iced tea. I always left my door to the hall ajar for ventilation reasons.

About midnight, as I sat sweating in the only light coming from the TV, the door creaked open. And when I looked up, there was the hunk who lived down the hall. He, too, was wearing only a pair of jockey shorts to beat the heat, and held a brown sack in one arm.

"Hey, neighbor! Could ya stand some company and a couple quarts of beer?" he asked.

"Hell, yes!" I answered, and he came inside.

He pulled out one quart, and handed it to me. Then, a second one for himself. He also dropped a cigarette lighter and three joints on the coffee table that I had my legs resting on. He discarded the sack on the floor, and sat down on the couch, beside me.

"What's on?" he asked.

He was well-built and handsome. I could smell the aroma of his body sweat, and liked it.

"A World War II movie," I told him.

"Wanna share a joint? It's good stuff!" he offered.

"Sure," I said, and observed the big bulge in the crotch of his shorts.

He lit up, and we shared the joint, and watched the tube, and drank our beer in silence. But I was every bit aware of his presence.

"War movies suck!" he commented, looking over at me, after we had finished the first joint.

Our eyes met, and I noticed the glaze in his. One of his hands moved at his crotch, and drew my eyes away from his. I watched as his hand pulled at the leg of his underwear and exposed his huge, flaccid cock and big balls, freeing them from their entrapment. His other hand suddenly gripped my shoulder.

I looked back into his eyes. His eyes were not smiling, and

neither was he. They were cold and serious. I *knew* what he wanted, and had to make my choice. I bent down, and kissed his thick, sweating piece of meat.

I felt his hand on my head as I began licking the tasty roundness of his raw meat. He leaned forward slightly, and spit on the back of my neck and shoulders. He spread his legs wide, and pressed my face down on his wet, sweaty crotch.

My nose pressed into his pubic bush, its perspiration wetting my face. I inhaled him, and was enraptured by the magnetism of his crotch. His big hand slid off my head and gripped the edge of the leg of his underwear, and ripped the whole crotch of it away from me. It was erotically hostile and attractive to see his whole crotch exposed in the surrounding shreds of his ripped-open underwear like that.

He was so dominant and animalistic in his actions. He controlled and manipulated me with an air of confidence.

I tongued at his huge balls, amazed at their size, aroma, and sweating masculine, raw taste.

I licked the sweat off the man's balls. I slurped them with the lusting saliva of my mouth, then sucked them, and swallowed his tasty ball-sweat.

His hand stroked my head, and again, he spit on me. Suddenly, he lifted one leg and put his foot on the knee of the leg I was bent over while licking his crotch. His hand shoved my head away from his crotch, along his big thigh, and to his foot. I slid off the couch to a kneeling position between it and the coffee table, and instinctively began licking his big, naked, sweaty, wild smelling foot.

He picked up his quart of beer, and sat watching me lap wetly at the meaty bottom of his foot while he drank. He fondled his meat in one hand, and held his bottle of beer in the other.

I licked about the heel and ball of his foot. His feet were slightly dirty from the floors, but I licked it away. His foot was big, and the odor of it was enticing and erotically exciting to smell and taste as I lapped it.

His toes wiggled, and I licked my way to them. He spread them apart by flexing, and I wedged my nose and tongue between them. I sniffed, whiffed, and inhaled his raw feet-stink. I loved the raw, masculine aroma. I licked the tasty, sweating flesh between his toes, and moaned my excitement at their smell and taste.

134

I had never licked a man's feet before. I don't know why I was doing it now. There was something about this man . . . his presence . . . his sweaty-smelling body that so easily attracts me sexually to it like a magnet. His cock and balls, his big meaty foot, his actions—all dominantly manipulative. His B.O., his raunchiness, his beauty—all seem to control me and ignite my lusts.

His feet were powerful. I wanted to smell and taste them. I loved sucking, and going down on his toes was exciting to me. Doing it to this guy's foot really turned me on.

And just as I was really getting turned on, he guided me back to the crotch, and to his cock. Again, I was licking his bone. A big, hard, excited "love bone" that needed taking care of.

I sucked on his cock as he spread his legs apart. He was raw and had a delicious, hot, sweaty fuck-meat. He closed his eyes, and just felt me and my mouth as I greedily worked his dick with sucks.

Ohh, I liked him in my mouth! His cock was so suckable, and big for my mouth. I bobbed on it, loved it, and couldn't enjoy enough of it.

Then he cummed, heavy and forcefully inside my mouth, and I ate him. Afterwards, he left as abruptly as he came.

It happens!

"YOU LIKE THESE SOCKS OF MINE?"

I was sweaty, raunchy, dirty and raw-smelling. I peeled off my dirty, stinking work shirt, my dirty Levis and raunchy jockstrap, and left them lie. I stood there in my worn, old workboots and dirty socks, giving Rod plenty of body to look at.

I climbed atop the chaise lounger he sat in, naked, straddled him, and shoved my big, smelling, sweaty, hot cock in his mouth.

Rod's a queer who knows what I want and expect sexually from him, and likes it. Rod's one good cocksucker, and he loves my crotch. And I love that wet, sucking, queer mouth of his sliding on my sweaty fucking dick.

It's my Wednesday night visit to Rod's house for satisfaction. I come here right after I get off work, and am at my raunchiest. When I have sex with chicks, I like being clean. But with a queer, like Rod, I dig being dirty, raunchy, and reeking with B.O. when getting serviced sexually.

Rod calls it being sleazy. He likes to smell, kiss, lick, suck and rub all over my sweaty-smelling body.

I treat Rod like a low-life, sleazeball faggot. I dominate, humiliate, degrade and verbally abuse him, and he likes that.

I like to get him indoors, and down on the floor, and get into seriously feeding him my dick.

It really turns me on to make a guy suck my cock. I like to watch my big dick slide in and out of Rod's mouth as he smells and sucks on it. He's so fucking cock-hungry for my sweaty-tasting meat. I'm so fucking big-dicked that Rod sucks about two thirds of it. Rod's a fucking cunt-mouth that I like to lean over, and fuck into awhile, then let him suck it awhile. Rod's such a dick-sucking pervert into raunch that I feel so fucking superior and in control of him, I just *have* to use and abuse the fucker.

I think every straight guy should own a queer like Rod. You can spit on him, piss on him, cum in him, and make him lap the sweat off yer body. He's so into me sexually, I can make him do anything I want. And right now, all I want is to have him blow me like a faggot loves to do to guys.

"Suck on that fuckin' meat, Rod. Yeah, you like a man's meat in yer mouth. You like smellin' that sweaty, raw crotch while you're suckin' on dick. Ahhhhh, slurp on it, Rod. Let me feel that wet mouth of yers. Faster, man, faster!" I coaxed him. "Ahhhh . . . you fuckin' son-of-a-bitch! Taste that meat. I'm gonna cum in you, Rod. I'm gonna blast that faggot, fuckin' throat of yers with sperm!" I told him.

And I can cum, too! Rod knows that because he's swallowed my thick "fuck" before. He's queer for my cum because I give him lots of it.

"Ahhh, do it! Gimme yer suck, baby. Suck it, suck . . . suck . . . suck . . ." I coaxed at his every, wild stroke.

We were sweating, and the room reeked of our masculine B.O., and resounded with his slurping wet sucks on my cock.

Ohhhh, I was *there*. Straddling over him on all fours, and my cock erupted down his throat and into his mouth. My thick, creamy, slimy, fucking cum was everywhere. My thick, juicy sperm was all over his face. He sucked and swallowed my fuck-slime, cum-juice with uncontrolled gluttonish lust.

I knelt up, and held my cock with one hand. Grabbing his hair with my other hand, I pulled his head up. I slid my dick over his cheeks, and let him lick the slimy head of my cock.

Rod gave me a good blow job. And I gave him one of my good loads. I sat on his chest, and watched him savor his reward . . . licking, sucking, and swallowing my cum. I let him enjoy it, knowing that he would soon be licking my boots while I rested up to feed him more of my sperm later.

"Lick it up, you fag!"

When it was over, we had a beer together. Both of us naked and sweaty, except for my dirty workboots, and grey and orange worksocks.

They had a special interest to Rod, my boots and socks. And my feet, too. Right now, what he's waiting for, as we sit having our beer, is for me to take control and make him get down.

You see, Rod is a queer with a perverted fetish for footwear and feet. And that's why I didn't remove them. In past experiences with Rod, I've come to enjoy his fetish at my feet. There's a certain ego-serving, superior satisfaction to having a queer down at your feet, worshipping you.

"It's time, asshole," I told him, and he knew what I wanted.

I sat atop the kitchen table, letting my lower legs dangle above the floor. He got to his knees, and bent to grab and kiss my dirty fucking boots. And it was the beginning of another perversion of Rod's that I take advantage of.

The fucker kisses all over my boot, then begins at the top of the boot, and licks the dirty leather clean.

"You're a scumbag, Rod," I tell him. "But if you want to suck on my sweaty butt, and lap out my stinkin', smelly armpits, and lick and sniff all over my muscles and body, eatin' my B.O., you'll clean them fuckin' boots good for me. Yeaahhh, lick 'em, you dirty-mouthed bastard," I abuse him, as he really gets into me.

A ring of dirt begins to form around his mouth. Rod is very much into licking my boots, mentally and physically, in total sexual worship for me and my body.

I'm a straight, dominant, big-dicked, well-built, raunchy, smelly, raw, sexy man that Rod needs to worship. A queer sleaze, like Rod, is a low-life scum male that belongs at a man's feet. Think about it—my big, meaty feet sweat all day, trapped inside my boots and socks, as I work outdoors under the sun. There's nothing more satisfying than to watch and feel a scumbag, low-life pervert that loves to lick and smell, kiss and suck yer raunchy, dirty, stinking, smelly boots, socks and feet, because they're yours.

You can't treat or talk to Rod anyway but down, ya know? I mean, he's queer sleaze who eats B.O. He licked my entire boots from top to the soles and heel.

"Take 'em off, and smell and chew my stinkin' socks, asshole," I tell him.

I know he'll wipe his dirty mouth off on my socks. As he sniffs, and chews, and licks my sweaty moist, stinking socks, he'll moan his hungry sexual greed for them. He's a real "dick wipe," man!

"You like those socks of mine, Rod?" I asked as I sat, drinking my beer. He just moans because he's so into them. "Chew that sweaty foot odor outta them, creep! And pretty soon, you can lick them bare, raw, scuzzy-smellin' feet of mine. Yeah, you want that," I teased him as he chewed my thick, tasty, dirty worksock.

I finished my beer, and laid back on the table, resting my head atop my folded arms. I would now relax, and let Rod do it all to my feet.

Rod smelled, kissed, licked, and massaged both my entire feet, with my socks on them. He was "high"on their aroma and moist stench.

To lick my dirty socks and rough leather boots was a symbol of his dedication to me. He ate dirt, and licked wet filthy socks. And now, he was peeling them off my feet, and exposing the true goal of his affections.

It felt good to me to be finally rid of boots and socks, and my feet be free to breathe. I was totally naked, and felt his hands massaging them for me. I could hear him moving around, getting in different positions for access to them. My boots and socks were gone. He was now down to the meat of the matter.

Now, I got me two big meaty, strong feet. And they sweat and reek with raw odor more than the rest of my body because they're trapped inside my boots and socks.

It's that raw-sweaty masculine aroma, like from my ass, or armpits, or my crotch, that Rod also smells and inhales off my feet . . . but only stronger. He gets intoxicated by the smell of 'em, and it turns him on. His heart starts pumping with excitement, his head whirls in the raw scented bliss from my smelly feet odor, and his cock . . . that's *always* hard when I'm around . . . throbs with excitement over my feet.

I felt his lips kissing the top of my foot from the end of my leg, down the heavily veined flesh to my toes. His kisses are affectionate and lustful, making a point of his worship of it.

Ol' Rod's really got it bad for feet. Smellin' 'em, rubbin' 'em, and kissin' all over 'em like he does. And ever since the first time he done it to me, it's what I want and expect from him. I mean, hell, I like havin' an inferior male being lickin' all over my stinkin', sweaty feet for me.

He must be on his back because he's kissing and rubbing his face all over the bottom of one of my feet. Now he starts licking the sweat off them with the wet tongue sliding and slurping around my heel. He moans with delight at the taste of it. And it feels good to me as I lie atop his kitchen table, relaxed. My cock stirs some, and I know when it gets real excited and hard, I'll have him back sucking it for me. But for now, I'm just contented lying here, and having my dirty stinking feet cleaned by my own raunch-loving, foot-licking queer faggot.

He licks and sucks at the meaty sole as he strokes the top with his hand. He's a million miles into a fetish fantasy on my foot.

Funny thing about Rod—he'll spend endless hours all over my body when I visit. He licks, sucks, smells, and rubs me all the time. It's as if I'm a feast, and maybe the last meal he'll ever have. The guy's a rare breed of queer, I think! Anyway, he's kinky enough for me.

Ohhhh, I like it when he licks between my toes like that . . .

BOOT SLAVE

"I don't *ask*, I fuckin' *tell!* If you choose me, you're choosin' to be slave. Slaves are inferior scum who *obey*, or they don't *get!* You want me? You get down and kiss my dick!" he said.

And I obeyed!

"Now get yer fuckin' ass down, and lick my boot, asshole!" he commanded me, and I obeyed.

He shoved my head down, and I licked boot.

"Scarf on 'em, ya creep. You lick 'em like a dog. You're a boot-lickin', asshole, mother-fuckin', sleazy fag, man! You're dirt! You're scum! You're my slave. You want me so fucking bad, you'll scarf the dirt off my boots.

"Do it, you foot-worshippin' slave. My dirty socks and sweaty feet are in them boots, creep. And you're gonna chew my fuckin' dirty socks clean for me, just like you'll clean my boot!

"Damn! What a nice fuckin' butt you got! You got an ass worth fuckin', homo!" he said, gripping and squeezing my buns while I lapped at his boot.

He was a stud, and was right about being dominant and taking what he wants. Damn, if he didn't grope my ass. He got naked, except for his boots.

"Git on all fours, like the dog you are, faggot!" he ordered.

I obeyed. He went to his knees behind me.

"I'm gonna fuck your butt, slave," he said.

He spit on his hand, and rubbed it on my hole. He spit again, and wiped it on my hole. Then again. My ass dripped with his thick saliva, and I felt his cockhead probe my hole. It was going to be a vicious, heartless, callous fuck, and I *want* him.

"Eiiieeee!" I screamed as he shoved into me unmercifully.

He slapped the back of my head, and I fell forward and down.

"Shut the fuck up!" he said.

I muffled my mouth against the mattress as tears came to my eyes. His cock hurt, and he didn't care. But I *wanted* him.

He had me down, and his cock probed inside my ass. Halfway in, his cock hit an obstruction. He lifted slightly, pressed harder, and my whole insides gave way. He buried his whole dick into me. My pain changed to pleasure.

"Feel it, you bitch dog! I'm gonna fuck a 'man' into you. Ohhhh . . . yeaahhh . . . gonna fuck me a faggot butt. I'm gonna fuck yer socks off, baby!" he said as his cock began pumping my ass like a piston.

"Ahhhhh . . . give it to me, master, plleeeaasssse . . ." I begged.

His butt and hips pounded back and forth like a jackhammer against my ass. And inside me—that masterful, hard, horny, dominating, male sex organ. I cannot resist as it thrusts its pleasure into me.

He is a naked, savage, glorious, beautiful, human, male animal fucking me in my butt. He fucks into me with vengeance and greed for his own pleasures.

Our bodies sweat, and raw aromas of masculine, animalistic sex fill the room. Our moans and groans, and the squish-smacking rhythms of savage cock pounding male ass fill our ears.

His pleasure is taking me . . . conquering another into submission. He gives what he takes—pleasure. And he fucks me like the masterful stud he is.

"Feel it, you bitch! You faggot-assed wimp!" he abused as he pumped splash after splash of his warm, thick, slimy cum into every cavern of my insides. His cock fucked his load into me. And his stiff cock squished and smacked my ass with creamy, lubed strokes of pleasure.

When his climax subsided, he popped his slimy-coated cock from my ass, and twisting and turning me around, he found my face, and thrust his meat into my mouth.

"Suck it!" he demanded, and I obeyed.

I sucked my master's slimy, hard meat that had just fucked my ass. I looked up at him with my mouth full of cock, and our eyes met.

"You're a pig!" he told me. "I just fucked yer queer ass, and you're suckin' my slimy fuck-stick in yer mouth!" he reminded me.

He watched as I sucked it clean for him.

"Hey, man . . ." he said, pulling out of my mouth, and sitting on the bed. "Get these boots and socks off me. I'm gonna feed ya my feet. You *do* want to smell and lick my sweaty ol' dirty feet, dontcha?" he asked.

"Oh, you bet I do!" I said as I tugged at his boots and socks with mounting, anticipating excitement.

I love to get down on a good pair of smelly feet. Especially on a good-looking hunk like him.

I pulled off the last sock, sniffed it, and went down on one of his feet.

"No!" he said. "Sit up!" he instructed.

I sat up, atop my own feet. He laid back on the bed, raised one leg, and rested his foot on my shoulder. He raised the second, and shoved his foot in my face. I grabbed his ankle with both hands, and began kissing his wet, smelly, meaty sole at the instep.

"Yeah, homey, that's it. Kiss all over my foot. Get 'high' on that ol' feet-stink ya like off another guy's foot. Scarf 'em down, you creep. Kiss, and lick, and eat my feet!'' he commanded.

He lay before me, his head cradled in his folded arms behind it. He watched me smell and savor the aroma of his foot. He watched me kiss them in homage to him. He watched and felt my wet tongue slide along the meaty flesh as I cleaned and licked its stink away.

"Ahhhh . . . do it, pig! You sleazy, fuckin' bastard,'' he abused at me.

I drooled for such a man and his feet. My own spittle dribbled from my mouth, down his raw, meaty foot, only to be lapped back up in tasty slurps of his tangy foot sweat.

He watches me with contempt. He does not understand my perversions, but only uses and takes advantage of them.

I am slave at my master's feet.

"Suck my toes, slave!'' he commands.

I obey, scarfing his sexy, hot toes into my mouth.

RAUNCHY STUD

The minute Mark came into the basement, I knew it was him. The 23 year old, 9th grade dropout had worked another hot day under the sun in a sleeveless Army shirt, and smelled of raunch. He worked for a battery company for minimum wage.

Mark was young and dumb, and wandering the streets when I first met him. I had propositioned him when he was 20, and he came home with me. He's lived here ever since. You see, Mark may be young and dumb, even antisocial with most people, but he's tolerable to me because he has one hot body and youthful sex drives that are wild, imaginative, and unharnessed. He is power and strength to me. Mark is "the sleazed.'' He is a young, dumb, dirty, sweating, smelly, raunchy, dominating, raw, untamed, energetic, sexual male animal.

I meet him every day in the coolness of our dirty old basement, where raunchy surroundings supply atmosphere for raunchy sex. I wear only my cut-offs, and lie atop a leather gym wrestling mat on the floor. It is surrounded by storage boxes and old furniture, and other rubble, collecting dust.

"Hi, I'm home,'' he greets me, with his shirt unbuttoned and hanging open, and his big dick hanging out the fly of his dirty Levis.

"Hi," I replied, getting up and going to him. I grab his thick, huge meat in one hand, squeezing it, and touch his shoulder with the other. I then kiss him lightly on his lips. "I've missed you," I tell him.

"Me, too!" he said, then stepped away from me.

"How'd work go today?" he asked as he peeled off his shirt and tossed it on the floor. He then sat down on the old, dirty love seat at the edge of the mat.

"Wasn't as hard as you probably went through," I said, kneeling on the mat before him, and unlacing his dirty, old workboots.

"Fuck, no! You work in air conditionin'. Me, I sweat all day," he teased.

I pulled off his boots, and tossed them aside. I then peeled off his thick wet, sweat-soaked, dirty, dingy socks, and brought them up to my face, and inhaled their odor.

"Whew!" I responded. "Yes, you do sweat, Mark. And I love it when you come home smellin' like a man." I then bit into his dirty, stinking socks.

He grinned at me. He was so beautiful and rugged-looking, sitting before me, his hairless muscular frame glistening with that wet sheen of sweat. His huge, thick cock protruding flaccidly out of the fly of his dirty Levis, onto the cushion between his thighs. And chewing his funky, tasty socks, I looked down at his feet, and stroked the veined tops of them with my fingertips. I could smell Mark's sweaty body over the stench of the socks already so close to my nose.

"And I stink so bad that you wanna give me a bath, right?" he asked, with that ornery look on his proud face, as he grinned.

I pulled his socks from my mouth, and tossed them aside. I then traced one of his big, meaty feet with the fingertips of both my hands.

"Yes. I love it when you come home dirty and sweaty, and smellin' all raw like a working man. You're so rough and rugged, and muscular . . . I just want to lick your whole body clean for you," I said, bending down and kissing his foot. He stood up and unfastened his Levis, and shoved them down his legs.

"I wanna be naked. You get naked, too," he said.

I helped him out of his dirty Levis, tossed them aside, and re-

143

moved my cut-offs. The mat was cluttered with his dirty clothes and boots, and I laid down amongst them at his feet. He sat back down.

"Awww, do it, man! Smell and lick them dirty feet of mine for me," he commanded.

Already I was licking all down the ankle and side of one of them. It was so raw and smelly, I hungered and tasted its saltiness.

"Ahhhh . . . I like it when you do that. When I sweat all day at work, it never bothers me 'cause I know when I get home, I got you to lick my feet and lap the sweat off my whole body. Roll on yer back, and let me put my feet right on yer face," he told me.

I rolled over, and he stepped on me with both his big, wet feet, pressing their meaty bottoms atop my face. Ohhh, what godly feet he had. So beautiful and young, raw-smelly and dominant. I licked at the tasty, meaty flesh as I held them at their ankles above me.

"Mmmm . . . lick that fuckin' sweaty-smellin' raunch off my feet, baby. Let me feel that wet fuckin' mouth all over them. Ahhhh, you like my feet. Eat 'em! Suck on them big, sweaty sexy feet, baby! Ohhh, yeah, that's it! Do it! Eat your man's feet!" he coaxed and teased.

His dirty talk was a turn-on to my already excited hungry attack on his wild, tasty, hot feet. He was grinding and rubbing my face with them as I wetly slurped at the meaty flesh. I loved it.

The Sleazed One slid his ass to the edge of the love seat. His legs were spread wide apart, the lower legs angled inward to his feet, both of which were on my face. He squeezed at his heavy, huge, flaccid meat just above his feet.

"Gotta get raunchy, baby! Gotta be animal!" he said.

Suddenly, his kidneys burst, and he was pissing like a stud horse all over his feet. Piss flooded my face and hair.

He slid his feet off my face and stood up. He pressed his cock against his stomach, and piss fountained from his fleshy hose onto it. Piss flowed down over his body, crotch, thighs, and rained off him to the floor.

"Ohhh . . . get up here!" he demanded, and I was up on my knees before him.

He fisted my wet hair in one hand, cocked my head back, and began showering my face. With closed eyes, piss hosing my face,

I gripped his thighs with my hands. I opened my mouth, and he filled it. I raised up on my knees, and spit it all over his chest as he pissed down the front of me.

I sat back down on my legs, and took another mouthful, and swallowed it. As he pissed, his cock grew hard. He filled my mouth again, and I held it. I stood up, and he closed his eyes as I spit it out all over his face.

I grabbed my cock just as it burst with my own piss. I stepped back, and he went to his knees. I grabbed behind his head with both hands, and pulled his face into my crotch. With my cock pinned upward between his face and my groin, my piss fountained and flowed down us both. I could feel his piss splashing my feet.

He then pulled me down, and we wrapped onto each other's body with arms and legs, pissing into each other's crotches as we kissed.

"Ahhhhh . . ." he sighed as we rolled and rocked our bodies in puddles of our piss.

"Animal! Raunchy, fuckin' raw 'animalism' is the way to go, baby!" he shouted.

Our pissing subsided, and we humped and grinded into each other's wet body, fucking at each other's hard, muscular flesh.

"Ahhh, man, I *gotta* be blowed! I want my pisser in yer mouth, baby. Ya wanna suck on my big dick, huh? It's gotta taste good, all sweaty and piss-soaked. Come on," he said, pulling from our embrace and lying on his back, spread-eagle, in our piss on the leather mat.

I moved between his legs, and laid on my side, straddling his thigh with one arm. He sat up, and piss dripped down his body. I leaned forward, and licked the rivulets of piss off his belly.

"Suck my cock, ya piss-lickin', raunch-lovin' cocksucker," he demanded. I grabbed his shaft at its base with my free hand, and sucked onto it.

"Mmmm . . ." I moaned at the taste of his salty, sweaty, pissed-drenched meat. I love Mark's meat in my mouth. *Meat—* hot fucking meat I loved to suck raw!

"Ohhh . . . do it! Blow me! I wanna cum in that faggot mouth of yers. Ohhh, yeah . . . faster, baby. Suck!" he coaxed dirty, grabbing my head between his hands.

I bobbed on his thick, slick meat with wild, wet sucks. He was delicious, and erotically raw. My mouth squished loudly and wetly up and down his round, big, thick throbber.

"Uhhhhh . . ." he sighed. "Eat my . . . 'fuck' . . . baby!" he groaned as his cock filled my mouth with warm, thick, creamy, jismic spermy cum-slime.

Wildly I gulped and swallowed the pungent, salty, spunk-syrupy male cock fuck-slimy cream. He shoved my head down on his fuck-slimed, throbbing dick.

"Ahh . . . suck it all! Swallow my cum, scumbag!" he jeered.
I obeyed.

"YOU'RE MY COCKSUCKER"

He looked so hot in just his jockey shorts. He had called me a "dirt bag" earlier that day, and when I asked him what it meant, he invited me to his place tonight, saying he'd show me.

He sat down beside me, and put his arm around me. He pulled me to him to take his kiss, and my hand slid into his underwear.

"Mmm . . . ya like that cock of mine, do ya?" he asked softly, kissing me again.

"Ummm . . . yes . . ." I said, breathing excitedly at the feel of his body against me . . . his kisses . . . and his hot meat in my probing, rubbing, and squeezing hand.

"You been wantin' to get in my pants for months," he said. "I knew you were queer the day they hired you at work. That was the first day you stared at my crotch. Ummm . . . yer hand feels good on it. Go on, pull it out, and get a good look at it. And don't stop playin' with it. It feels good!" he told me.

I brought his beautiful cock out of the top of his underwear, and gazed upon its beauty.

"That's the way you like it, ain't it? I mean, all nice and hard to play with, and do whatever queers do with another guy's cock?" he teased at me.

"You're so big and horny, I wanna suck it for you," I told him, stroking its beauty in my hand.

"You mean you wanna take my dick, and put it in yer mouth? You wanna 'blow' me?" he asked, talking down and dirty to me.

"Oh, yes. I wanna go down on you, and suck it all inside my

mouth, and please you. Yes, I wanna 'blow' you," I said, drooling to have him in my mouth.

"I wanna be licked. Lick all over my chest, and suck my tits with that wet, hungry mouth of yours." he instructed, manipulating me.

Obediently, I began tasting his wild, raw flesh. He stroked my back and shoulders as I tongued and sucked at his tits.

"I want ya to hear me good, baby, while ya lick down my bod. From tonight on, you're gonna be my 'dirt bag,'" he said. "You're gonna get 'down and dirty' with me, doin' whatever I want. Yer mouth and yer ass are mine! If I so much as want my armpits or ass ate out, you'll do it. If I want ya down on the floor, lickin' on my stinkin' feet, you'll do it. 'Cause you're a 'dirt bag,' asshole! *My* 'dirt bag'!" he made it clear to me. Oh, how I liked to hear him talk as I licked down his tasty stomach.

So now I knew what a 'dirt bag' was to him. Now I'm not offended. And if I had been offended, I kinda liked that, too.

I drove my tongue hard over his navel. I could feel the heat of his crotch against my face. The thought of licking his feet upon demand intrigued me. I have never licked a guy's feet before. I licked slowly down his groin, and from the sighs, and throb of his cock in my hand, I knew he was ready for "head."

I licked into his pubic bush, and inhaled his sweating crotch aroma.

My moment was *now* when I open my mouth and take his cock into it. For a few months, I have fantasized this moment. And now, I was sliding, down slowly onto his meat. His hard, round, thick, beautiful, fleshy, raw, hot, sexy cock. I filled my mouth full of it, with every cocksucker's dream of reality.

"Mmmm . . ." I moaned at the delicious tasty satisfaction his cock was to me.

"Ohhh, yeahh! Taste that cock of mine in yer mouth, baby," he sighed. "Suck on it! I love it in yer mouth. It feels good. Mmmm . . . suck it, honey! Give yer ol' buddy one hot blow job," he coaxed and teased at me.

I bobbed up and down slowly on it, savoring the taste of its flesh. I felt his hands on my back and head, and his hot meat in my mouth.

"Ohhh . . . yeahhhh . . . you love my cock in yer mouth, baby. You're my 'cocksucker.' I like bein' blowed by yer faggot-ass mouth. Dirt bag!'' he called me.

His meat expanded harder and bigger in my mouth. His hands gripped my head, and pumped it up and down, pacing the rhythm on his cock. The room was hot and pungent with the smell of our sex and sweat.

"Ahhhh, give me that suck! Suck! More and more wet *suck*," he demanded.

The word itself being repeated was a turn-on. I purposely began giving loud, squish-smacking sucks for effect in response to his demand. It instantly made him throb and quicken his pace for more glorious wet, sucking mouth on his hot, quivering meat. And I'm a hungry meat-sucker 'dirt bag' who loves a man who fills and feeds my mouth full of his phallic beauty for sucking.

In one violent pull of my hair with one of his hands, he jerked me up off his cock. With his other hand, he fisted his wet slippery cock, and began pumping long strands of his thick, juicy sperm all up his body, which already glistened with sweat.

It was so erotic to smell and watch his cock eject the long, ropey, generously-portioned squirts of his cum. I drooled and licked my lips. My mouth watered, and I hungered to taste it. His hand in my hair held my head steady to watch while he moaned his joy at every round he pumped onto his ribs and stomach.

His hand came off his cock and joined his other hand on my head. Violently, he pulled me down and smacked my face onto his hard, wet, slimy stomach. Gripping my head in both hands, he began grinding my face up and down his body, smearing me into his cum and sweat.

"Ohhhhh . . . you 'dirt bag'! Feel that slimy 'fuck' and sweat all over yer fag-ass face," he moaned as he slid my face up and down the slippery flesh.

He made his climax an erotic, slimy mess for me to feed upon and wear on my face. My face squish-smacked on his flesh. He shoved his slimy-coated cock into my mouth.

"Suck and eat me clean, ya 'dirt bag'!" he demanded . . .

FEET FAG

"You like feet, do ya?" he asked.

"Yes," I answered.

"Here's what I think about queer feet-fags," he said, giving me the "bird." He also gripped the bulge in his underwear.

He was young, cocky, and hard-bodied. I was instantly attracted to him. I went to my knees.

"You are *everything* and I am *nothing*," I said, hoping to appeal to him.

"Ya want my feet, do ya? Ya gonna worship me and kiss 'em like a slave?" he asked.

"Yes, I worship you," I told him.

"Crawl yer ass over here and kiss my feet, fag!" he demanded. The floor was dirty, but I crawled to him. Again, I was at another cocky, young stud's feet—kissing at their beauty.

My cock was hard, and I was excited kissing and smelling the aroma of his sexy, hot, sweating, meaty foot.

"Ya like my feet, fag?" he asked from high above me, stepping on my upper back with one foot, as I kissed at the other.

"Ohhhh, yes, yes!" I answered, kissing and inhaling its odor.

"How bad do you want to lick 'em for me, ya sleazy foot-freak?" he asked.

"Ohhhh . . . please . . ." I begged to him, "your feet are so sexy . . . so smelly . . . and so dominating and muscular like all of you. I want to lick your sweat off them and swallow it. I want to lick and suck on them, clean and worship them for you. Pleeaasse! I beg you. Let me have your sexy, hot feet!" I pleaded, kissing at it.

"You fuckin' low-life, queer-assed bastard!" he called me, breaking his foot free from my clutches, and walking farther into the room. He sat down on the dried, cum-stained, sheeted mattress that lay in the corner on the floor.

"Crawl yer ass over here," he commanded as he removed his underwear and tossed it aside. He sat with his back against the wall. His legs spread wide—one straight out across the mattress, and the other bent at the knee. He had his hard cock fisted in one hand as he fondled his balls with the other.

"If ya want my feet so bad, ya best earn 'em by blowin' on this awhile," he grinned cockily at me crawling to him.

I crawled onto the mattress, between his legs and sucked onto his cock. He grabbed my head with both hands, and forced me down as he arched his hips upwards, burying his six-incher into my mouth.

"Ya like sweat . . . taste and smell that, ya cocksucker!" he jeered, holding me onto him. My nose inhaled the raw-sweaty crotch smell of the hair it nestled in.

His pubic hair was wet, and its pungent vapor entered my nostrils each time I inhaled. He laid his leg out over my shoulder, down my back, his heel resting just above my ass at the spine.

"Give me a blow job, foot-freak! I wanna cum all over yer faggot-assed face, and wipe my feet on it," he said, releasing the pressure on my head. "Blow me!" he demanded. I came up for air, and sucked back down on him.

"Ohhh, yeah . . . you love that cock, too! Just like ya love feet. Suck it, you faggot whore!" he said, spitting on my head, thrusting his cock. "Ahhhh, yeahhh . . . suck on that cock of mine. Think of my cum all over yer face, and me slidin' my feet all over yer mouth. Yeahhh, ya can eat sperm off my feet like the pig-ass foot-fag ya really are. Ahhh . . . suck!" he coaxed me on.

I sucked for his load, and his feet. I wanted them both *bad*. And the cocky young punk gave it to me! Grabbing my hair, and holding up my head with one hand, he milked his warm, splashing load onto my face.

"Ohhhh, fuck! Cum, all over . . . yer . . . fuckin' fag-face . . ." he moaned as he jacked off onto me. His cum was thick and oozed down my face in slow tracks.

When he finished, he brought his feet up and shoved them both in my face, and pushed with all his strength. My body moved away from him, off the mattress, onto the dirty floor. He sat with his legs spread out, and he could slide his feet on my cum-gooey face. His meaty soles and heels squish-smacked his creamy fuck-slime loudly all over my face.

"Grab them feet, you fuckin' bastard, and *eat* that fuckin' cum off 'em!" he demanded.

I grabbed hold of his ankles, and grinding my face on his soles, I began lapping his gooey slime off them. His cock, sperm, and hot sexy feet triggered my hunger and lust to a wild, erotic, animalistic sexual worship to his feet.

"You gross, fuckin', feet-eatin' pervert! Lick my 'fuck' off them feet!'' he demanded, spitting at me as he squeezed at his cock. "You're nothing!" he said with complete disgust at my perversion.

"I know, I know," I thought to myself as I slurped at his wildly delicious feet. I'm *just* a feet-fag.

BUTCH HAD BIG, STRONG MEATY FEET

"Hi," I think, was the first word he ever said to me. And he sat down on the grass beside me.

"My name's 'Butch,' what's yours?" he asked.

"Phil," I answered. "What do you want?" I added, being somewhat curious and defensive.

Butch was a rough and rugged, sleazy-looking kid with dirty shirt and faded jeans, and old torn sneakers. He was long-haired, handsome but slightly unkempt.

"I just need somebody to talk to. You don't mind, do ya?" he said, grinning as our eyes met.

"I guess not. So what's on your mind?" I asked.

"Are you a homosexual?" he asked. The question wasn't staggering or a surprise to me since it's a known fact that gays frequent this park, which would include me.

"Why do you ask, Butch?"

"I'm horny, for one reason. And I'm lookin' for an older, mature queer that will appreciate what I have to offer. I'm a hot number!" he boasted.

"Are you hustling me, Butch?" I asked.

"Just for somethin' to eat, and a place to stay tonight. I'm passing through town on my way to the west coast. I been payin' my way by offering my big dick and hard body to any fag who wants to queer me." he said, and peeled off his shirt to show me his well-muscled, hard, hairless upper body. "This is part of what I got to offer. And I'm dominating, too. Are you interested?" he asked, grinning at me as I eyed his body.

"Yes," I answered, "Keep talking." I smiled.

"I'm raunchy, and I'd like to get naked, and make you get down to kiss, smell, lick, and suck all over my body. I'll talk down and dirty to ya. I'll let ya be my queer, and make ya please me.

We'll be friends whenever we're not havin' sex, and yer ass belongs to me when we are. That's the way it's gotta be. My pack is hidden in them bushes back there. Ya wanna take me home, and see the rest of me?'' he grinned.

"Let's go, stud!'' I said, and helped him with getting his pack on.

At my place, Butch wasn't shy getting naked. He was an exhibitionist and egotistical young hunk who enjoyed enticing me with his body.

"Ain't I enough to make ya drool, Phil baby? C'mon, get naked and down on the floor on yer back. I wanna sit on that face of yers. A queer lickin' my balls, and suckin' on my asshole gets me excited, ya know?'' He instructed and teased me.

I wanted all of him I saw, and he certainly knew it. I liked his self-awareness, his dominant uninhibited appeal, and his easy ability to control me to be obedient to his commands.

I got naked, laid on the floor, and he straddled my face while on his knees. His crotch, ass, and thighs filled my nostrils with his raunchy-raw, heated aroma of sweating flesh. His balls were huge and heavy and he laid them at my lips while his hand milked at his huge piece of meat.

"I been on the road for 36 hours, man. With no chance of showerin'. Ya like the smell down there?'' he asked.

"Ahhhh, yes . . .'' I moaned. "You're raw and stink like a man. I love your body odor. I want to lick you, taste you, worship you!'' I moaned as I rubbed my own balls, and squeezed at my cock.

"Yeah, I know!'' he said. "Lick my balls, baby. Taste me! Ahhhh, that feels good,'' he chimed.

His balls were tight and swollen, and I scrubbed on them wetly with my tongue. Butch was a hot number—the type I'd lick the sweat off his balls.

"Ya like me dirty, dontcha, asshole? Yeah, I've had yer type before. Kiss my ass, baby, and let ol' Butch know you appreciate him,'' he instructed me.

I began kissing his hairless, sweaty, firm buns. He reached back and spread his buns.

"Kiss my hole, faggot!'' he said.

I kissed the puckering orifice, and he sat down, pressing it to my lips. I tongued it while he sat on my face and fisted his meat again.

"Ohhhh, fuck! Eat my sweaty, fuckin' shithole!'' he moaned,

shoving his ass against my tongue.

There was no shit at his hole, just sweaty hot body odor. I puckered his smooth hole and sucked on it.

"Ohhhh, you butt-suckin' bastard! Do it!" he shrilled as he beat his meat frantically.

Suddenly, he got up off my face, slid away from my head in just enough time to squeeze off splashing, thick, ropey strands of his cum all over my face.

"Ohhhh . . . yeahhh, my fuckin' cum . . . all over yer faggot-assed face," he jeered as he squeezed his thick jism all over my nose, cheeks, lips, and neck.

I had my mouth open, and caught some with my tongue. Its salty, pungent, spunky taste triggered my own climax, splashing up my body.

When both our climaxes had ended, Butch pulled a chair over to near my head. He sat down, and stepped onto my face with his big, meaty feet.

Now, I love a good man's cum, and I do have a fetish for big, meaty, male feet. If you could imagine Butch's big, strong feet, you would understand why I appreciated him sliding them all over my face, allowing me to lap the cum off them.

The bottoms of his big, fleshy feet were dirty, sweaty, dripping with his slimy sperm, and smelly-raw. I smelled, whiffed, inhaled, licked, and sucked on them with hungering, mouth-watering, lusting greed. That's how a sleaze-loving foot-freak like me likes to get down on man-feet.

"How it is, man," he said down at me with that cocky attitude, "you are meant to serve other guys like me. I know what you want and need from ol' Butch. You're scum at my feet, Phil. Only a scum low-level pervert would lick sweaty asshole, scrotum and dirty, stinkin', cum-smeared feet like you do. Tell me, Phil, why do you like to lick my feet like that? I mean, when they're so dirty, sweaty, stinky, and even got my sperm all over 'em?"

"Ohhh, Butch . . ." I moaned as he stood up, and began sliding one of his big feet over my chest and stomach, coating its bottom with my own sticky, gooey cum. "You're so gifted with that beautiful body, big cock, and huge feet. You're so raw and raunchy like a wild stud animal who appears to dominate and take your pleasures from the domesticated. Your feet are powerful and strong, like you. They are the lowest part of your body, and the altar of a worshipper. The more one has them at their raunchiest, the more you know one's dedication to you as the superior being," I preyed on his ego.

"I know," he said as he sat back down, and covered my face with his feet again. "Queers in different towns on my trip have become so hot over me. And every once in awhile, I get one like you who don't want me to shower first. I like yer type . . . especially a good, foot-lickin' toe-sucker like you. You appreciate a good pair of dirty, sweaty, stinkin' feet," he said with teasing, belittling tone.

I liked hearing him talk as I licked and inhaled the meaty, raw aroma of his feet. Never had I had a more beautiful pair of huge, ripe-raunchy feet that smelled and tasted so masculine. They were young and strong, and so dominant and demanding of worship.

"Yeah, it's gonna be a long evening," he said. "Maybe later, I can dig all my socks out of my pack, and you can launder 'em clean with yer mouth. Maybe even try cleanin' those sneakers of mine. They used to be white. Tell ya what, Phil, you go whip me up somethin' to eat . . . and I'll feed you some more of my feet and this big dick of mine. You would like that, wouldn't you?"

I got up and hurried to the kitchen.

He stayed with me for three days. That was six months ago, and I envy any gay he might have now. I gave him my name, address, and phone number, but have not heard from him since.

But since then, I have found myself searching for someone with that same personality, that easiness, that natural dominance and sexually uninhibited charm, which Butch had, and . . .

I met Tony. He's a tall, young, handsome, long-haired, hot-blooded Italian stud. Tony is attractive, and can easily be sexually magnetic. He is that tall, tight-bodied, lean, long-legged, naked, raw-raunchy type Adonis who dons himself in high, black boots, and prefers the outdoors for his sex.

"I wanna be one with nature," he told me. "I want to hike the secluded countryside in only my boots. You'll come with me the same way, as my slave. We'll hike, and sweat in the sun, and you'll carry wine and food in a pack on your back like an ass. You'll be my slave to use as I please. Do you understand where I'm coming from?" he explained and questioned.

"Yes, master," I answered.

It was a sexual fantasy with merit and imagination. I gathered wine, cheese, bread, and grapes . . . apples, oil, and towels. I packed the fruit and bread in Tupperwear™, and packed it all to carry on my back.

It was Sunday morning, and we drove to a favored, secluded countryside known to Tony. We stripped naked, except for boots, and with pack on my back, I followed my young master into secluded nature.

We hiked an hour before Tony wished to rest. Our bodies sheened with a layer of sweat. Tony sat upon a rock, and I removed the pack from my back.

"Bring me wine!" he instructed, and I obeyed. I brought it to him, then sat on the ground at his feet. He cupped his palm and poured some wine into it, then lowered it before my face.

"Drink!" he demanded, and I tilted my head back with open mouth, and he poured it into me.

I then began licking his hand and fingers clean of the wine while he drank from the bottle.

"You are really a filthy bastard, Phil. You're so weak, so fuckin' easy," he said as I sucked on his wine-tasty finger in my mouth.

"You sweat, slave," he said as he raised one leg upward until the toe of his boot rested tight into my sweating armpit. "You smell so stinking raw, and sweat all over my boot."

In several wiping angles, he scraped my sweating wet flesh with his boots, coating the leather with my perspiration. He then brought one boot up near to his crotch, and rested the heel on the edge of the rock, before my face.

"Lick it!" he demanded.

I could see the wetness of my own sweat on the rough leather surface. I began to lick at the toe of my master's boot. He took a long draw of wine with arrogance and disinterest at my action. I was just his boot-licking slave.

I could smell and feel the heat of his crotch as I tasted his leather and my own sweat. Tony was so raw, so intoxicating to inhale.

He lowered his boot to the ground, and I followed it. As I knelt, bent over, licking his boot, he stepped on my back with his other foot.

"Take off my boot, Phil," he ordered. I obeyed. I was surprised that he wore no socks. His feet were beautiful, too.

I was made to hold his boot up to his crotch as he pissed into it. He filled the foot portion of it, and made me hold it as he slipped his foot back into it. Then, I was ordered to do the same with his other boot. When I got his second boot back on his foot, he made me remove my own boots, and he pissed into them, too. I put them back on, and stood there feeling the soothingness his piss brought to my feet.

He stood up and took me in his arms, and we kissed in passion. I pressed and ground against his wet, slippery body with my own. Our kiss was long, and I came off it gasping for air.

"Ohhhh, Tony . . ." I moaned my pleasure of him, and we kissed again. His powerful arms slid down my sides and back, and he grasped and squeezed at my wet, sweating buns.

We were two naked males, standing in piss-filled boots, wrapped in each other's arms. Two sweaty bodies grinding and belly-fucking each other with excited, hot, hard cocks.

"Ahhhh . . . Tonyyy . . . you're an animal! A beautiful, raw, fuckin' *wild stud!*" I moaned in excitement.

"I know, baby!" he said, grinding his hips hard into mine. "Open your mouth," he said, bringing his hand up and grabbing my hair. He jerked my head back, and spit into my mouth. "Swallow it!" he demanded, jerking my head. "Ya like that, baby?" he asked.

"Ohhh, yes. I like everything about you. Give me more, please!" I begged, opening my mouth to him.

He spit into me, and I swallowed it. He spit all over my face, and into my mouth again. My toes squished in my piss-filled boots as I fucked against his belly and drank his slimy spit.

"Tonnyyy . . ." I called as my cock erupted between our tightly pressed, sweating, wet, slippery bellies.

"Oh, yeah, baby. Cum all over us! Sweat, piss, spit, and cum is what we're all about," he breathed heavily as he fucked his cock through my slimy cum and our sweat between our bellies. "Slide down me, Phil. Wipe all down the front of me with your face, and squat," he said.

Slowly, I moved downward, wiping my face over his sweaty chest, ribs, and around his cum-sweaty, slimy, hard stomach. My face squish-smacked loudly against his cum-coated muscles and navel. My face slid and was coated with the slime. As I came to full-squat in my piss-filled boots, he shoved his hard, round, slimy, cum-coated cock past my slimy, dripping wet lips, into my mouth.

"Yeahhh . . . that's it, baby. Suck your own slimy 'fuck' off my sweaty meat. Ohhh, yeahh . . . you like that!" he teased and enticed me. "I got me one fine piece of fuck-meat, man. Hot . . . sweaty . . . smelly-raw meat that a cocksuckin' faggot like you can appreciate," he boasted proudly as I slid its length back and forth with my mouth.

"Ohhh, you slimy-faced, cunt-mouthed bastard . . . suck on my fuckin' dick," he abused at me. "Mmmmm . . ." he moaned, "you love givin' me suck. Mmmm, yeah, I like that! Suck on it, baby!"

His dirty-talk talk enticed me more.

"You're a dick-sucker, Phil! You're so fucking queer ya make me wanna cum right down yer cocksuckin' throat!" he jeered at me as I greedily sucked his tasty, throbbin' cock.

His hands gripped my shoulders.

"Ahhhh, suck it! Suck, and suck, and suck," he commanded on every inward stroke his cock made as it burrowed into my mouth.

"Ahhh, you bastard!" he moaned as his cock erupted with his salty, pungent, spunk-starchy, wild-tasty, thick sperm splashing my throat.

I swallowed, and he shoved his cock into my throat as I did. His hands pulled on my head from behind, holding me on his cock as my throat milked on it.

"Eat it! Eat my fucking sperm, you bitch!" he demanded as his thick, creamy jism pumped down my throat.

He fed me his load, and finally pulled from my mouth. I gasped for air desperately to fill my lungs. He almost choked and drowned me with his cock and sperm!

"Maaan, you are gross! Sit down!" he said as he raised his boot to my chest and shoved me back.

I fell into a sitting position, and he made me take off my boots with orders not to spill any of his piss from them. He took them, and set them side-by-side on the ground next to him.

"Now yer socks, asshole," he commanded, and I peeled the piss-soaked sweatsocks off my feet. "Give 'em to me," he said as he stepped up to straddle over my body.

He took the socks in one hand, and grabbed my hair with the other. He jerked my head back, and holding the socks balled up in his hand, over my face, he wrung the piss out of them and all over me. Piss ran down my closed eyelids, nose, cheeks, lips, chin, and neck. He then shoved the socks into my mouth.

"Chew the piss out of 'em," he laughed as he stood up and stepped back.

He picked up one of my boots, walked around behind me, and poured it over my head. Again, he laughed at me. He then fetched my other boot, and poured the piss in it all over his hairless chest, pouring it down the front of his body.

"Pull my boot off, Phil. And don't spill the piss out of it!" he instructed. I held the boot as he pulled his foot out. "Now the other," he said, and I repeated the process. He picked up his boots, and walked over to the rock and sat down. "Maan, I need me a good fuckin' foot-lickin', ya know? Get over here, and lick my feet, Phil!" he ordered.

Immediately, I went to him and began licking one of his dirty, sweaty, pissy feet. Tony raised one boot to his lips, and filled his mouth full of piss. He then looked down at me, licking his feet, and spit the piss in a spray all over me.

"You fuckin'-assed foot-freak," he cussed at me. "Lick that fuckin' piss and sweat off my goddamned feet!" he demanded as he stepped on the back of my head with one foot, and pressed me down on the other.

"You're disgusting, Phil! You're fucking gross!" he said as he tipped one boot and poured his piss all over his feet and my head. When he emptied it, he dropped the heavy boot on my bare ass.

Tony then began pissing all over me as he began drinking his old piss out of his remaining boot. Barbarically, he overpoured as he gulped, and let his piss run down his chin and neck, and down the front of his hairless body. All the while, he took a leak all over me, his legs and feet.

"Piss on you, fucker!" he jeered, and threw his boot down at my butt. "Roll over so I can put my feet on yer faggot-ass face, queer!" he demanded.

I rolled over on my back in the wet, pissed grass. He slid his dirty, wet feet over my face. I gasped with excitement.

"Ohhh, yeahhh, you like lickin' guys' feet, dontcha, baby? And mine are all wet and stinky with my piss. Wallow in my piss as you lick my big feet, ya fuckin' pig! You're dirty, man! You're filth!" he belittled me.

I liked Tony's dirty talk and verbal abuse. It really added to the joy I was getting by licking the meaty, tasty flesh of his soles and heels when he rubbed them all over my face.

He found the bottle of wine he left on the rock, and began drinking it. He took his time, and took his foot-licking worship from me as he drank.

"Maaan, it takes a real scumbag low-life to go down on another guy's stinkin' feet like that. You're a real slimeball pervert, you are! Hey, man, why don't ya jack off while ya slurp all over my feet like that? Yeah, that's it! I wanna see ya cum all over yerself while lickin' my feet like a dog," he said, grinning. "I ain't the only fuckin' animal here. Give me some suck on my toes, asshole," he demanded.

I was so turned on by him. I cocked my head back, and let him shove his toes into my mouth. At the same moment, I began milking ropey strands of cum from my cock, all over my stomach.

"Oh, fuck man! Look at that slimy, fuckin' queer cum. Ahhh, scoop that sperm up with yer hands, and rub it on my feet. Ohhh . . . yeah, now ya can lick yer own cum off my feet, asshole," he grinned, as I smeared his feet with my thick, creamy load.

I rolled over onto my stomach, grabbed his two hunky feet, and began licking one, then the other. I wanted them *bad*, and greedily licked and sucked at the flesh.

"Damn, man . . . be perverted! Suck on feet!" he teased at me. He liked it, though, and let me go at them.

He was getting a buzz-on from the wine. As I licked at his feet . . . as we sweated in the sun . . . he stared at my sweating ass. "Yeah," he thought, "I'm gonna fuck that."

"Hey, you foot-licker, in a little while I'm gonna *fuck* you! I'm gonna bury this cock of mine in yer ass. I'm gonna make a woman outta you. Yeah, I'm gonna fuck me some ass!" he fantasized, staring at my firm, hairless butt.

I sucked his toes, and thought how nice it would be with beautiful, hard-bodied Tony fucking me. His toe was big and meaty, and so fucking suckable. Tony stood up, and pulled his feet from my hands.

"I wanna fuck!" he said. He spit on my hole, and on his dick, and fucked into me. "Ahhhh . . . yeah . . ." he moaned, sliding his arms around me.

We were two wet-sweaty, hot male bodies. Naked and raw. Reeking in odors of piss, cum, and our sweat.

"Feel my dick, baby! Yer butt's tight. Ahhh . . . yeah. Fuck you, baby," he moaned his strokes into me.

"Ohhhh, To-onnyyy! Fuck me! Don't ever stop . . ." I begged.

He was another Italian stallion with boiling balls and a thunder cock, who knows how to fuck. He fills my ass with joy. He takes me, uses me, abuses me, degrades me, and humiliates me. But, why not?

FEET-LAPPIN' COCKSUCKER!

"Hey!" he said as I passed his cell. I turned to see him rub at the crotch of his prison-issue pants. I was mopping the tier floor as I eyed his hand, then looked up into his eyes.

"Sure do need some 'head,' man," he told me. I looked up the tier and saw the guard watching me.

"And I sure would like to go down on you, but . . ." I said, nodding my head toward the guard. He picked up on my point, and smiled.

"Ya like suckin' on dick, do ya?" he asked as he stepped back into his cell, out of the guard's view. He unzipped his fly, and pulled out his cock.

"All night long," I sang as I mopped the floor, and eyed his beautiful cock. My own cock began to harden.

He jacked at it, and puckered his lips like he wanted to kiss. He was teasing and exciting me. Then he spoke one word silently, but I read the lips. He called me "faggot." I smiled at him, and ran my tongue over my lips.

He grinned, and milked his load all over the cell floor.

Two days later, I was being returned to my cell from my work detail, and found that the same convict had been assigned there. He was now my cellmate.

"Well, well, ain't it a small world." he said as the guard searched me before I entered the cell.

After I was searched and locked in, I felt a certain tinge of fear of him. He had those powerful arms with his sleeves rolled up over the hard biceps. He had to be well-built under that uniform of his.

"Welcome home, baby," he said, patting my ass as I stepped past him.

I felt weak, and my legs shook and trembled. It's true I've had the hots for him ever since that day I'd first seen him. But now, no bars separated us. We were cellmates, and I sensed his power in his presence.

He began removing his shirt as I sat on the lower bunk, which was mine. His eyes stared into mine as he peeled off the shirt, and tossed it atop the upper bunk. I dropped my gaze to behold the hairless, hard, smooth, tight-muscled upper torso of his body. Instantly, my cock began to stir.

He sat down on my bunk, and offered me a cigarette. I took it, but not without letting him see my hand shaking.

"What's yer name, baby?" he asked, lighting my cigarette.

"Rick," I answered, inhaling smoke deep into my lungs, then exhaling.

"My name's Nick," he said as he moved to a lying position on my bunk, placing his shoeless, but socked, feet atop my lap. I grabbed his feet with my hands the moment they rested atop my bulging crotch to relieve the pain he brought to my balls as he set them down roughly.

His feet felt strong in my hands. I gripped them with one hand as I removed the cigarette from my mouth with the other, and exhaled the smoke.

"It's hot in here, ain't it?" he said. I looked into his eyes and grinning face, not even realizing I was stroking his foot with my hand.

"Yes," I managed to say with difficulty. His upper body already seemed to take on a wet glow of sheened sweat.

He tossed his cigarette into the cell toilet, and I did the same. He folded one arm back under his head, atop my pillow, and rubbed at the crotch of his pants with the other.

"Ya like my feet, do ya?" he asked. I looked down at his feet, crossed one atop the other in my lap. I was stroking both of them with my hands. I liked rubbing them for him.

"Lift one up to yer face and smell it, baby. You're gonna like what ya smell," he enticed me. I lifted his foot up, and inhaled the aroma of his smelly sock.

"Ohhhhh . . ." I moaned as the masculine aroma filled my nostrils. It was instant, cock-throbbing, sexual euphoria.

"Yeahhh . . . whiff it, baby. Smell that feet sweat of a man, and feel that foot inside that stinky sock. Smell it!" he spoke sexy at me.

"Ahhhh . . . the smell," I moaned at the intoxicating aroma of his socked foot. "I've never got into a guy's feet before," I said, pressing my face against his soft, cotton, cushioned sweatsock.

"Oh, you'll like it, baby. Just like the fag cellmate I had doin' time in Iowa a couple years ago. Pull off my sock and get yourself a real treat—smellin' and lickin' my bare foot," he told me.

I peeled off his sock, revealing his strong, meaty foot. It seemed so sexual now, as I had never looked upon a guy's feet this way before.

"Ya like it?" he asked.

"Yes," I answered as I stroked its shape, feeling its flesh.

"Hey, Rick," he said, making me look up at him. He had gotten his fly open, and released his beautiful, hard 7" of cock, and held it in his hand. "Remember this?" he asked.

"Ohhh, do I! Can I have it?" I asked.

"Kiss my foot, faggot!" he said, grinning as he shoved his foot hard against my face. "You kiss, and smell, and lick, and suck on my sweaty fuckin' feet, baby, and maybe I'll let ya have this hot dick in that mouth of yers," he demanded.

I began licking the meaty sole of his foot, and instantly found the raw-masculine, sweaty flesh a wildly erotic sexual experience. The taste only made me greedy for more.

I couldn't believe I was licking hungrily on another con's sweaty feet like I was. This dominant stranger cellmate, named Nick, had me servicing him sexually within the first 15 minutes we were together in our cell.

He made me remove his pants and other sock, then lay back before me in all his naked beauty, with me licking his feet and sucking his toes.

"Yeah, you're gonna work out OK for me as a cellmate, baby. You're gonna be my feet-lappin' cocksucker," he said, laughing. The more he talked to me, the more I liked tonguing wetly between his sweat-tasty toes. I guess I've needed someone to take control, and Nick seemed to do it natural. Licking his feet was so natural for me, and I was surprisingly attracted to them.

"Ahhh, man . . . give me a toe job with that wet faggot mouth of yours," he instructed. I sucked onto the first man's toes ever to be in my mouth.

I tongued, licked, and sucked each one like I have on guys' cocks. I knew that from now on, *feet* would be a part of my sexual attraction to men. And Nick's feet, the most important of all.

"Hey, man," he said. "Get yer ass up here and blow me!" he demanded.

Oh, god, how I fell upon that man and devoured his manhood! I forgot who I was, what I was, and where I was.

"Ahhhh . . . feel me in yer mouth, homey. Let me feel them wet fag-sucks up and down my dick. Ohhh, yeah, that feels good, baby. Suck it! Slurp that meat!" he coaxed and enticed.

Nick was a hard-core con who knew how to pick out and manipulate the weaker, sexually submissive males in prison. Already, he had begun his stretch with me during his first week here. And like all rough and rugged, hard-bodied, muscular, tough cons, he needed and sought out his sex.

He took my sucking lying back, but after enjoying it for awhile, he made me get on the floor. He stood before my kneeling frame, and shoved into my mouth. He held my head in his hands and he fucked my mouth.

"You learn my cock, baby, 'cause you're my property now. You're my 'prison lady,' and I *love* gettin' sucked. Do it, fag! Suck for that slimy fuck-sperm of mine!" he demanded, letting me take over the action on his cock.

Ohhh, to be down on such a man. To feel and taste his man-meat in my mouth. Never have I loved so much to suck . . . to blow . . . to wetly polish a cock as I did Nick's.

I bobbed on it, sucking its raw-sweaty, masculine, round, tasty length. I could smell that sexual aroma of sweating crotch. His pubic hair, his hard-muscled shaft, and his raw-smelling flesh and balls ignited in me a drive for the smell of his excited manhood.

"Ahhhh . . . you like that cock, do ya, homo?" he asked, amusing himself. I sucked off it, rubbing my face against the phallic beauty of it.

"Ohhhh, Nick . . ." I moaned my excitement over him. "You're a sex god to me," I praised as I ran my hands up his smooth hips and sides, to his chest.

"Ohhhh, yeah . . . feel my body, homey. Feel a *real* man's muscle and flesh. Suck my dick and worship me," he coaxed. I sucked back onto his cock as I traced down his curved, muscularly-formed body.

"Go for it, man! Suck for the 'joy juice,'" he demanded. I put my whole head to the task. "Ohh, yeah, that's it, cocksucker! Go for it! Suck!" he demanded. I built my pace—fast and wet—sucking for his load.

"Ohhh . . . you bitch! I *love* it!" he moaned his pleasure, meeting my sucks with thrusts of his hips.

"Suck sperm, asshole! Eat me!" he cried out as he pumped thick, creamy gobs of cum-slime into my mouth. I gobbled and gulped, and drank his manhood. It was everything to me . . .

"I LOVE TO SMELL YOUR FEET"

"Hello, sleaze," Danny surprised me when I entered the manager's small locker room, and turned on the light. "Where have you been, asshole? I been waitin' here twenty minutes now," he demanded.

"Oh, Danny, I'm sorry. I got held up closing up the place," I explained, hastily undressing as I stared at the gorgeous hunk sitting posed on the bench in front of the lockers.

I stood naked and humble before him. I was not allowed to touch his naked body without approval. I knew my place with him.

"I stand before you, master," I said. "What will you have me do?" I asked. He wore only a worn, old, funky jockstrap and dirty sneakers with no socks. He peeled off the jockstrap and tossed it to me.

"Smell it, dummy!" he degraded me, demanding it. I lifted it to my face and pressed into it.

"Ahhhh, maan . . ." I moaned at its raw, stenched pungence that filled my nostrils.

"It's a month's crotch funk, pervert . . . *my* crotch!" he told me, egotistically. "Them's piss and sweat stains from my dick, man. Smell it!" he ordered.

I whiffed its pungent scents loudly for him.

"You like that smell of my B.O. and piss, queer?" he asked.

"Ohhhh, Danny, you know I love your raunch," I told him as

I inhaled his gamy jock.

"Then chew it, scuzball! And get down, and take off my sneakers while you do," he demanded.

I bit into the jock, tasting his funk, as I knelt on the floor. I removed one of his dirty, worn sneakers.

"Lift it to yer nose and smell inside it," he said, amusing himself at my perverted interest in all things raunchy about him.

I pressed the wide opening of his sneaker over my face, driving my nose deep against the inner bottom of it, and whiffed the raunchy, masculine, moist-sweaty aroma of Danny's feet inside me. Ahhhh, I was getting turned on, my cock growing stiff as I chewed his jock and whiffed wildly at his sneaker, while staring at that beautiful, muscled body of his.

"I worked out hard for you today, sleaze. I'm really dirty and filthy with the sweat and B.O. you like to smell and eat off me. Spit that dick rag outta yer mouth, and get my other sneaker off," he told me.

I spit out his jock, and tossed the first sneaker aside to get to the other on his foot. As I slid it off, I ran my hand over his moist, sexy foot.

"Ahhhh, Danny, you always have the sweatiest feet," I complimented him.

"You know it, man. And you want 'em, too! Toss that sneaker, and grab my ankles, baby, and stand up," he ordered me.

I stood up, lifting his feet and legs into the air before me.

"Stand there and just smell 'em, you dumb bastard. Let me hear it, about my feet," he grinned up at me with teasing orneriness.

His B.O. rose in warm waves up into my face . . . my nostrils. Holding his ankles, I closed my eyes and moved my head side to side over each foot, just inhaling each one's odor as it rose to my face.

"Ohhhh, Danny," I moaned in sheer erotic ecstasy of his feet. "I love to smell your feet! Ohhhhh . . ." I inhaled loudly as I moaned, drawing their raw aroma into me. My cock throbbed, and I smelled that power his feet had over me. "Danny, you are *the man.* I worship you!" I moaned. "I wanna kiss your big, beautiful feet! I wanna lick 'em and eat your sweat off 'em, for you," I said. "You got the best fuckin' stud-feet a queer could ever lick on," I told him.

165

"Yeah, I know, fag. And you're the perverted queer that *would* lick dirty-smellin', sweaty feet, too," he teased and degraded me. "Let go of my ankles, and play with my cock while you smell and tell me more," he said, intending to torture me more by not allowing me onto his feet just yet.

I leaned closer to smell his feet as I began fondling his rigid, hard cock with my hands. With my own cock, rubbing against the crack of his ass, I could feel his wetness on it.

"Ohh . . . why do you torture me like this, Danny?" I groaned inquisitively.

"Because you're a faggot, for one reason," he explained, "and I turn you on so much with my body that you'll obey, or you know what you won't get." He grinned up at me, then touched my nose with one of his toes. "C'mon, you filthy pervert, let me hear you beg to kiss and lick my dirty-smellin' feet in yer face, while you play with my dick," he demanded.

"You're 'sex smart,' Danny," I told him in praise. "You recognized my homosexuality, and quickly learned how to take advantage of me. Do you like me at all? What is it between us?" I asked.

"I *don't* like you. I like *what you do*, man!" he degraded me with a sadistic intent to hurt my feelings. "I like yer filthy, fuckin' queer perversions, ya know? I mean, you're a sleazy, scuz, raunch-lover . . . and I like using and takin' fuckin' advantage of you," he said, then shoved the bottoms of both his feet on my face, pinning my nose between them. "Here, faggot, feel them fuckers on yer face. Smell 'em, now!" he said.

"Mmmm . . ." I moaned with instant ecstasy. I whiffed him into me, and jacked wildly on his super-hard cock in response.

"Ahhhh . . . beat my meat, you bastard, and beg for dirty feet!" he ordered.

"Ahh . . . Danny, Danny . . . please!" I moaned. "I'm beggin' you . . . ahhh . . . pleeaasse, I *need* your big, sexy feet!" I practically yelled through his feet.

"Ah, let go of my cock, you asshole. Take my feet in 'em and do it!" he told me.

Danny's feet—the most beautiful, smelliest, dirtiest, strongest athletic feet I wanted to have. He slid one foot off my face, onto my chest, and I took the other into my hands. I pressed my lips to the pads of his toes, and kissed them. I wasn't just kissing toes. I was kissing Danny. I was in love with him, and my kiss was passion and worship.

I moved slowly down the meaty bottom of it, breathing his sweaty, manly odor into me, as I felt him on my face. I stroked it as I kissed.

"Yeah, get *high* on that fucker, baby. Taste it!" he told me.

I began licking the meaty bottom, and sighed with excited, rushing heart. The taste was immaculately raw-raunch delicious to me. My eyes were closed, and my head spun with lightness. My cock throbbed with ecstasy as his sweat saturated my lapping tongue. I was making love to my straight, heterosexual stud, Danny, through his feet. I lapped about the firm, hard, rounded flesh of his heel.

"Ahhhh, yeah . . . do it, sleaze. I like you queerin' on my feet like ya do. It's low-life, ya know?" he teased and enticed at me.

I submitted to his abuse with masochistic romance. I was his queer, if not his lover. I licked about his ankle, and forced my fingers between his moist-fleshed toes. I could feel his wet, raw sweat on my fingers, and knew I *had* to taste him there.

I licked down the top of his veined, Adonis foot, smelling and tasting and anticipating . . . with a need to *suck*.

"Go get them toes, fucker! Gimme a toe job like a true queer," he enticed.

"Ohhh, Danny . . . yes . . . yes!" I moaned, sucking into his big, hard, meaty, sweat-tasty toe, all the way down. My mouth watered, and I whirled my tongue about it, suck-cleaning its raunch into me.

He lay watching, feeling me sucking his toes off. My perversity amazed him as he stroked his throbbing cock. His mind thought many dirty, imaginative, sexual things that fed his ego.

"Ahhhh . . . you filthy bastard," he called me. "Suck!" he demanded. And I did . . .

SWEATSOCKS AND HOT FEET

I guess none of it would have happened if I hadn't decided to be absolutely honest in filling out the psychiatric questionnaire that was given to all third year students at Oklahoma State College. Thanks to the G.I. Bill, I was enjoying the pursuit of a college degree at that prestigious university, and, wanting to do everything "right," I took things like questionnaires more seriously than the other, mostly younger, students.

So it was that when I came to the question asking about any unusual sexual interests or fetishes I could lay claim to, I wrote a long, detailed, very damning confession of the particular peculiar tastes I had acquired. It was a dumb thing to do, and looking back I can't figure out *why* I didn't lie, or put down something noncommittal. But no—like a fool, I outlined my whole trip . . . like how I get super turned-on by sneakers and socks, feet and toes. . . .

Soon's I wrote it down, I flung the pen away and leaned back in my chair, my cock stiff and throbbing in my crotch from just thinking about such things. Shaking my head, I muttered, "Oh, no. . . . I'm not sending *that* in!" I made up my mind to throw away the questionnaire and get a new one the next day.

Meanwhile, I had gotten myself so turned on, writing about my favorite "trip," that I got up and went to the bathroom for a hot jack-off. I pulled my stiff prick out of the confining fly of my cut-off Levis and started pounding it furiously over the toilet. My mind was filled with visions of warm, smelly sneakers and stinking sweatsocks; spinning with images of big, hot, sweaty feet shoved in my face, and I threw my head back and closed my eyes, giving myself up to my fantasies but determined to prolong my pleasure as long as possible. . . .

I had been working away for several minutes—till the pre-cum juice was practically dripping off the slimy end of my dick—when a sudden noise made me look up and there in the doorway was my roommate, Stosh Sandusky!

Stosh was one of those big, muscular, raw-boned blond Slavic types. Twenty years old, but with the brute power of a more mature guy, he was a natural athlete and the star of the school's basketball team. Unbelievably handsome, but not too smart, he had a latent streak of sadism that sometimes got dangerous—both on the court and with former roommates who got him angry. For-

tunately we had hit it off well, and—while not the best of friends—
we were at least cordial.

Caught like that in the act of self-pleasure, I could only smile
weakly and mutter, "H-Hello . . ." in my embarrassment.

He grinned noncommittally and leaned against the door jamb,
his blue eyes flicking between my red face and the now-softening
sausage sticking out of the open fly in my jeans. He had just come
in from basketball practice, and was still in his shorts and team
shirt, sweatsocks and big Converse sneakers. (He liked the
shower in our room better than the ones at the gym, and so
usually came home to clean up.) Rivulets of sweat ran down his
golden muscular limbs, and his blond hair was plastered to his
skull with wetness.

Suddenly I panicked, remembering the incriminating papers I'd
left on my desk in the other room! Had Stosh seen them, I wondered, feeling my stomach turn to butterflies? Had he read that
stupid confession of mine? I wasn't long in doubt. . . .

Casually, the giant athlete leaned down and pulled off one of
his hi-top canvas sneakers, exposing his very large, wide foot,
sheathed in grimy, woolen sweatsocks that accented every sweet
curve and hollow of his shapely Slavic feet.

"Hey, buddy," he smiled in feigned innocence, "I gotta get me
another pair of sneakers—these are really raunchy! You ever smell
anything so stinky?"

He held the soiled and ripped shoe toward me, but I backed
away, a cold sweat forming on my upper lip.

Stosh snorted derisively. "Shit, it won't hurt you none, Dwight
—it's only some sweat and stink from my feet . . . the way you're
acting, someone'd think you don't like my feet or something."

I didn't answer. To tell the truth, I *couldn't* have spoken then if
my life depended on it.

The brawny blond athlete made a pretense of looking inside the
frayed white shoe. "Gee, I can't make out the size in here . . . it's
all rubbed out and smeared. . . ."

He stepped in close to me. I felt the sink pressing against my
back. I couldn't get away from the overpowering closeness of
Stosh's big hot body. "Here, pal . . . maybe *you* can read it for
me!"

Slowly, teasingly—and with a big cruel grin—he lifted the
sneaker up to my face. It was like some huge shell, with a beat-

up star patch on one side. The laces completely loose and partly out, the tongue up, the dark, mysterious opening gaped like some special, fragrant cave. . . .

It was this very opening that Stosh lined up with my face, barely an inch away, so that my face and nose were practically inside the sneaker. Vaguely I noticed that the shoe size stamped inside was clear and readable, not in the least smudged or wiped away. Big, bold black letters proclaiming proudly to fit a royal size thirteen! Shit, the kid had *miles* of feet!

"Can ya make out the size, pal?" he grinned cockily. "No? . . . Well, maybe it's not *close* enough for you to read good!" His grin widened even more as he brought the raunchy sneaker still closer, jamming the thing right against my face so that I was breathing no air except that inside the cavernous shoe! My lungs filled with the heavy, damp, warm, powerful odor that Stosh's big foot had left . . . the hot stink was overpowering, and I drank it in greedily . . . the sounds of my sniffing and snuffling were loud and vulgar and primal, like a pig rooting for truffles.

"Hey, man . . . whatcha doin' inside there? Huh? You smellin' my shoes—my gamy, stinky, smelly, sweaty sneakers—huh?? Is that what you're doin'? Is it? Do they smell good, Dwight, ol' buddy? Hot and strong and raunchy? I bet they smell just like my hot feet, don't they?!"

While he was talking and grinding his foul, well-used sneaker in my face, Stosh ripped open the buttons on his basketball shorts, and kicked the satin garment off, revealing his slim, full-buttocked hips adorned with a plumply bulging jockstrap, the wide white elastic straps standing out sharply against the deep golden tan skin, wet with man-sweat. He pried off the other big sneaker, and shinnied out of his athletic shirt, so that he finally stood there on the bathroom rug, naked except for the dingy, moist jockstrap and his floppy wool sweatsocks.

He took the sneaker away from my face and tossed it off into a corner. Grabbing the other big athletic shoe he had just pulled off, he said, "Hey, pal, how about this one? D'ya s'pose it smells as bad as the other one? Or maybe even worse? Here, take a good whiff and lemme know!" and with that he shoved his other moist, gamy sneaker into my face! "Shit, man, you really know how to smell a guy's sneakers, don't you! I guess I know where to go now, whenever I need my sneakers sniffed good!"

Finally he released me, walked to the commode and put down the seat, and sat on it, legs spread and outstretched, resting on their wool-clad heels. My mouth hung slack and open and my eyes were glazed. I was literally drunk with the orgy of sneaker-sniffing I'd just enjoyed inside Stosh's large, wide basketball shoes. Their heavy athletic aroma still lingered in my nose, fresh and strong, raunchy and virile.

"Boy," he said, studying his socked feet, "my sweatsocks sure are dirty. . . . They need to be washed real bad. How'd you like to take your tongue and use it to launder my filthy socks for me? Think you'd like that, huh?"

My eyes fell to the sweatsocks in question. The once-white wool was dingy grey and hanging limp around his golden-haired ankles, the sheath of the socks wrapped wetly in clinging folds around the two huge, meaty feet. He'd obviously been wearing them for more than just one workout in the gym. Still, the suggestion he'd put forward that I clean those soiled and smelly socks with my tongue, sent a shiver of anticipatory delight down my spine! Stosh noticed the slight shiver that vibrated through my body, and he broke into a confident grin. Correctly interpreting my silence for assent, he taunted me further:

"Been storin' up a whole lot of dynamite juice from my funky feet there in them socks . . . real good, tasty stuff! Bet you'd like it, once you tried it. . . . G'wan, why doncha? Give my funky socks a good cleanin'!"

Numbly, I crossed the small space that separated us and dropped down to my hands and knees, lowering my head to one of Stosh's beautifully shaped size 13 feet. The socks were soggy with foot-sweat and permeated through with the ripe, pungent stink of sneaker-smell and the moist musky aromas of his wide, high-arched manly feet. The strong blast of intoxicating foot-perfume that I had experienced while my face had been buried inside his sneakers was mild in comparison to the powerful onslaught of repulsive odors that filled my nostrils as they approached the sculptured arch of his wool-covered toes. I felt my senses reeling. . . .

My tongue extended and began to lap the blond jock's smelly socked foot, over the hard, full instep and around to the sides, licking and gnawing at the ankle and the delicious hollow underneath the ankle. Then downward over the fleshy side-ridge on one side and the shapely arch on the other . . . then the tops of his sock-clad toes. I could feel the separations between each strong, firm toe, and the hard bones lifting like a line of miniature mountains on the broad, flat plain of his toe-tops. Shifting my position on the floor, I was able to reach the bottoms of his socks. They were filthiest here, with the imprint of his naked big foot clearly marked in dark wet grey, the large expanse of gracefully curved sole and five circles of toe-prints like a border at the top curve of the sock-bottom.

My tongue was dry and coated with wool by now. I swallowed a few times and worked up some spit as best I could, and got to work licking off the dirt from the bottom of his sock.

Stosh encouraged me. "Yeah, that's it, ol' buddy. . . . Get those socks real clean for me. You're doin' real good, yeah, real good. . . . Looks like I found me a first-class laundromat!" He chuckled cruelly, "Yeah, with *you* as my roomie, it looks like I'm gonna have the cleanest, whitest socks on the team! Every night after practice, I'll use your mouth for a washing machine to clean my socks . . . and maybe I'll throw in a pissy jockstrap or two . . . sweeten it up a little. . . ."

It took a long time, but after about thirty minutes of licking and chewing, gnawing and sucking, and licking some more, the sweatsock so stuffed with the big hot foot of that blond college jock was finally clean! My tongue felt like it had been scraped raw, and the sock was literally dripping wet with my saliva—but, by God, it was *clean*!!

Stosh raised his hairy, muscular leg, lifting the foot off the floor. With his thighs spread as they were, this movement served to spread open the twin mounds of his muscular, firmly-packed, alabaster white buttocks, exposing the pinkish-brown rosebud of his hair-ringed asshole. As he studied his lifted foot approvingly, checking on his newly laundered sock, I devoured with my eyes —the rare glimpse of his most secret and private mystery—his warm, moist, and tender man-hole! Like a hypnotist's eye, the winking button lodged between the powerful, melon-shaped cheeks held me in a servile grip, and there was no escape.

"You did a pretty good job on that sock, fella," Stosh said, lowering his foot back down to the floor, his sweet, puckered, moist rectum-hole vanishing from sight, locked between the two pale muscular butt-mounds. "Now let's see how good you can do on the other one. . . .'' He shoved his other foot into my face, mashing my nose with it and rubbing the smelly sole of it in a grinding circular motion.

I took the big thing in my two hands and began licking it with long, hard strokes of my tongue. Somehow it seemed *important* for me to get 'em both completely clean—the smelly socks of this handsome young blond giant college-athlete! After about another thirty minutes, the second sock was as immaculately clean and white as the first—and drooping just as wetly.

"O.K., buddy,'' Stosh grinned, "you did your job real good and you deserve a reward.'' He stood up and turned around so that his back was to me. Then he spread his legs wide apart and leaned over from the waist, resting his hands on the toilet lid. "So here it is, pal!''

His full, beefy butt, lightly fuzzed with golden hairs, was framed in the white elastic straps of his athletic supporter, and I could see the heavy-laden pouch dangling between his wide-spread muscular thighs.

"Dig my ass, man . . . dig it . . . good, hot ass . . . can you dig it, baby? You know what's tucked in there between my cheeks? Huh? Something *juicy* and *sweet* and *tender*!! Something real *tasty*! . . . an asshole, buddy, that's what . . . *my* asshole! Yeah, my hot, fuckin' asshole, and if you wanna, you can *eat it out!* Go on—take hold of my buns and open 'em up so you can get your mouth into my hairy old bung-hole . . . you'll go apeshit when you taste how good it is!!''

I did as he directed. Gripping the rock-hard, powerful buttocks, one firm cheek in each of my hands, I pried them apart, like opening a clam-shell to expose the ''pearl''—and found myself staring into the tight, pinkish, buttonlike asshole of that muscular young athlete.

Eagerly I thrust my face into the warm, sweaty crevass and put my mouth down squarely over Stosh's asshole. I licked at it, stroking the soft, tender manmeat with my tongue. I sucked it up into my mouth and nibbled at it gently with my teeth. I sucked and chewed on his rectum, tasting all the manly sweat and virile sour-mash from inside his hard male bod. I inserted my tongue into the tight hot opening, probing deep inside, tongue-fucking him good! Stosh moaned and squirmed against me, saying, "Shit, yeah . . . french-kiss my shitty asshole, you fuckin' sneaker-sniffer!''

My hands released his butt mounds as I burrowed in his ass, and they snapped back into place, squeezing my face between them, holding me like a vise, locking my face in place. My hands swept up and down his tanned, muscular legs, tracing the bold curve of his column-like thighs, the hard edges of his knee caps and the hollows behind them, the voluptuous thick slabs of his calf muscles, and the hairy length of shin, and all the while I kept eating out his fantastic asshole!

''Told you you'd like it once you got a taste of it!'' Stosh said, ''You ever eat out a basketball player's ass before? Well, you're eating out one now!''

Suddenly, without warning, he straightened up and pulled his rump away from my face. ''O.K.—you've had enough of my ass-hole!'' he said abruptly. My face was smeared with my saliva and his funky ass-sweat and brownish shit-stains. I watched as he put on a pair of old grey sweatpants. Then he stripped off his wet, dripping, soggy socks. But before I could catch more than just a fleeting glimpse of Stosh's *naked* feet, he had stuffed them into his frayed old sneakers, lacing them up securely.

He grinned at my look of disappointment. ''Oh, don't worry! he laughed, ''You'll get to see my feet later—and more! But they're too clean and washed now. I'm gonna go for a long, hot run on the track, so's when I bring 'em back to you they'll be all gamy and ripe and sweaty and smellin' like *real feet* again!''

He sauntered to the door and out into the next room, his voice trailing back over his shoulder as he walked with a loose-jointed, hip-rolling gait. ''Whyn'cha wash all that shit from my asshole off your face—then get yourself stripped naked and on the bed wait-ing for me.'' Then I heard the door open and slam shut, and he was gone.

I thought I should get the hell out of there while I had the chance, but the tantalizing promise of getting at Stosh's big, tanned feet again drove all thoughts of flight away. So, instead, I did as he had instructed: washed my face, stripped off my own sneakers and socks, and the T-shirt and cut-off jeans I was wear-ing, and went and laid down on one of the beds totally nude to wait for him to come back. Meanwhile I amused myself by rub-bing my stiff dick while chewing and sucking on one of my own smelly socks, my nose buried deep inside one of my own raunchy sneaks—always one of my favorite activities, but now I knew the taste and smell were nothing compared to Stosh's funky gear!!

It seemed like an eternity—my raunchy socks were sucked nearly clean and I had nearly shot my wad several times—but in reality it wasn't more than half an hour before I heard a key in the door and it opened to admit the young, Nordic athlete . . . his golden, muscular limbs literally *dripping* with sweat, his mouth hanging open to gulp in air as his powerful chest heaved with heavy breathing.

Ignoring the sweatsox which I hastily pulled from my mouth and tossed to the floor as well as the stiff prick jutting up from my groin with clear sticky juice gushing from the slimy slit on the end, he walked to the bed and collapsed down on it on his back, his long, muscular legs sprawled wide. Arching his lean hips up off the mattress, he peeled down his sweatpants and kicked them off. Then, flopping his naked, jockstrap-framed ass back down on the bed again, he nodded down toward his feet.

"There they are . . . all hot and steamy inside my sneaks for you . . . like bread fresh from the oven. . . . Love 'em, man! Love 'em to death!!"

Hastily I scrambled downward to his hair-haloed ankles. My fingers nervously untied the shoelaces of the first shoe. Grasping the bony ankle in my bare hand, with the heel of his warm, moist sneaker in my other, I removed the funky athletic shoe slowly . . . almost reverently . . . like unveiling some exquisite treasure . . . which, indeed, I was!

Slowly . . . slowly . . . my eyes devouring each new inch of naked foot as it came to view, I slid the sneaker off Stosh's wide, sunbronzed foot. Soon, only his long, shapely toes remained inside the sweat-drenched canvas. Then, like a cloud passing away from in front of the moon, the large, heavy sneaker was completely and fully removed, and I was staring, only inches away, at the rugged jock's moist, bare foot! The exercise had done its work well, and restored the familiar, strong manlystink to his filthy sneaker . . . and, I hoped, to his feet even more! A light film of sweat glistened over the entire foot, and tiny droplets of sweat had gathered in the hollows between his toes. The flesh was a deep sun-browned tawn, and the toe-tips pinkish and pale like jewels.

He allowed me to contemplate his graceful, tapering bare foot for a few moments. Then he brought his other sneakered foot to my face and had me remove that shoe also. Now *both* of his magnificent feet were naked before my eager eyes! I held these damp, hot prizes, one in each hand, and wiped them across my cheeks, like applying some funky sort of after-shave. . . . with one large, fleshy foot on either side of my head, it was like stereophonic smell! The familiar smell of his feet hit me from both sides, and I felt like I was getting stoned.

"You really get off on my feet, huh, Dwight?" His voice was low and sexy; his eyelids drooping, and his pouty, full-lipped mouth open. "They really turn you on every which way, don't they? Good, strong feet, ain't they? . . . hot, funky smelling feet . . . with a rich, ripe *taste*, too—just what you'd expect a basketball player's smelly feet to taste like!"

Like a blind person reading Braille, my fingers caressed every part of Stosh's sweat-slippery feet . . . squeezing the fleshy sides, stroking the sinewy tendons and metatarsals, running my fingers along the thick, wet sole. The moisture on his rubbery flesh gave the giant size thirteen feet a slightly clammy feel. I caressed each of his delightful toes individually, running my fingertips across the hard edges of the shining toenails and down in the deep groove between the toes.

"Hey, Dwight, ol' buddy—how's about if I feed you something *real special*. . . . A little State U *feet soup*! All you gotta add is the saliva . . . I got a lot of that funky goop on those two big feet of mine that you're holdin' . . . probably make a right nourishing soup out of it . . . and *lots* of it, too—good, strong stuff, enough to keep you well-fed for days!!"

I nodded my head, dumbly staring in worship at the two bare, smelly feet I was holding in my hands.

"Well, then . . . it's chow time, partner! Start eating out my sweaty, funky feet. Get 'em while they're hot, ripe, and gamy!"

With a strangled sob, I dropped one of Stosh's feet, and used *both* my hands on the other foot, clutching the massive, fleshy thing as though I feared it might escape. Hungrily, like a starving dog, my mouth slobbered over the blond athlete's beautiful, strong-toed foot, sucking up all the salty sweat on it. My tongue discovered the strongest concentrations of the sour, smelly stuff collected in the crevices between the suntanned toes, packed in the delicate webbing between the bases of the toe shafts. I scooped up the intense tasting toe-jam with my tongue, like a shovel digging out the lode, let the salty residue mix with a mouthful of spit in my mouth, rolling it around and squishing it, till it was thoroughly mixed—till the saliva was flavored through and through with the rank, strong flavor of Stosh's feet! Soup—a pungent, rich, and meaty soup, made out of Stosh's feet! Then I gulped down the delicious mouthful, and proceeded to suck up another. And no matter how much I licked off, there was still more . . . the two superbly arched feet never completely lost their heavy flavors, in spite of my determined efforts to eat off *all* of his smelly foot-juices. . . . mouthful after mouthful of thick, gamy foot-soup went down my hungry throat as I eagerly licked and sucked, tasted and chewed, and finally *swallowed* his ripe, gooey toe-gunk and raunchy foot-juices! They were like two miraculous, bottomless reservoirs of virile male smells and tastes.

"Hey, buddy boy . . . it's time for the second course. . . . you've had *lots* of soup, now how about some nice juicy meat?"

My mouth stretched wide with a span of four thick toes jammed in it, I looked up the length of his hard, sculptured body to see him, his jockpouch pulled to one side, and my gaze was filled with the sight of his blond young cock standing at rigid erection, plump and pulsating and steely hard, the bulbous, mushroom-like head blushing a dark, angry purple, and dripping forth big clear droplets of stud-juice! He held the monstrous man-club with two fingers at the root, tangled among the profusion of fair curls that shadowed the flat groin. I had thought Stosh was pretty well hung, but my surreptitious glances had never caught him fully hard—I had no idea how much *bigger* that heavy fuckmeat of his got! As that giant shaft of manhood throbbed before my eyes, I knew I had never seen a prick as big and thick, as long and massive, as Stosh's. . . . To one side of the tall, bony column I saw that his square-jawed, clean-cut, all-American jock-face wore a confident cocky grin. He waggled his engorged fuck-stick at me playfully.

"How about this for a dynamite piece of meat, eh, baby? Ever see anything look so good?! That's *real dick*, buddy boy . . . grade A, choice-cut, prime dick! . . . the biggest hunk of meat on the whole fucking basketball team, and the sweetest, tastiest, and *juiciest* fuckpole on campus! It's really too good for you, you know, but I'm feeling kinda generous . . . besides, my crotch's too juiced-up for comfort—need to drain off some of that hot butch milk packed away down there! So you're in luck! You *did* suck a good job on my hot feet, so I'm gonna let you chew on my big stick for a while . . . let you polish the ol' knob for me. C'mon, buddy—Come 'n get it!''

I looked up from those sweaty, tasty jock-feet in my hands, to the tall throbbing column of fuckmeat jutting up from his hairy crotch, then back to his sexy feet again. My mind was in a turmoil of indecision. I couldn't bear to tear myself away from that muscular jock's handsome feet, yet the invitation—or was it an order? —to get my face into that heavy stud-crotch, wrap my lips around his throbber and give him some head was just too tempting to resist! Seeing my reluctance to abandon his perfect young feet, Stosh reassured me.

''Shit, don't worry about it, man . . . you can eat some more of my feet for *dessert—after* you've finished your *meat!*''

Reassured by his promise to let me return to his delicious feet later, I scrambled up the bed to his lean young hips where the drooling, dripping fuckstick was standing rigid and arrogant like a thick rod of steel growing out of a bush of cloud-like golden hair. The pouch of his gamy jockstrap was tangled around the base of his hot, pulsing cock, and one of his massive nuts was still caught inside the sweat-soaked elastic mesh, the other dangling outside like some giant, hairy egg.

I pressed my face against the crumpled fabric and inhaled the jockpouch aroma. It was saturated with the heavy smells of his meaty crotch, warm from the heat of his thick, beefy genitals, wet from all the funky stud juices his hot jock-bod had pumped out into it! A faint, acrid aroma of male piss added spice to the dirty fabric. Stosh smirked down his muscular torso at me as I lay there, eagerly sniffing the rank jock-stud odors that had permeated his athletic supporter. ''Ya kinda like the way my ol' jock smells, huh?!'' he snorted contemptuously.

''Hmmmm-mm-mmm. . . .'' I answered, obviously meaning a big *yes*!! It was definitely the strongest, foulest, rankest jock I'd ever smelled—and I'd sniffed a lot in my time!

''Well, I tell you what, ol' buddy,'' he said, ''you do a good job on my dick and I'll let you chew on my smelly jockstrap afterwards—give you a little jock-broth to go with that raunchy foot-soup you liked so much!'' He made the offer like he was conferring some great, royal honor on me. "Now get on it, man! I wanna see your lips around my pecker . . . I'm gonna fuck your mouth till I blow my wad down your throat!!"

He reached down and stuck his long thumb and two fingers into my unresisting mouth, and spread the lips apart, opening my jaws to receive his drooling meat. With his other hand, he guided the massive club of hard flesh to the open cavity he had made of my mouth. I felt the fist-like, mushroom-shaped head of his prick probe, then push inwards, stretching my jaws wide—as wide as they've ever opened. For a moment I thought my mouth was going to rip at the corners as the huge knob forced its way further into my head! Then, with an audible *slurp* it slipped in past the widened flange collar, and my lips closed on the rock-hard shaft behind the head.

"Yeah . . . yeah . . . that's a good little cocksucker," he crooned in a low, sexy voice, his eyelids half-closed, his handsome mouth in a sullen pout. "You got my whole goddam plum in there now, fella. . . . lemme feel you lick on it, tongue that slimy slit and taste the sticky juice oozin' out for you!"

It felt like a fucking baseball jammed in my mouth, but I managed to massage the tender underside a little with my tongue, feeling at the same time a big glob of slimy fluid gushing out of the hot meat far back in my mouth . . .lubricating my throat, I knew, because I knew it was only a matter of seconds before he'd begin the long slide to give me all his shaft too! Slowly, gently, he reared his narrow muscular hips upwards, pulling my head down simultaneously upon his giant cock, spearing my face with that incredible weapon. It poked against the back of my mouth, stopped a moment, and then, lubricated by sex-slime, it slipped past the ineffective barrier there and pressed onward, breaching my throat! I gagged, and thrashed and kicked, but I was skewered and there was no way I could get off. The thick shaft went on and on, stretching my throat wide, as he drove the monster implacably all the way in to the hilt, and only stopped when my nose was buried deep in his pubic hair, pressed hard against his hot sweaty groin.

He held my head there for what seemed an interminable time, squirming and moaning in ecstasy, till I thought I'd pass out for lack of air. Then, just as I started to black out, he pulled my head up, holding me by the ears, and letting his fuckrod slip out of my throat for a moment.

But not for long—up and down, up and down, he manipulated my head, sliding it to and fro along the rigid length of his athletic cock, timing the savage thrusts of his slim muscular hips with the forceful shoving of my head so that my face slammed up hard against his hairy crotch with each vicious plunge, making an audible "plop."

Suddenly he jerked up against me harder than ever; his magnificent body went taut and trembling; the washboard muscles of his flat belly contracted in spasms; he gasped and started cursing like a madman; and I prepared myself to receive his flood of hot nut-juice!

Bolt after bolt of the steaming, stringy, slimy cream shot from his tube like jets from a firehose and splattered down my throat into my stomach! After he'd shot off about six volleys, he pulled his jerking, pumping cock part-way out, so that the spurting knob was lying against my tongue. In this new position, all his jism was squirted into my mouth instead of down my throat, and I was able to taste the bitter slugs of oyster-like slime as they came blasting out of the slit.

Stosh went on cursing and swearing: "Eat it, man! Drink my slimy cum, you fuckin' cocksucker! Swallow every fuckin' drop of my hot fuckslime, you sockchewin' sneakersniffin' bastard! Suck my prick and lick my smelly feet! I know you *want* it, you jock worshipper—you actually *want* me to fuck your face and cum in your mouth!! Shit, now you've *got* it, so *eat* it—eat it *all*!"

I *drank* it all right—every slimy drop of hot fuckjuice he pumped into me—but finally he ran out of ball-milk, and with a sigh, he released my ears and went limp, the giant sausage of man-meat in my mouth softening and shrinking enough for me to let it slip out from my lips and flop down wetly on his sweaty belly.

Remembering his promise, Stosh stirred himself enough to lift his hips and pull down his jockstrap, freeing the straps from his legs and peeling off the rank, wet supporter. He tossed the limp, sweaty, smelly thing into my face.

"Here . . . I think this is what you want now," he said as I caught the warm, moist strap off my face. "Chew on it a while if you want to so much . . . you've earned it . . ."

He watched me, idly toying with his wet, sticky dick, as I eagerly stuffed the repulsive pouch into my mouth and started sucking out the rich male juices from it, rank and virile. . . . there was the taste of locker rooms and crotch-sweat, piss and cockdrippings on it, and it went well with the flavor of hot cum that still lingered on my tongue.

Suddenly Stosh swung his long muscular legs over the side of the bed and got up, striding to the bathroom as he absentmindedly scratched one of his big, gumdrop-like tits. I watched his creamy, compact butt dimple and ripple as he took step after step toward the john door.

"C'mon in here," he said without looking back, "and bring my ol' jockstrap with you."

I jumped out of bed and did what I was told, the legstraps and waistband of his filthy jock swinging obscenely from my working mouth. When I got into the bathroom, he was standing at the toilet, his meaty pisser, still gigantic though now soft, in his hand pointed toward the bowl. He stuck out his other hand toward me and snapped his fingers: "The strap!" he growled.

"Hmmmm?" I muttered, muffled with that jockpouch stuffed in my mouth.

"C'mon, c'mon!" he said, impatiently snapping his fingers again. "The strap, man, my fuckin' *jock*. Give it to me, c'mon!"

Hastily I handed him the well-chewed athletic garment I had been sucking on. Holding it by the waistband, he placed it between his cock-head and the toilet, dangling the pouch directly in the line of fire where his massive young dick was aimed! I watched fascinated as the slit on the end of his big dong widened and a drop or two of amber liquid squirted out. . . . then the torrent came!

Like a firehose, his juicy prick gushed out an arc of steaming yellow piss, splashing against the dangling jockstrap and dripping into the toilet bowl below it! Soon his funky supporter was thoroughly soaked with the hot male urine, hanging heavy with its load of fresh, strong piss. Stosh stopped the flow, shaking off the last golden drops, and held the sopping, dripping jockstrap out to me.

"Now *here's* a jockstrap for ya—full of good, strong, hot jockpiss! Fresh from my hot stud bod—just the thing to sharpen up the appetite before dessert course!"

Dessert course?? My ears perked up and my heart quickened as I understood his meaning. I remembered he'd said, "You can eat some more of my feet for *dessert*—*after* you've finished your *meat!*'' But I could see he was going to make me work for the privilege again. . . .

MARRIED: "I WANT MY FEET CLEANED"

I watched his mouth slide back and forth on my cock, his mouth leaving the wetness of where it had been on my shaft with every backstroke he made. His lips were locked tightly around my meat. He was one good cocksucker, and had me excited.

I was going to cum, and shoved him down onto his back, replacing his mouth with my hand. This was one queer I wanted to cream all over his lips and face.

I pumped the same fast pace on my meat as he did with his mouth. I looked down at him, and began pumping my thick, creamy fucking sperm all over his face.

He lay still, and held onto my thighs as I straddled him on my knees. He moaned with excitement at being cummed all over his face. The fucker loved sucking guys' dicks, and taking their sperm any way they gave it to him.

I wanted to splash his faggot face with my slime, and watched it run down his nose, cheeks, and chin. I then leaned forward, and rubbed my dripping dick all over his lips and lower face, smearing my cum all over it. I then pressed my slimy cock to his lips, and shoved it into his mouth.

"Eat it!" I told him, and he slurp-sucked the cum from my dick and swallowed it.

I repeated my wiping his face with my cock, and feeding it into his mouth to eat. Yeah, faggots love that.

I climbed off of him, and sat up with my back against the wall, sitting on the floor.

"Did ya like my fuckin' load, fag?" I asked.

"Yes, sir," he answered. I crossed my feet, one atop the other.

"I want my feet cleaned, homey. Get yer ass over here, and lick 'em for me," I demanded, and he obeyed.

And there I sat, looking at this queer hugging my feet in his arms as he licked all over the bottoms of them. How do you explain a guy like that? I mean, even though I am a good-looking guy who has a hard-muscled body, and a man in my 30's, I haven't showered in at least thirty hours. So here's a queer who not only likes his men hunky, but likes them raunchy, too. He likes to smell me, and lick all over my sweaty body. He sucks on my cock, and eats my sperm. And now, the fucking pervert's down on my dirty, sweaty-smelling feet, making fucking love with them. If my wife saw me now, I wouldn't blame her if she shot me.

"Hey, man," I said, shoving my top foot on his forehead, pushing his face off my other foot. He looked up at me. "Why do you smell and lick my sweatin', dirty feet like that?" I asked. His eyes dropped to my feet, and he stroked them with his hand.

"Because they're yours. Your feet are sexy, strong, and dominating like the rest of you. I like to smell and inhale them because they've a raw, sweaty smell only a man can have. There's something animalistically sexual about a man's body odor that makes me hunger for his muscles and flesh when I smell him. Like now!" he said, pressing his face against my feet, and licking them.

The guy's honest, and he really turns on to me. I could never make love to another guy, suck a cock or lick a guy's feet like this dude does.

But having him do me has been a trip every time. Besides being married and straight, I also got me my own queer to do the raunchy things with. This fucker worships me.

He's a good foot-licker, too! And I don't know anybody else who digs feet like he does. And I like making him do it to 'em, too. It feels great, even if it is kinda gross to me to do.

I got up and walked across the room, and sat back down on the floor with my back against the wall. I crossed my feet again. He rolled over, and was watching me.

"I know I got the feet you want. Ya wanna smell and lick 'em some more, faggot?" I asked, watching him stare and drool over them.

"Yes, I do!" he said.

"Enough to beg for 'em?" I asked.

"Yes," he answered.

"Beg!" I told him. I could see him tremble, and be uneasy with it.

"Please . . . I . . ." he paused.

"Beg, damn it!" I yelled at him.

"I want your feet!" he cried out. "I wanna smell and feel, and lick your sexy feet for you. Please, I beg you, let me have your toes in my mouth. I want to suck 'em. I want yer whole foot in my mouth. Ohhhh . . . please . . . ppllleeaasse!" he seriously begged.

"Crawl, asshole!" I told him, and watched him crawl across the floor to my feet.

What a queer.

DREAM INTERVIEW

Hey foot slave of mine, your pics are hot. You are one good looking dude. But I sense a cocky attitude which needs to be worked on by me. I can just see you waiting at the directory for your job interview with me. I recognize you from your photo and your resume, but you don't know me. I stop and stare, and you stare back. I see your eyes look me over, and then rest at my shoes. Then I know I've got you when you get into the interview.

You've told me in your resume that you need this job and you haven't found any other because people won't hire you because you're overqualified and they feel you'll leave as soon as something better comes along. So now I've got the upper hand. I know I'll have a lot of fun with you.

When I get to my office, I let my two office workers, Tony and John, know what's happened. I tell them to play up to you when you get in and to really lay the feet bit on thick. Shortly after I go into my office, they buzz me and tell me you are here. I tell them to entertain you because I'll be tied up for another 10 or 15 minutes. Then I leave the intercom on so I can hear what's going on. They start out lightly with just idle talk. Then they get started on you. Tony says that his foot is killing him, takes off his shoe and checks it out. He puts it close to his face to check it out but can't find anything, so John takes his shoe and looks into it, commenting about the smell from it. They banter a bit about it, and then John takes off his shoe and tells Tony to smell it, because it has a good smell to it, and it's not raunchy like his. Tony puts his fingers in John's shoe and says it's all wet from his feet sweat and is disgusting.

I smile to myself because I imagine that you must be going nuts now, seeing all this stuff taking place right in front of you. I figure you're nice and primed now, so I buzz the outer office to bring you into my office. When they show you in, I sit you down in front of my desk and I sit on my desk with one foot on the floor, close to yours, and the other dangling about halfway down. Just about the level of your cock.

I make certain to move it around at times, kicking the desk. I ask you a couple of general questions, and tell you to tell me why you want this job, and what you'll bring to it.

I think to myself that any time I want to, I can just lean over, grab you by your hair, push you down to the floor and have you get to work on my shoes. While you're talking away, nervously glancing at my foot, I begin rubbing my shoe. Then it dawns on you that you have seen me downstairs and that we had stared at each other. You get red. I know you're embarrassed and I'm going to get you good.

I then interrupt you and tell you that I hurt my foot and need frequent massaging on it so I call in Tony and tell him to massage my foot. He takes my shoe off and begins massaging my socked foot. You stop talking and I let you continue while he's massaging my foot.

I look right into your eyes while you're talking and smile to myself when I see you trying to not look at what Tony is doing to my foot. I also make the appropriate moans and groans of pleasure to really get you going. Then I tell you that you would be expected to do the same for me, because I demand unconditional obedience from my staff.

Tony tells you to kneel down in front of me, and shows you how to massage my foot. You begin slowly and reluctantly, and nervously. I tell you that it's pretty good and to continue and tell Tony to start on the other foot.

Both of you are going to town on my feet real good, and I know Tony has a hard-on, but I'm not sure about you. Then Tony tells me that he learned a new technique in relaxing feet and would like to try it on me, but it's a little different. I tell him to go ahead, and show you in case I like it.

He then goes down on my feet with his mouth, licking the instep and working all around it and really licking long strokes on my well defined arches. He then darts his tongue between my toes and finally puts them all in his mouth and comments how smelly my socks and feet are. You start out slowly, and then get even more energetic than Tony about it.

Then I get up, sit on the easy chair, and spread my legs out so you guys can get to work on my feet. Tony takes off my sock and so do you and start getting to work on my bare feet. I purposely keep my feet down on the floor. That forces the two of you to get down on your bellies to suck and lick my feet. I then tell you that you're going to get your clothes dirty and messy, and that's not good for business, so I tell you to take your clothes off.

Now, both of you are in your underwear, on your bellies, and working my feet over, and I see that you have a fantastically large hard-on. Then I tell you to kneel in front of me and really work on my feet, as though you were worshipping them. I tell the two of you that my legs are also hurting and to massage them, and lick them with your tongue. I put my feet right on your cocks and dig them in. You begin to slow down a bit. I grab you by your hair and push your face down at my feet again. I ask you if you really want this job and you tell me that you do. I tell you that it's yours if you please me enough and do whatever I say. You answer "okay," and I take off my belt and swat your ass with it and tell you whenever you speak to me, you will always use the word "sir" and use it with respect and fear. Then I tell Tony to tell John to lock the outer door to the office and get his ass in here, because we are going to initiate our new employee.

Because of our interest in leather and domination scenes, Tony, John and I always keep extra leather and toys at the office in case things get slow and we have a need to fulfill. I tell you to start working on John's feet, shoes and socks while I change. I drag Tony in the back with me while I change into my leather vest, chaps, jockstrap and biker's hat.

Then I come back into the room to see you bent over John's feet. I kick you off balance onto your back. Then I stand over you with my foot on your belly and tell the boys to rip your shorts off of you. I then take my foot, rub it all over your cock, on your balls, between your legs, and then when I get back to your cock and balls again, I push a little harder to see you groan in pain and pleasure.

Then I work my foot up your body to your tits and then grab your nipples with my toes and pull hard. I walk around you and stand over your head with my bare feet and the leather chaps pressing against the side of your head. You probably can just get a faint smell of my feet.

Meanwhile, both of the other guys have stripped down naked and come over to us. I make them get on either side of you on their bellies and begin to work on my feet.

I have a cat-o'-nine-tails and whip their asses and backs. You are still on your back with your head immobile between my feet, under and between my crotch. I then pull out my cock and start to piss on the three of you. As I'm straining to get the piss out, I'm farting at the same time, and I hear you groan with pleasure. Then a real turn on for me, I sit back and the three of you start sucking my cock, licking my balls and eating out my crotch while I use the cat-o'-nine on you fuckers.

I also use my smelly socks and push them in your faces and rub them all around your necks and heads and while you're down there eating out my crotch, I'm probably farting some really ripe ones. Then we're getting very close to coming, all of us, so I make the three of you stand up while I tie your cocks and balls up with rawhide. I then tell you to start jerking off. I want all of your hot cum on my chest, belly and cock and balls at the same time, so I start jacking off while I'm pulling those rawhide strips and watch you three grimace in pain and pleasure.

Then I talk dirty to you pricks while you're getting hotter and hotter and I spit at the three of you and get you more and more excited and finally the three of you shoot all over my hairy chest and belly and my balls and cock. Then I pull the three of you down to lick your cum off my body. Now I'm motherfuckin' ready to come.

As the initiate, I only let you smell my feet, and then work your way up my legs by licking my legs but I won't let you lick or kiss my feet, only smell them. Then I grab you by the hair and make you start sucking my cock and gently licking my balls, and working on my crotch.

"Get it all wet and sloppy."

Meanwhile, Tony and John are working my feet over real good, licking my arch, sucking my toes, really going to town on them. I tell them to get on their backs, I put my feet on their faces and let them lick the dirt out from between my toes while you are going to town on my cock with alternating long and slow strokes and quick strokes, getting me real close and ready to come.

As I get closer and closer, I keep calling you motherfuckin' foot lickers and shit-eaters and I tell you guys to work harder or I'll beat the fuckin' shit outta you. I use my whip on your ass and back to make you work better, and then I take my socks and push them in your face, and shove them at your nose as hard as I can. That gets you really hot. You really start working on my cock, getting it harder and harder and closer and closer to coming all over you fuckin' scums of the earth.

I'm getting real close to coming now. I tell you to get my cock real wet with your worthless shit spit and then push you away and tell you to get on your no good fuckin' back between the other two cunts and get ready to take my come.

I beat off real good while I'm cussing you three fuckers out and listen to you three punks beg for my come. I'm getting closer and closer until I finally start shooting all over your mouths, your fuckin' faces, especially yours, because you've got the best motherfuckin' face of the three of you, and now you're almost my boy to do with as I please.

While all this is happening, you worthless cocksuckers are beating each other off. Then I take my feet and rub them all over your faces, spreading my come all over your faces and getting it between my toes and then rubbing my feet all over your chest and nipples, into your pubic hair, cock and balls while you try to lick the backs of my legs and stroke my feet. Then I bring them back to your faces again and have you lick them clean from the come and the sweat from your bodies, especially taking care to get it all from between my toes.

I push you away then. Usually I take a shower with my boys and let them lick my body dry before we go back to work. But today's activities took longer than usual so we just stay dirty and smelly. It's almost lunchtime now, but we're going to stay in the office to catch up on some work. You ask me if you were good enough to be rewarded with the job and I say that you were, and you tell me that it's great, because you'd really like to work here and be a part of all the job requirements.

While we're getting dressed you ask me when you can start, and you say that you really feel a part of the group and can't wait to start. Meanwhile, Tony and John are smiling. Then I lay it on you. Fucker, you did fine in a nice close knit group like this. But are you really going to regard me as your boss and show the respect I deserve no matter where we are? You say, "Yes, sir, no matter where we are or what you want." Tony and John are really pleased now, and say, "Motherfuckin' okay!"

I tell them I think you will be able to start tomorrow morning at nine o'clock but I will let you know for sure tonight, because you will meet us at the Hitching Post bar at ten-thirty sharp.

"And here. Make sure that you're wearing this slave collar. None of us will clean ourselves up for the rest of the day. When you come in through the doors of that bar, you'd better be psyched up to do whatever I tell you to do, whenever I tell you to do it and to whomever I tell you to do it, because this will be your final test of submission to see if you will unconditionally obey me in front of a group of people who are strangers to you. Believe me, this will be the ultimate test to see how bad you want this job and how obedient and submissive you'll be to me.

"Isn't that right, fuckers?"

"Oh, yes, sir," they dutifully snap out. "Yes, sir."

"So, you asshole worthless piece of shit, you'd better get your gorgeous sweet ass out of here, go home and get some rest. Tonight, you're going to wear out your fuckin' tongue doing my bidding and your fuckin' ass is going to ache good tomorrow morning. I'm going to use that beautiful stud body and that fuckin' cocky attitude of yours to fulfill my every whim and fantasy. Is that clear, cunt?" You answer with a weak,

"Yes, sir." And I tell you,

"Hey, shithead, I can't hear you." And then you say nice and loud and clear:

"Yes, sir!" And then I say,

"Well, fuckhead, you want to know what's going to happen to you tonight?" And you say pleadingly,

"Oh yes, sir, please sir!"

"Well, fuckin' pisshead, you be at the Hitching Post at ten-thirty sharp and you'll find out. Now, get your no-good fuckin' faggot ass outta here fast. And one warning: don't be even a minute late tonight. If you are . . ."

BOOKS FROM LEYLAND PUBLICATIONS / G.S PRESS

- [ ] **KISS FOOT, LICK BOOT**. Foot, Sox, Sneaker & Boot Worship/Domination Stories. Edited by Doug Gaines / The Foot Fraternity. $16.95.
- [ ] **MUSCLESEX A collection of erotic stories** by Greg Nero. $16.95.
- [ ] **CRYSTAL BOYS** The first modern Asian gay novel by Pai Hsien-yung $16.95.
- [ ] **PARTINGS AT DAWN: Anthology of Japanese Gay Literature.** Edited by Stephen Miller. Brilliant collection covering 800 years of Japanese culture. $17.95.
- [ ] **MEN LOVING MEN: A Gay Sex Guide & Consciousness Book** by Mitch Walker. New revised edition. 40 + photos. $16.95.
- [ ] **MEATMEN Anthology of Gay Male Comics.** Tom of Finland, Donelan, etc. Large sized books / $17.95 each. Circle books wanted. Volumes 1, 3, 4, 5, 6, 7, 8, 9, 10, 11, 12, 13, 14, 15, 16, 17, 18.
- [ ] **ENLISTED MEAT / WARRIORS & LOVERS / MILITARY SEX / MARINE BIOLOGY / BASIC TRAINING: True Homosexual Military Stories.** $15.95 each. Circle books wanted. Soldiers / sailors / marines tell all about their sex lives.
- [ ] **SEX BEHIND BARS / BOYS BEHIND BARS / THE BOYS OF VASELINE ALLEY** (3 Vols.) by Robert N. Boyd. True stories of male-male prison sex, and street hustling. $16.95 each. Circle books wanted.
- [ ] **MANPLAY / YOUNG NUMBERS / 10½ INCHES / BOYS BOYS BOYS! / STUDFLESH / BOYS WILL BE BOYS / EIGHTEEN & OVER:** True Gay Encounters. Circle books wanted. Hot male-male sex stories. $12.95 each.
- [ ] **LUST** and **HUMONGOUS** True Gay Encounters. Vols. 1 & 5 $16.95 ea.
- [ ] **LEATHERMEN SPEAK OUT** Vols. 1 & 2. Ed. Jack Ricardo. 50 leather dads & sons, slaves & masters reveal their S&M sex encounters. $16.95 ea.
- [ ] **SIR! MORE SIR! The Joy of S&M** by Master Jackson. Complete guide to S&M / leather sex with sections on bondage, spanking, etc. $16.95.
- [ ] **THE KISS OF THE WHIP: Explorations in SM** by Jim Prezwalski $17.95.
- [ ] **TRASH / TRUCKER / SEXSTOP / HEADSTOPS / HOT TRICKS / MEAT RACK: True Revelations from 18 Wheeler** Vols. 1 to 6. Ed. by John Dagion. True sex stories. Circle books wanted. $12.95 each.
- [ ] **ROUGH TRADE: True Revelations** Vol. 7. Hot sex stories. $16.95
- [ ] **ROCK ON THE WILD SIDE: Gay Male Images in Popular Music of the Rock Era** by Wayne Studer. Illustrated. $17.95.
- [ ] **GAY ROOTS: Anthology of Gay History, Sex, Politics & Culture.** Vols. 1 & 2. Edited by Winston Leyland. More than 100 + writers. Illustrated. More than 1000 pages total. Vol. 1: $25.95; Vol. 2 $22.95.
- [ ] **HIGH CAMP: A Guide to Gay Cult & Camp Films** by Paul Roen. Illustrated reviews of gay camp films over the past 50 years. $17.95
- [ ] **MEAT / CUM / JUICE / WADS / CREAM True Homosexual Experiences from S.T.H.** Boyd McDonald $14.95 each (5 vols.). Circle books wanted.
- [ ] **MILKIN' THE BULLS and other Hot Hazing Stories** by John Barton. Stories of military school, sexual hazing, etc. $16.95.
- [ ] **ORGASMS / HOT STUDS / SINGLEHANDED:** Homosexual Encounters from *First Hand*. $12.95 each (3 vols.). Circle books wanted.
- [ ] **GHOST KISSES Gothic Gay Romance Stories** by Gregory Norris $14.95.

TO ORDER: Check book(s) wanted (or list them on a separate sheet) and send check / money order to Leyland Publications, PO Box 410690, San Francisco, CA 94141. **Postage included in prices quoted.** Calif. residents add 8¼ % sales tax. Mailed in unmarked book envelopes. Add $1 for complete catalogue.

AIDS RISK REDUCTION GUIDELINES
FOR HEALTHIER SEX

As given by Bay Area Physicians for Human Rights

NO RISK: *Most of these activities involve only skin-to-skin contact, thereby avoiding exposure to blood, semen, and vaginal secretions. This assumes there are no breaks in the skin.* 1) Social kissing (dry). 2) **Body massage, hugging.** 3) **Body to body rubbing** (frottage). 4) **Light S&M** (without bruising or bleeding). 5) **Using one's own sex toys.** 6) **Mutual masturbation** (male or external female). Care should be taken to avoid exposing the partners to ejaculate or vaginal secretions. Seminal, vaginal and salivary fluids should not be used as lubricants.

LOW RISK: *In these activities small amounts of certain body fluids might be exchanged, or the protective barrier might break causing some risk.* 1) **Anal or vaginal intercourse with condom.** Studies have shown that HIV does not penetrate the condom in simulated intercourse. Risk is incurred if the condom breaks or if semen spills into the rectum or vagina. The risk is further reduced if one withdraws before climax. 2) **Fellatio interruptus** (sucking, stopping before climax). Pre-ejaculate fluid may contain HIV. Saliva or other natural protective barriers in the mouth may inactivate virus in pre-ejaculate fluid. Saliva may contain HIV in low concentration. The insertive partner should warn the receptive partner before climax to prevent exposure to a large volume of semen. If mouth or genital sores are present, risk is increased. Likewise, action which causes mouth or genital injury will increase risk. 3) **Fellatio with condom** (sucking with condom) Since HIV cannot penetrate an intact condom, risk in this practice is very low unless breakage occurs. 4) **Mouth-to-mouth kissing** (French kissing, wet kissing) Studies have shown that HIV is present in saliva in such low concentration that salivary exchange is unlikely to transmit the virus. Risk is increased if sores in the mouth or bleeding gums are present. 5) **Oral-vaginal or oral-anal contact with protective barrier.** e.g. a latex dam, obtainable through a local dental supply house, may be used. Do not reuse latex barrier, because sides of the barrier may be reversed inadvertently. 6) **Manual anal contact with glove** (manual anal (fisting) or manual vaginal (internal) contact with glove). If the glove does not break, virus transmission should not occur. However, significant trauma can still be inflicted on the rectal tissues leading to other medical problems, such as hemorrhage or bowel perforation. 7) **Manual vaginal contact with glove** (internal). See above.

MODERATE RISK: *These activities involve tissue trauma and/or exchange of body fluids which may transmit HIV or other sexually transmitted disease.* 1) **Fellatio** (sucking to climax). Semen may contain high concentrations of HIV and if absorbed through open sores in the mouth or digestive tract could pose risk. 2) **Oral-anal contact** (rimming). HIV may be contained in blood-contaminated feces or in the anal rectal lining. This practice also poses high risk of transmission of parasites and other gastrointestinal infections. 3) **Cunnilingus** (oral-vaginal contact). Vaginal secretions and menstrual blood have been shown to harbor HIV, thereby causing risk to the oral partner if open lesions are present in the mouth or digestive tract. 4) **Manual rectal contact** (fisting). Studies have indicated a direct association between fisting and HIV infection for both partners. This association may be due to concurrent use of recreational drugs, bleeding, pre-fisting semen exposure, or anal intercourse with ejaculation. 5) **Sharing sex toys.** 6) **Ingestion of urine.** HIV has not been shown to be transmitted via urine; however, other immunosuppressive agents or infections may be transmitted in this manner.

HIGH RISK: *These activities have been shown to transmit HIV.* 1) **Receptive anal intercourse without condom.** All studies imply that this activity carries the highest risk of transmitting HIV. The rectal lining is thinner than that of the vagina or the mouth thereby permitting ready absorption of the virus from semen or pre-ejaculate fluid to the blood stream. One laboratory study suggests that the virus may enter by direct contact with rectal lining cells without any bleeding. 2) **Insertive anal intercourse without condom.** Studies suggest that men who participate only in this activity are at less risk of being infected than their partners who are rectally receptive; however the risk is still significant. It carries high risk of infection by other sexually transmitted diseases. 3) **Vaginal intercourse without condom.**